A CONCISE FIELD (
TO POST-COMMUNIST

Bálint Magyar – Bálint Madlovics

A Concise Field Guide to
POST-COMMUNIST REGIMES

Actors, Institutions, and Dynamics

Central European University Press
Budapest – Vienna – New York

©2022 by Bálint Magyar and Bálint Madlovics

Published in 2022 by
Central European University Press
Nádor utca 9, H-1051 Budapest, Hungary
Tel: +36-1-327-3138 or 327-3000
E-mail: ceupress@press.ceu.edu
Website: www.ceupress.com

All rights reserved. No part of this publication may be reproduced, stored in a retrieval system, or transmitted, in any form or by any means, without the permission of the Publisher.

Cover design and layout by Éva Szalay

ISBN 978-963-386-587-3 (paperback)
ISBN 978-963-386-588-0 (ebook)

Library of Congress Cataloging-in-Publication Data

Names: Magyar, Bálint, 1952- author. | Madlovics, Bálint, 1993- author.
Title: A concise field guide to post-communist regimes : actors, institutions, and dynamics / Bálint Magyar, Bálint Madlovics.
Description: Budapest ; New York : Central European University Press, 2022. | Includes bibliographical references.
Identifiers: LCCN 2022025086 (print) | LCCN 2022025087 (ebook) ISBN 9789633865873 (paperback) | ISBN 9789633865880 (pdf)
Subjects: LCSH: Post-communism—Europe, Eastern. | Post-communism–China. Europe, Eastern—Social conditions—1989- | Europe, Eastern–Politics and government—1989- | China—Social conditions—2000- China—Politics and government—21st century. | BISAC: POLITICAL SCIENCE / Political Ideologies / Communism, Post-Communism & Socialism | SOCIAL SCIENCE / Sociology / General
Classification: LCC HN380.7.A8 M3423 2022 (print) | LCC HN380.7.A8 (ebook) | DDC 306.0947—dc23/eng/20220714
LC record available at https://lccn.loc.gov/2022025086
LC ebook record available at https://lccn.loc.gov/2022025087

Table of Contents

FOREWORD: A new paradigm for understanding post-communist regimes by Oleksandr Fisun vii
User's guide to the book..xi

I. The Conceptual Framework: 120 Propositions 1
 Trapped in the Language of Liberal Democracy... 3
 Dissolving Axiom #1: Stubborn Structures and the Region's Development 9
 Dissolving Axiom #2: Formality and Informality... 19
 Dissolving Axiom #3: From Constitutional State to the Mafia State.................... 35
 A Sui Generis Phenomenon: the Adopted Political Family................................... 45
 The Formal Institutional Setting: Changing Patterns of Legitimacy 61
 Legislation and the Legal System: From the Rule of Law to the Law of Rule...... 81
 Defensive Mechanisms: Stability and Erosion of Democracies and Autocracies...... 93
 Relational Economics: Corruption, Predation, and the Redistribution of Markets 109
 Market-Exploiting Dictatorship: Coexistence of the Three Economic Mechanisms in China 131
 Clientage Society and the Social Stability of Patronal Autocracy 141
 Populism: an Ideological Instrument for the Political Program of Morally Unconstrained Collective Egoism... 151
 Beyond Regime Specificities: Country-, Policy-, and Era-Specific Features 163
 Post-Communist Regime Trajectories: A Triangular Framework...................... 185

II. Trajectories of Twelve Post-Communist Regimes 193
 Estonia: Regime Change to Liberal Democracy 195
 Romania: Regime Change to Patronal Democracy 198
 Kazakhstan: Regime Change to Patronal Autocracy.. 201
 China: Model Change to Market-Exploiting Dictatorship 205
 Czech Republic: Backsliding Toward Patronal Democracy................................. 209
 Poland: Backsliding Toward Conservative Autocracy.. 213
 Hungary: Backsliding to Patronal Autocracy from Liberal Democracy............ 217
 Russia: Backsliding to Patronal Autocracy from Oligarchic Anarchy................ 222
 Ukraine: Regime Cycles with Color Revolutions.. 227
 North Macedonia: Regime Cycle with Intra-Elite Conflict 231
 Moldova: Regime Cycles with Foreign Interference... 234
 Georgia: An Attempt to Break the Regime Cycle 239

Notes 243
About the Authors..252

FOREWORD

A new paradigm for understanding post-communist regimes

On February 24, 2022, Ukraine was invaded by Russia. The military aggression perpetrated by Vladimir Putin brought death, destruction, and the displacement of hundreds of thousands of people from the war-torn zones—myself included, whose home and university in Kharkiv was leveled. Russia's aggression not only destroyed the international order but also forced us to look for a new answer to the question: How can we explain the nature of post-communist regimes such as Putin's Russia? What are the conceptual tools for explaining their behavior?

The lack of understanding, particularly the inability to see the actual nature of Putin's regime, contributed to the escalation of events leading to this point. In mainstream political science, the regime has been described using a system of categories rooted mainly in the West, such as 'illiberal democracy' or 'hybrid regimes'. Such categories are inadequate to make sense of the nature of post-communist actors and institutions, their motivations, and modes of action. The lack of appropriate language leads to deficient understanding, and deficient understanding leads to misconceptions about the acts and plans of people like Putin. The tragic events in Ukraine must compel Western observers to seek a more authentic language, words, and concepts that can explain the post-communist world, its peculiarities, and tendencies.

The conceptual framework devised by Bálint Magyar and Bálint Madlovics, presented here in 120 short propositions, provides just such a language. Their post-communist regime theory offers a fresh and original perspective on explaining the nature of post-communist dynamics. We are talking about a new paradigm for explaining post-communist regimes, which considers the role of formal and informal institutions. A significant shortcoming of the previous concepts of analysis of post-communist regimes was that they used the conceptual language developed to analyze classical transitions from authoritarianism to democracy from the point of view of formal institutions undergoing transformation. However, the post-communist world cannot be understood through the language of formal legal and constitutional norms, rational-legal actions, and the language of bureaucratic rationality. This language addresses only the visible part of the political reality, which cannot grasp the real nature and motives of the actions of post-communist leaders. In fact, what is a deviation from the point of view of the classical mainstream is the main principle of the operation of these systems.

This concise book by Magyar and Madlovics proposes a new language for describing post-communist regimes, one which integrates informal institutions and makes it possible to see how, where, and why they are the main basic principle of operation in post-communist systems. The basic hypothesis of the authors is that the post-communist political trajectory after the fall of communism is leading to 'informal patronal' systems of rule, and by no means to the establishment of Western-style legal-rational liberal democracy. This approach represents the third stage in the evolution of paradigms for understanding post-communist regimes, following the transitology of the 1990s (when transition from communist dictatorship to liberal democracy was taken for granted) and 'hybridology' (the combination of authoritarianism and democracy). But these paradigms tried to place regimes on a democracy-dictatorship axis and focused primarily on political institutions while treating everything else as external or 'tutelary' interference. In contrast, Magyar and Madlovics start their exposition by questioning three basic axioms of the mainstream comparative paradigm and develop a triangular conceptual space with six ideal types of political-economic regimes: three polar types (liberal democracy, communist dictatorship, patronal autocracy) and three intermediary or hybrid types (patronal democracy, market-exploited dictatorship, conservative autocracy). Finishing the 120 propositions, the reader will gain a clear understanding of these types, their differences, and most importantly their inner workings in terms of politics, economics, and society.

The book contributes to the development of a new language for the description of post-communist realities. According to them, post-communist regimes are characterized by a concentration of power in the hands of a *chief patron*, a patronal president or prime minister who maintains control by distributing rewards and punishments to a network of various rent-seeking actors from *an adopted political family* (oligarchs and *poligarchs*, regional barons and loyal elites, relatives and *front men*). The connection between the center, i.e., *the patron's court* and political participation is exercised through joining the *single-pyramid patronal network*, different corporatist arrangements, or a formal *transmission-belt party*. The adopted political family holds the key position in the polity and controls profitable industries of the national economy. The central element of this network is a system of personal ties, centered on the chief patron and based primarily on regional or "clan" unity, as well as on current rent-seeking interests. The ruler, the chief patron *does not govern but disposes over wealth and people*: they completely dominate and control the political, administrative, and economic elite around them.

This approach is very close to my neopatrimonial interpretation of post-communist development. The mainstream of democratization studies has largely ignored the role of Max Weber's theoretical heritage, especially his magnum opus *Economy and Society*, for understanding post-communist processes. Max Weber widely used the concept of 'patrimonialism,' which he contrasted with both feudal and bureaucratic rational-legal forms of government. The main feature of patrimonialism is the private appropriation of a governmental sphere by those who hold political power, and also the indivisibility of the public and private spheres of society. This is essential for understanding both post-communist politics and regime dynamics: post-communist politics is not a struggle of political alternatives in the context of parliamentary contestation, but a struggle of different factions of rent-seeking entrepreneurs to monopolize the main segments of patron-client networks.

Magyar and Madlovics understand the concept of neopatrimonialism and incorporate it in their framework as one of four sides of patronal autocracy. Combining the political concept *(neopatrimonial state)* with a sociological concept *(clan state)*, a political economy concept *(predatory state)*, and a legal concept *(criminal state)*, they come to define the complex entity of the *mafia state*. This term represents one of the key messages of the book, namely, that political, economic, and communal spheres of social action are not separated in post-communist regimes, and they must not be analyzed separately if one is to understand this part of the world.

Beyond neopatrimonialism, the paradigm presented by Magyar and Madlovics finds its roots in Weber's three types of domination (traditional, charismatic, rational-legal), Karl Polanyi's types of exchanges (market, redistribution, reciprocity), as well as the work of Henry E. Hale on post-Soviet patronal politics. Hale wrote one of the blurbs for the authors' previous book, *The Anatomy of Post-Communist Regimes* (CEU Press, 2020), for which the present book is a condensed companion. There, Hale wrote: "This ambitious book provides not only a better vocabulary, but a whole new grammar for describing the political regimes that emerged in communism's wake." Masha Gessen, journalist of *The New Yorker*, stated: "Reading this book feels like having the curtains opened, letting the bright light come in." And Iván Szelényi, Professor Emeritus of Yale and an important intellectual figure of the Eastern bloc, wrote: "This book is better and more important than anything I have done during the past 30 years." The accolades apply to this book just as much—if not more so, as it is shorter and probably more accessible to today's readers.

While *The Anatomy of Post-Communist Regimes* was a breakthrough in post-communist studies, *The Concise Field Guide* brings the innovations of that breakthrough to a wider audience. The highly structured theoretical exposition of the 120 propositions is accompanied by 12 short country studies in the second half of the book. These studies are not just enlightening in their description of the last 30 years of development of Ukraine, Russia, Poland, Hungary, and other countries, but they also illustrate how appropriate language can result in insightful analyses. This is what makes this book so important amidst the difficulties of today's world.

Oleksandr Fisun

Department of Political Science,
V.N. Karazin Kharkiv National University, Ukraine

User's guide to the book

This book serves as a concise summary of the main theoretical contributions presented in the authors' previous book, *The Anatomy of Post-Communist Regimes: A Conceptual Framework* (Budapest–New York: CEU Press, 2020). While the *Anatomy* is a massive, 800-page volume with over 2.000 footnotes and 50 pages of bibliography, this short book aims to be an easy-to-use conceptual toolkit for the analysis of actors, institutions, and dynamics of post-communist democracies, autocracies, and dictatorships.

The book is divided into two parts. The first part consists of 120 propositions, summarizing the conceptual framework, its main concepts and typologies. This part contains only in-text references to books and papers, with the title, date of publication, and the name of the author(s). No footnotes are included in this part: a QR-code at the beginning of the Notes points to the bibliography of the *Anatomy*, containing the literature used to develop the conceptual framework presented in this book.

QR-codes will be placed along the text. The first one, on this page, points to the website of the authors, *www.postcommunistregimes. com*. Courtesy of Knowledge Unlatched, the *Anatomy* is open-access, and it can be downloaded for free from the website. The website also contains further related materials, including a 3D model of regime trajectories and the draft of a seminar with PowerPoint presentations for MA or PhD level. QR-codes in the book will point to either a presentation of the seminar, or the 3D model.

The theoretical framework consists of ideal types, in the mold of Max Weber. While empirical examples will be provided to orient the reader, the main point of the concepts in this book is to serve as points of reference. They are models: "pure," utopic depictions of actors, institutions, and dynamics, which can be used to describe their real world counterparts in terms of congruence and deviance. For example, we will associate Estonia with "liberal democracy," and Russia and Hungary with "patronal autocracy." This does not mean these countries always work according to their ideal types, or that their actions conform to the model with no exceptions. But using an ideal type for them means to underline the *dominant* logic and forms of political, economic, and social organization in these countries. Indeed, the concepts in this book are created, not by taking into account every feature of real world phenomena but only some of the distinctive ones, which are arranged in a pure and ideal form—as Weber writes—into a unified analytical construct.

This book provides, not simply concepts for understanding post-communism, but aspects of analysis. Each typology in the book should be seen as attempts to find, between the various types, the relevant dividing lines which by themselves are just as important for comparative analysis as the types. The importance of clear-cut analytical concepts is highlighted in the book by the high number of tables and figures, each containing main concepts and the analytical aspects that distinguish them.

The second part of the book is an application of the conceptual framework, with the modelled trajectories of twelve post-communist countries. These trajectories are painted with a broad brush; we explain how they were constructed in brief "country studies," but these should not be seen as real case studies, only as illustrative sketches. They were made for the purpose of orientation and illustration, to show the reader how the analytical framework can be used to describe post-communist developments in the last thirty years. A precise, quantitative description of the trajectories can be found on the book's website (Supplementary Material / Appendix).

I.
The Conceptual Framework: 120 Propositions

Trapped in the Language of Liberal Democracy

1.

AFTER THE COLLAPSE OF THE SOVIET EMPIRE, an illusion prevailed that communist dictatorships would be necessarily replaced by Western-type liberal democracies. The obvious conclusion from the disintegration of the bipolar world order of the Cold War was that the countries that had been associated with the falling pole—the Soviet Union and communist dictatorship—have no other choice but to go to the winner pole—the United States and liberal democracy. Democracy remained "the only game in town," which also coincided with a normative, liberal position: the moral impetus for the universal extension of human rights, and a moral inhibition toward taking into full account the historical and cultural background of post-communist societies.

As a result, there was a consensus that post-communist countries are part of a linear, progressive process of development in the direction of liberal democracy, and *ad hoc* deviations from democratic norms initially seemed to be "teething problems" rather than "adult" personality traits of regimes. The political science literature of the 1990s was dominated by various branches of transitology: the study of how transition countries walk the road to liberal democracy, and how they cope with the difficulties they face on it. Post-communist regimes were seen as mere transitional systems, rather than terminal stations.

2.

SINCE THE TURN OF THE MILLENNIUM, post-communist countries have been regarded as "hybrid regimes" somewhere between democracy and dictatorship. It was realized eventually that the "neither dictatorship nor democracy" regimes that emerged after the regime changes do not necessarily evolve toward the Western ideal. This was the point when, in political science literature, transitology was replaced by "hybridology": when it was accepted that the institutional elements of the new regimes are capable of constituting stable, *sui generis* systems. These systems are interpreted along the democracy-dictatorship axis, where between the two polar types—the Western-type liberal democracy and the overtly oppressive, totalitarian dictatorship—a permanent "grey zone" is recognized (Figure 1).

Descriptive language experiments of hybridology have tried to interpret the political processes of individual post-communist states as part of this grey zone: illiberal democracy, defective democracy, managed democracy, etc. on the one hand, and semi-dictatorships, electoral authoritarianism, competitive authoritarianism, etc. on the other hand. The adjectives in these labels express a certain kind of deviance from the ideal types of democracy and dictatorship. Hybridology, and the interpretive framework of the democracy-dictatorship axis constitute the mainstream comparative paradigm today.

Figure 1: The democracy-dictatorship axis, with a grey zone between the two poles.

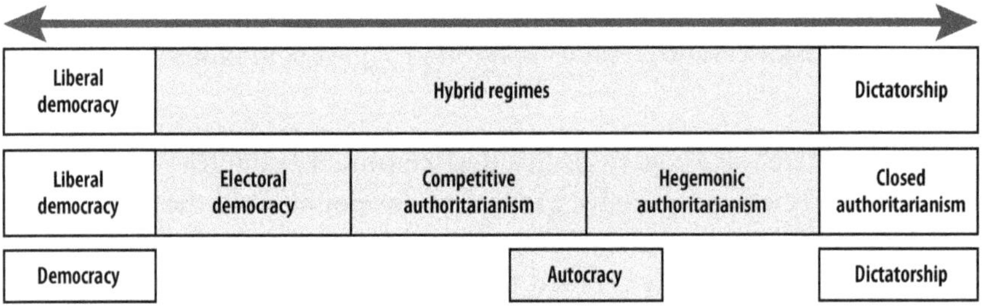

Liberal democracy	Hybrid regimes			Dictatorship
Liberal democracy	Electoral democracy	Competitive authoritarianism	Hegemonic authoritarianism	Closed authoritarianism
Democracy		Autocracy		Dictatorship

3.

Hybridology has only changed the regime labels, not the regime framework. On the one hand, hybridology is clearly a positive step from transitology. Hybridology escaped from one set of false presuppositions, and showed that "transitional stations" can indeed be terminal ones. It is based on the idea that the new regimes are not what they present themselves to be: behind a democratic façade, there is anti-democratic politics. It is this discrepancy hybridology builds on, breaking with the transitologist approach that would have explained this phenomenon as a teething problem of "uncultured politics," or a temporary deviance resulting from "underdeveloped institutions."

On the other hand, the plethora of new labels for the regime as a whole is still accompanied by the concepts that were developed for the analysis of the elements of liberal democracies. Hybridologists speak about "governments," "parties," "politicians," "checks and balances" and so on. When Russia's Vladimir Putin or Hungary's Viktor Orbán are called politicians, they are immediately put in the same group with the likes of Joe Biden, Emmanuel Macron, and Angela Merkel. Whereas they are completely different kinds of actors who fulfill different positions in their regimes, and exercise different powers over a different scope of actors and institutions.

The indiscriminate use of the language of liberal democracies brings in a number of implicit assumptions, or axioms which are neither questioned nor realized at all. Just as if a zoologist tried to use the language developed for describing fish—such as "gills," "scales," and "fins"—to describe an elephant: saying that is has no gills and fins does not say much about what the elephant substantively is, and recognizing it as a "defective" or even "illiberal fish" that does not live in water also makes little sense.

4.

THE MISLEADING TERMINOLOGICAL FRAMEWORK perpetuates misunderstanding, and replaces exact analysis with endless storytelling. Hybridology argues that, in the hybrid regimes, democratic institutions are reduced to a façade role. In other words, this means that there is *something* in the background that defines the actual dynamics of the political system. But this something cannot be captured properly by the mainstream, Western categories. Within the language of liberal democracy, a scholar can explain specific phenomena of post-communism only through approximations: they must tell their readers the "story" of the phenomenon, that is, the specific context and all the components for which they can use Western terms with specifying adjectives and prefixes only. It is this storytelling method that leads to the excessive use of qualitative methodologies like process tracing, trying to bridge the gap between Western assumptions and post-communist realities. And while qualitative assessments can provide authentic descriptions and valuable insights into the functioning of post-communist regimes, their results are often non-comparable as they are not ordered by statistically interpretable, comparative data.

On the other hand, quantitative data collection is also distorted by the misleading terminological framework. When institutes like Polity and Freedom House publish so-called continuous measures to indicate the state and trend of "democraticness" of the countries of the world, the institutional criteria they focus on are based on Western terminology. These criteria are used to assess the extent of deviation from liberal democracy, on the basis of which each country is assigned a place on the democracy-dictatorship axis. First, here we can see how the open teleology of transitology is being replaced by the hidden teleology of hybridology. While necessary progress toward democracy is no longer presumed, post-communist regimes are still judged against a democratic ideal. Recognizing "the lack of" certain democratic features implies an expectation, introducing normative bias into positive, descriptive analysis. Second, focusing on a predetermined set of democratic features conceals possible structural differences of the analyzed regimes. The language of liberal democracy prevents the recognition of real *sui generis* features, and it allows for the analysis of post-communist regimes just as if they were Western ones.

5.

THREE AXIOMS NEED TO BE DISSOLVED to lay the foundations of a conceptual framework for the analysis of post-communist regimes. The first axiom of the mainstream comparative approach holds that the separation of spheres of social action is completed. In his study "Political Corruption" (2004), German sociologist Claus Offe distinguishes three spheres of social action: political, economic, and communal. When hybridology focuses only on political institutions, it implicitly presumes that the center of a regime is, as in Western societies, a political sphere with its own, autonomous logic. If the separation is completed, economic logic is separate from political one, and it refers to the specific rationale of entrepreneurs, who may cooperate with politicians as autonomous actors through transparent, regulated, and normative channels. What if there are no autonomous economic and political spheres, and the actions and motivations of political actors are not confined to the political sphere?

The second axiom holds that the *de jure* position of persons and institutions coincides with their *de facto* position. When hybridology recognizes actors like Putin and Orbán as "president" and "prime minister," respectively, it implicitly presumes that they can be described by their legal titles, or that the powers they have and the function they fulfill in the regime are those assigned to their *de jure* formal position in the constitution. Similarly, concepts like "entrepreneur" or "capitalist" used for post-communist economic actors implies they can actually use their capital, or exercise their *de jure* property rights freely. What if one's formal, legal standing does not coincide with sociological reality?

The third axiom holds that the state is an actor pursuing the common good. When hybridology speaks about "right-wing" or "left-wing" actors, it implicitly presumes that they are ideology-driven, and aim at carrying out a social vision, which in turn may lead to public policy "mistakes." At the same time, corruption is also treated as a deviance: a result of wrong or deficient legal frameworks that dishonest administrators and private actors exploit. "Opportunity makes the thief," we may say. What if the case is the other way around: if the thief makes the opportunity, that is, if the ruling elite organizes corruption, and therefore "policy mistakes" and corrupt acts of "misconduct" are not deviances that the government tries to eliminate but system-constituting features?

Dissolving Axiom #1: Stubborn Structures and the Region's Development

6.

REGIME TYPE DEPENDS ON the separation of spheres of social action as it manifests in the culture and norms of the actors who populate the regime. The level of separation of spheres appears differently on the level of actors and the level of institutions. When we talk about actors, the separation of spheres means their informal understanding of their roles, actions, and motives being confined to certain spheres. For example, in a liberal democracy, there exists a distinction between a politician's obligation to the state and obligation to the family.

This kind of separation is reinforced on the level of institutions: the formally assigned role of a politician is to engage in the acquisition and use of legitimate authority, whereas entrepreneurs engage in the contract-based pursuit of acquisitive interests within the framework of legal rules. The relationship between the two spheres is regulated, and the actors also act by their separate logic: the politician focuses on political power, the entrepreneur focuses on profitability.

Yet it needs to be seen that the regime is operated by the actors themselves, and its institutions can function only as far as they are respected by the actors who need to operate them. If the norms of the actors predominantly reflect the same separation as the formal institutions of the regime, the regime is sustainable. Otherwise, actors will operate formal institutions according to their own informal norms—as it often happened when formal institutions of liberal democracy were established after the regime change. If the prevailing regime presumes a different level of separation than its actors, then it will (a) either be weak and prone to degenerate into a more feasible type or (b) have to institute specific (effective) mechanisms to avoid degeneration. The lack of separation of spheres of social action appears in the form of certain, often only informally existing stubborn social structures in the countries of the region.

7. **STUBBORN STRUCTURES ARE DEFINED by the past: not just the legacy of communism, but the culture of the region's countries which is linked to their civilizational belonging.** When we talk about civilizations, we consider the boundaries described by Samuel P. Huntington in *The Clash of Civilizations* (1996), but we grasp the functioning of civilizations through the revised, more valid theory of Peter J. Katzenstein.

In *Civilizations in World Politics* (2010), Katzenstein explains that there are multiple civilizations in the world, but they are also internally plural and are in constant change. What still unites the countries of each civilization under the slogan of "unity in diversity" is two: (1) the specific interactions of the elites of different countries; and (2) the common civilizational identity shared by the population. For the former, Katzenstein highlights the role of civilizational actors (states, empires, political unions) and the techniques they use for "silent spread," copying, and export; for the latter, he shows that people who belong to each civilization develop a particular interpretation of reality, which draws them the lines between "us" and "the others," as well as between "good" and "bad behavior." Civilizational belonging thereby defines culture, and it is a strong determinant of the social norm of the (lack of) separation of spheres as well.

Applying civilizational theory to our region, we can follow the footsteps of the Hungarian historian Jenő Szűcs, who spoke of three historically defined regions of Europe ("The Three Historical Regions of Europe," 1983). In a similar way, we speak about three historical regions of the former Soviet empire: the Western Christian region, which included the Baltic and Central European states outside the Soviet Union; the Eastern Orthodox region, made up of the Soviet republics of Europe and Bulgaria, Georgia, Macedonia, Romania, and Serbia; and finally, the Islamic historical region, which includes the former Soviet republics of Central Asia (Figure 2). In terms of the separation of spheres of social action, the deeper we go into Orthodox and Islamic civilizations, the less a separation is observed between the rulers and the ruled assets (to use Weber's categories). The three historical regions adopted the communist system in different ways, and later, after its fall, they also had different adaptation potential for the establishment of the institutional system of liberal democracy.

Figure 2: Civilizations in post-communist Eurasia. (Legend: Right-to-left diagonal: Western Christianity; horizontal: Eastern Orthodoxy; dotted: Islamic; vertical: Sinic; left-to-right diagonal: Buddhist; grey: outside the post-communist region we consider.)

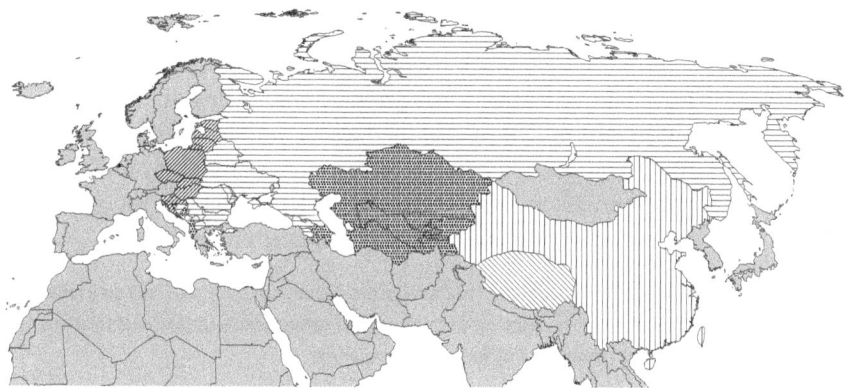

IN PRE-COMMUNIST TIMES, THE SEPARATION OF SPHERES followed civilizational boundaries. A comparison of the feudal societies that populated the three historical regions up until the 19th and 20th centuries reveals that the countries that belonged to Western Christianity showed a greater degree of the separation of spheres of social action than feudal states belonging to Eastern Orthodox and Islamic civilizations.

Absolutism could take firm root on the territory of imperial Russia, as well as the Chinese empire which was the core of the Sinic civilization. In contrast, greater respect of the autonomy of certain social groups (like the aristocracy, clergy, and merchants), individualism, and plural power structures (like the pluralism of spiritual and temporal authority) were constituent parts of most societies of the Western-Christian civilization. Hence the emergence of the omnipotent authority of a single lord was hindered.

On the other hand, the lack of separation of spheres of social action appeared in a formalized form in all feudal states of the region. These structures manifested in a series of interrelated and mutually supportive phenomena, depicted on Figure 3. On the left side of the figure, we can follow the chain of phenomena regarding personal relations: traditional (feudal) networks, which indicated a formalized version of the lack of separation of spheres with economic institutions still embedded in feudal political and legal structures; and patronalism, which refers to a pyramid-like hierarchy with the personalized exchange of concrete rewards and punishments through chains of actual acquaintance (as opposed to abstract, impersonal concepts such as ideological belief or economic class). On the right side of the figure, we can follow the chain of institutional phenomena: collusion of power and ownership, which means the lack of autonomy of the economy from the ruler, often based on the latter's monopoly on land; and patrimonialism, which refers to the treatment of society as a private domain by those who hold political power.

Figure 3: The logic of basic structures of pre-communist societies. (Dark grey represents the root cause, medium grey represents the consequences for personal relations, and light grey represents institutional consequences.)

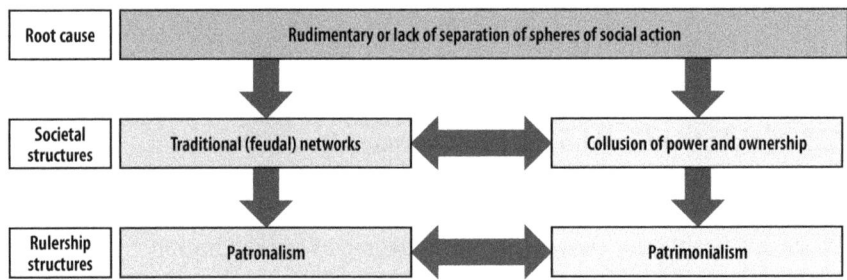

9.

IN COMMUNIST TIMES, COUNTRIES OF DIFFERENT CIVILIZATIONS were put under the "political lid" of dictatorship. The communist system brought its own series of interrelated phenomena that represented a merger of spheres of social action, reinforcing the preexisting patterns of (the lack of) separation (Figure 4). The framework of totalitarian communist ideology and established order liquidated the independence of the three spheres of social action, private property, the private sphere, and autonomous communities, uniting them in a single bureaucratic form. The traditional patronal networks of feudalism were replaced by a bureaucratic patronal network, the nomenklatura, whereas the collusion of power and property took the form of the monopoly of state ownership of the means of production.

Different kinds of communism developed in different civilizations, in accordance with Proposition 6. Most notable are the reform models of communism that appeared in the Western-Christian historical region: the Yugoslav model, in which most enterprises were notionally owned by employees' collectives, which also gained self-management rights in the 1950s; and the Hungarian model, where the private ownership of some small owners was tolerated and even property rights were protected to a certain extent after the reforms of 1968. Both reform models aimed at resolving the rigidity that followed from the bureaucratic coordination of the economy.

However, the one-party system and the unquestionably state-dominated, centrally planned economy induced similar social phenomena, and homogenized the countries to some degree. In terms of the separation of spheres of social action, while the establishment of the communist system impacted Central Eastern Europe as a regression, going further East it meant that the process of separation was arrested and frozen.

Figure 4: The internal logic of communist systems. (Dark grey represents the root cause, medium grey represents the consequences for personal relations, and light grey represents institutional consequences.)

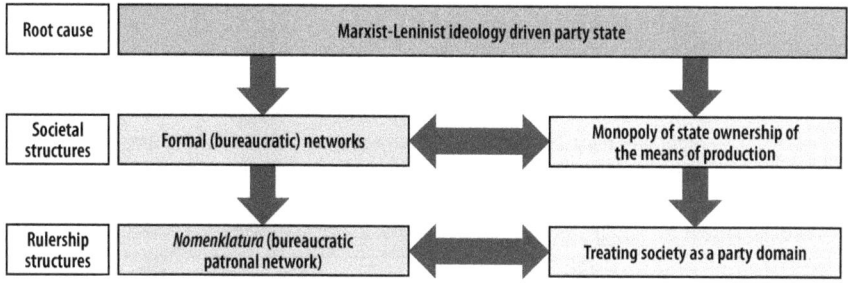

10. IN POST-COMMUNIST TIMES, REGIME CHANGES INVOLVED the change of the formal institutional setting but not of the actors' informal understanding of the separation of spheres of social action. The rudimentary or lack of separation of spheres of social action is the basic reason why post-communist regimes should not be treated automatically as if they were Western. Indeed, such an analytical viewpoint carries an illusion, a postulate of pastlessness, which disregards the social history of post-communist regimes and presumes that an ideal, Western-type political system of liberal democracy can be raised on any ruins of communism. The assumption is that, irrespective of prevalent value structures, such an undertaking would be merely a question of a propitious historical moment and political will. But the autonomously shifting "tectonic plates" of historically determined value structures do not support just any odd political construction one might want to establish.

Liberal democracy was feasible only in countries where the actors' informal understanding was to separate the spheres of social action (Proposition 6). The more unseparated spheres were produced by civilizational belonging (Propositions 7-8) and the influence of the communist regime on the level of actors (Proposition 9), the more stubbornly the social and domineering structures of the previous systems were present in the new system. Stubborn structures took on new forms in adapting to the institutional system of democracy: informal networks, as opposed to traditional and bureaucratic networks; adopted political families, which are informal patronal hierarchies as opposed to earlier patronalism that was linked to formal, feudal, and party nomenklatura; the collusion of power and property also continued to exist informally, in an illegal way, bypassing the legal framework; and patrimonialization, meaning the ruling elite treats public institutions as private domain while maintaining the façade of democracy (Figure 5).

Figure 5: Schematic depiction of the effect of the stubborn structures. (Dark grey represents the root cause, medium grey represents the consequences for personal relations, light grey represents institutional consequences, and the lightest grey represents the systemic distortion following the two lines of consequences.)

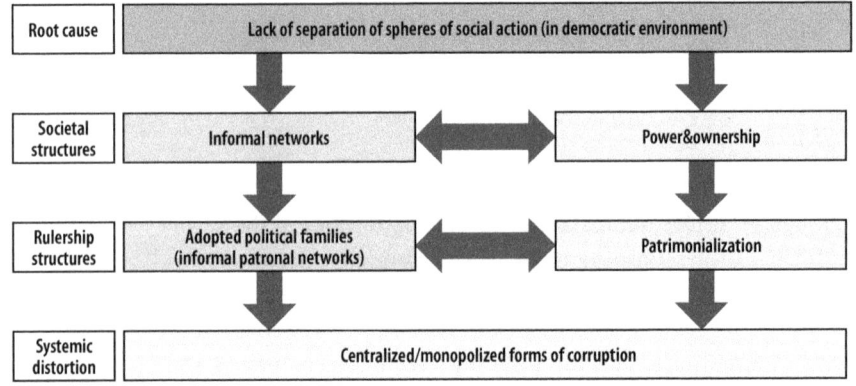

The lack of separation of spheres clearly manifest in the prevalence of power&ownership *(vlast&sobstvenost)*: there is no power without ownership and there is no ownership without power. As informal patronal networks dominate the political landscape, corruption is not eliminated or treated as a deviation from the norms but monopolized and operated centrally.

11.

THE STRONG PRESENCE OF STUBBORN STRUCTURES only determined the emergence of patronal regimes—not whether they are democratic or autocratic. A patronal regime can be "single-pyramid," which refers to one patronal network dominating with other networks being subjugated, marginalized or eliminated; or "multi-pyramid," where multiple networks compete, each representing roughly equal power and neither being strong enough to dominate the others. Single-pyramid patronal regimes, like Hungary, Russia, and Kazakhstan, can be regarded as autocracies; while the plural, multi-pyramid patronal regimes like Bulgaria, Romania, and Ukraine are democracies.

Which type a country moved to after the collapse of communism depended on various factors. On the level of institutions, two elements hindered autocratic breakthrough: the presence of divided executive power and proportionate electoral system. In contrast to the purely presidential setup, a system with divided executive power can offer more institutional possibilities for competing networks to keep each other in check, establishing more democratic conditions as they settle around the positions of president and prime minister as key seats of executive power. Similarly, a proportionate electoral system is normally able to make sure that no single political actor acquires a constitutional majority, or the exclusive opportunity to decide who staffs the key institutions guaranteeing the system of checks and balances.

Democratic development of some countries in the region was further supported by Western linkage and leverage, mainly through US democracy assistance, foreign capital inflows, and the conditions of EU accession. After accession, however, the EU's system of conditions lost their disciplinary power, and even before accession, they resulted in liberal democracy only in countries where stubborn structures were not strongly present. Where patronal legacy was dominant, Western linkage and leverage brought to life various techniques of camouflage rather than actual democratization.

12. A NEW REGIME TYPOLOGY IS NEEDED **for the post-communist region to simultaneously reflect on the order of political institutions and the stubborn structures.** To capture the form of political institutions, we can use the basic regime ideal types of János Kornai ("The System Paradigm Revisited," 2019): democracy, where the government can be removed through a peaceful and civilized procedure, and the institutions which concertedly guarantee accountability are well-established; autocracy, where institutions which could concertedly guarantee accountability are weak; and dictatorship, where no legal parliamentary opposition exists (only one party runs for elections). As Figure 1 showed, these ideal types can be placed on the democracy-dictatorship axis and used as points of reference for the identification of concrete regimes.

To reflect on the stubborn structures as well, we need to expand the democracy-dictatorship axis, which can be done by doubling Kornai's regime categories. Hence we reach a typology of six ideal-type regimes: Western-type liberal democracy based on pluralist power and the dominance of formal institutions (e.g., Estonia); patronal democracy based on pluralistic competition but of patron-client networks (e.g., Romania, Ukraine); patronal autocracy, dominated by a single-pyramid patronal network that breaks pluralism and embodies the unconstrained informal power of a chief patron in the political and economic spheres (e.g., Hungary, Russia); conservative autocracy where the political sphere is patronalized but the economic sphere is not (e.g., Poland); communist dictatorship that merged politics and the economy through the classical, bureaucratic patronal network (e.g., the Soviet Union before 1989); and finally, market-exploiting dictatorship that maintains one-party system but operates the private economy in various forms (e.g., China).

With the help of the six ideal types, we can expand the democracy-dictatorship continuum into a triangular conceptual space, in which the countries of the region can be placed (Figure 6).

Figure 6: The conceptual space of regimes, with six ideal-types and twelve post-communist examples (as of 2022).

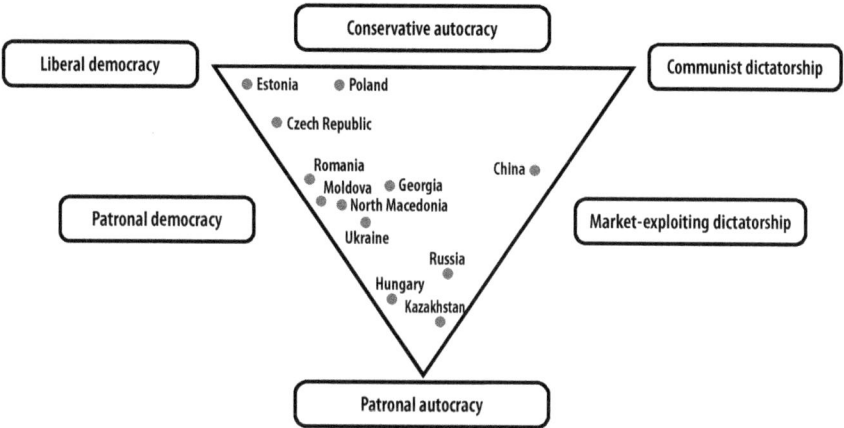

Dissolving Axiom #2: Formality and Informality

13.

DE JURE AND DE FACTO POSITIONS of post-communist elites do not coincide due to informal patronalism, which allows them to act beyond their formal sphere of social action. The separation of spheres of social action is guaranteed if the actors of different spheres mutually respect each other's autonomy. If the relations between the actors remain voluntary, neither of them is made to serve the will of another, and therefore they can follow their separate rationales. The situation is changed if horizontal relationships are replaced by vertical, patron-client relations. Table 1 summarizes the key dimensions by which post-communist patronal relations can be distinguished from Western-type non-patronal relations.

First, post-communist patronal relations are dominantly informal: they exist not by virtue of bureaucratic, legally defined dependence but the *de facto* power a patron disposes over and can use to extort their client. This leads us to the second point: non-patronal relations involve normative rules and impersonally provided benefits or punishments to certain groups, while patrons in patronal relations select between actors on a personal and discretional basis. Rewards as well as punishments are meted out with the exclusive, personal authorization of the patron and by targeting the client, a person or an organization directly.

Third, patronal systems place decision-making power into the hands of a single actor, the patron, and therefore authorization held or given in these systems is personal. This is in contrast to Western-type liberal democracies, which are characterized by collective authorization and decision-making (i.e., bodies decide instead of particular people) precisely to uphold impersonality and avoid arbitrary decision-making. Finally, in liberal democracies private or public organizations develop through bureaucratic, institutional chains with several levels of formally defined actors and corresponding procedures. In contrast, in patronal regimes the organizations characterized by informal patronal relations depend on clientelist, personal chains.

As a result of informal patronalism, actors who are *de jure* confined to the political sphere can act beyond their formal competences, and exercise power in the other spheres where their clients are located. *De facto*, such actors act as members of an informal network that coexists with formal institutions, and they follow the unwritten norms and interests of the network rather than the expectations of the formal, constitutional order.

Table 1: Contrasting non-patronal and patronal relations.

	NON-PATRONAL	**PATRONAL**
Institutions	formal	informal
Regulations	normative	discretionary
Authorization	collective (authorization)	personal (authorization)
Command	bureaucratic / institutional chains	clientelist / personal chains

14. Major economic actors become oligarchs if their formal economic power is accompanied by informal political power.

The oligarch is the most important player in the economic sphere, which is not separated from the sphere of political action. The oligarch uses their legitimate fortune to also build political power: the economic power is public, but the political power is kept hidden. While it is customary to refer to the lobbying major entrepreneurs of liberal democracies as "oligarchs," the two indeed sharply differ. First, the major entrepreneur uses a regulated, formalized framework to lobby, and enters into voluntary deals with the politician, in which both parties aim at solidifying their elite positions in their own sphere of social action. Such is the situation in the U.S., where business groups try to influence state regulations of the economy and provide campaign support for the parties in exchange in a formalized system of lobbying.

The relations dominantly influencing an oligarch's economic activity, however, are informal and patronal. In countries like Russia and Kazakhstan, oligarchs do not lobby and make competing offers to politicians but are given a position from the top down by the head of the network, the chief patron. Second, the major entrepreneur enjoys normative state regulations and non-excludable favors. In the case of a tariff, for example, every domestic producer gains from lower intensity of competition, and the regulation cannot be made in a way that it prefers only some chosen actors. An oligarch, in contrast, may enjoy discretional regulations and excludable favors, with special laws and informal practices targeted to certain people or companies (Proposition 81).

Third, the major entrepreneur on a free market becomes "major" through technical/organizational innovation, and remaining "major" does not depend on their personal allegiance to a *de jure* political actor: they can remain profitable without political favors, let alone the personal favors of a particular politician. Post-communist oligarchs often obtained leading positions in the economy irrespective of market innovation, securing monopoly grants with political/patronal support. In Russia, many of the early oligarchs were recruited from the former communist nomenklatura, whose members got exclusive rights in the first stages of economic reform. According to sociologists Iván and Szonja Szelényi ("Circulation or Reproduction of Elites during the Postcommunist Transformation of Eastern Europe", 1995), 81 percent the former economic nomenklatura were still in economic elite positions in 1993, while the corresponding numbers in the case of Poland and Hungary were 57 and 29 percent, respectively. Later, the oligarchs in Russia achieved (or could keep) positions in media, natural resource production, and other industries by the decision of the chief patron, Vladimir Putin.

Living in a single-pyramid system, the oligarchic position of these people depends on their patronal allegiance. In general, we can say that the more an economic actor's success is the result of discretional, patronal rewards rather than competitiveness and market performance, the less the actor is able to keep and build a fortune autonomously. When the profitability of an oligarch depends on political actors maintaining privileges, their informal political connections are necessary to maintain their economic elite status—and those connections can be revoked one-sidedly from the political sphere. In other words, oligarchs in a patronal autocracy are not capitalist in the Western sense: as the Russian joke holds, they are not billionaires but people working as billionaires.

The chief patron can "dismiss" them, stripping an oligarch of their privileges and *de jure* property. While oligarchs are formally autonomous owners, their *de jure* status does not coincide with the *de facto* sociological reality.

15.

Major political actors become poligarchs if their formal political power is accompanied by informal economic power. When political actors become patrons in informal patronal networks, their rationale is no longer separated political logic but the political-economic rationale of power concentration and personal-wealth accumulation. To paraphrase Max Weber, they handle their authority as economic opportunities they appropriated in their private interest. Hence the category of poligarch, which is a mirror concept to the oligarch: their political power is public, but their economic power is kept hidden.

Although their personal wealth is secured from their political position and decisions, the poligarch's illegitimate financial advantages far overstep the limits of privileged allowances that could be related to their position and revenues from classical corruption. In a democracy, a politician may be bribed and involved in various types of corrupt acts. Typically, such cases are initiated by private actors like (major) entrepreneurs in a bottom-up fashion, whereby the entrepreneur gets favorable treatment from the state and a bribe is given to the politician, who uses it for his own consumption or perhaps to reinforce his position in the public sphere. But the entrepreneur does not become a politician and the politician does not become an entrepreneur. They simply become corrupt.

In an informal patronal network, it is not the bribe that connects corrupt actors to each other. First, the poligarch does not receive bribe money to carry out corrupt acts but extorts protection money from the subordinated clients. They, in turn, may not receive any extra payment for carrying out the patron's decisions but simply avoid discretional punishments. Second, a powerful poligarch can engage in predation, taking over companies from disloyal or outsider actors and giving them to the loyal clients (Proposition 84). The benefit of the poligarch in the case of predation is the company itself, which becomes his *de facto* property in the sphere of market action via the clients he disposes over.

The poligarch receives money not as bribe but as dividend, a legalized rent reached through the application of illegal means.

De jure, the poligarch appears as a high-ranking politician, confined to the political sphere; *de facto*, the poligarch enters the economic sphere and also establishes land leases, real estate possessions, pseudo-civil organizations or foundations sourced from public funds, and a network of companies through economic front men who legally stand for his illegally acquired property and authority.

16. **THE ECONOMIC FRONT MAN is an actor who has formal economic power but cannot use it according to their own will.** Neither liberal democracies nor communist dictatorships necessitate front men. For in those regimes, everyone is simply who they are, be it as defined by the rule of law or by compulsion. The nature of power and its legitimation coincide: this was typical in the various historical predecessors of patronal systems as well. After all, the feudal landlord did not hang upon the acknowledgment of his vassals, and he could as a matter of course hold his goods and estate publicly to be his own. In a communist dictatorship, people in the positions defined by the nomenklatura were exactly what the official, formal position said. Neither one nor the other system required extra players to bridge the gap between the formal position and the actual competences.

In patronal regimes, however, front men are used both in the economic and the political sphere. Economic front men act in the economic sphere but they are clients in a patronal network, subordinated to the will of a patron who disposes over their formal authorization. Unlike voluntary relations between spheres in liberal democracies, patronal relations change the sociological character of political and economic actors: the *de jure* ownership of the economic actor's property is *de facto* exercised by their political patron (Table 2).

Several ideal types of front men can be distinguished, one of the key differentiating features being the rights they can exercise. In the case of low- and mid-profile front men, *de jure* and *de facto* property rights are completely detached: formal ownership remains little more than dead letter as the front man has no autonomy vis-à-vis their patron who actually exercises these rights. The main function of these front men is the legal personalization of the patron's accumulated wealth: to keep formally the wealth of a patron who could not legally own it. The situation is only slightly different in the case of a high-profile front man, who takes on the role of operating the patronal companies as well. By allowing to exercise certain *de jure* rights, the patron actually delegates his right to access and manage his *de facto* property. But the rights to withdrawal, exclusion and alienation remain in the hands of the patron, who exercises them through the front man via informal ties.

Table 2: Property rights of economic and political actors in a liberal democracy and patronal autocracy.

		Liberal democracy		Patronal autocracy			
		De jure ownership = *de facto* ownership		*De jure* ownership =/= *de facto* ownership			
Property rights		Entrepreneur	Politician	Front man (low/mid-profile)	Front man (high-profile)	Oligarch	Poligarch (chief patron)
Use rights	Access	+	-	-	+	+	+
	Withdrawal	+	-	-	-	+ -	+
Control rights	Management	+	-	-	+	+	+
	Exclusion	+	-	-	-	+ -	+
	Alienation	+	-	-	-	+ -	+

17. INFORMAL PATRONALISM OF THE RULING ELITE **is a regime-specific phenomenon that distinguishes post-communist patronal regimes from other settings.** The ruling elite is the power network that involves all the actors who have political power over the operation of the state machinery. If the axiom of the coincidence of *de jure* and *de facto* status is upheld, the ruling elite must be comprised of the formal holders of power. This is true in the case of two of the three polar type regimes from the above-mentioned triangular framework: liberal democracy and communist dictatorship (Table 3). Both being characterized by the dominance of formal institutions, the main decision-makers in these regimes are members of political parties, and belonging to the power network requires formal political ties to a party and/or the government.

However, the ruling elite in a liberal democracy is multi-pyramid and non-patronal. It is a constrained political elite with numerous autonomous factions, and the actors are bound to act within a constitutional framework. In a communist dictatorship, the Marxist-Leninist state party aims to engineer society by the means of state coercion, from which it follows the expansion of state power in the form of a bureaucratic single-pyramid patronal network. This network, the communist nomenklatura is a register of ruling positions, including party positions—the political decision-makers on national and local level—and administrative positions—decision-makers in state companies and other places where central plans are executed.

In the nomenklatura, it is formal positions that exist primarily and chosen people are assigned these positions secondarily. In other words, the bureaucratic setting is more permanent than the list of the people who are chosen to fill it. In the ruling elite of patronal autocracies, the case is the other way around: it is the patronal network, the so-called adopted political family and its members, which are primary. In fact, the network typically comes into being outside the state as a hierarchy of actors from various spheres, and once they seize power, formal positions are tailored to the family or the wishes of its members.

The adopted political family is a largely informal phenomenon, meaning not only that its effective hierarchy is situated outside (or above) the formal institutions of the state, but also that the adopted political family has no legal form. It is a conglomerate of political actors (party leaders, members of parliament, governors, judges, general prosecutors, leaders of the tax office etc.) and economic actors (oligarchs with key firms, banks, media, private and corporate philanthropic organizations etc.), all of which are tied together by an informal hierarchy based on unconditional personal loyalty to the chief patron, who enforces obedience by the discretional use of state authority. The actual decisions are removed from the—nevertheless strictly controlled—bodies of the "ruling" party and the government, and actors with no formal state power but strong informal ties to the chief patron may have more influence on state decisions than certain party leaders and ministers who are just political front men (Proposition 19).

Table 3: Main features of ruling elites in the three polar type regimes.

Constrained political elite (as in liberal democracy)	Adopted political family (as in patronal autocracy)	Nomenklatura (as in communist regime)
non-patronal network	informal patronal network	bureaucratic patronal network
multi-pyramid system	single-pyramid system	single-pyramid system
dominance of formal institutions	dominance of informal institutions	dominance of formal institutions

18. THE *DE FACTO* CENTER OF POWER is the chief patron, accompanied by the patron's court in a patronal autocracy. The chief patron is a poligarch and the ultimate decision-maker in a patronal autocracy. His word is law in political and economic matters, while others may decide on such issues insofar as they are authorized by the chief patron or act under his radar in mundane, less significant issues where the chief patron decides not to interfere. This central position stems not from his formal status but his informal one. Formally, the chief patron usually fulfills the position of head of executive, president or prime minister, whereas informally he is the leader of the single-pyramid patronal network.

Unlike the prime minister or president of a liberal democracy, the chief patron does not "govern": he *disposes over* people, status, and wealth in all three spheres of social action. His exercise of authority does not conform to or limited by his formal authorization. Naturally, a chief patron uses his *de jure* competences as well, but they are *de facto* extended as he colonizes state institutions in all branches of power with personal loyalists. Having them as clients, the chief patron can use state power by his whim, and distribute rewards and punishments in a discretional manner to political, economic, and communal actors.

Closeness to the chief patron, particularly direct contact with him can grant decision-making power to others, gaining the chief patron's trust and authorization. The "patron's court" is comprised of the closest circle of decision-makers, some of them with formal political positions (like poligarchs) and others without it (like certain oligarchs). An example is provided by a classic study of Stephen White and Olga Kryshtanovskaya ("Inside the Putin Court," 2005). The paper describes Putin's three "tables": first, the Presidential cabinet, attended by the President with members of the government, that is, a decision-making body reflecting the pattern of the formalized government structure; second, the Security Council, the composition of which does not coincide with bureaucratic boundaries, and it is attended by people from various branches of power: the presidential cabinet, government, secret service organizations, the prosecutor's office etc.; and third, the so-called "tea-drinking group," which consists of Putin's personal "friends," including both leading officials and people without formal authority or political position whatsoever.

Under such circumstances, the institutions of public authority cease to be the sites where real decisions are taken, those having been removed from the institutions and transferred to the decision-making pool of the inner circle, the highest level of the adopted political family. The patron's court is in sharp contrast to a royal court, a democratic cabinet, or the communist politburo as it lacks formal structure and legitimacy. As the adopted political family is an informal network, the patron's court is also an informal body, although "membership" in this inner circle is what matters in terms of *de facto* decision-making power, not one's *de jure*, formal position.

THE *DE JURE* HOLDER OF POWER, the ruling party becomes a transmission-belt party in a patronal autocracy. Before the collapse of the Soviet Union, the Marxist-Leninist party, as the holder of power, had transmission belt organizations by which it transmitted its will to the people and oiled the mechanisms of implementation (like the trade unions, women's association etc.). In patronal autocracies, the ruling party becomes a transmission belt of the informal patronal network, the adopted political family. Its function is to channel the decisions made in informal bodies into the realm of formal, legitimate institutions of political governance.

Laws are not made, policies are not formulated, and the country is not steered in a certain direction by the party. It ceases to be the regime's central actor: that role is taken up by the patron's court, an informal body which gains formal legitimacy to the realization of its will by means of the mediation of the party. After all it functions behind the scenes of democracy, where the party itself is a political front man—a subordinate, secondary entity where no autonomous decisions are made.

It follows from this that there are no internal factions or "cleavages" within the party as such. While factions are everyday in a democratic party, and even a communist state party might have sometimes a "reform branch" or other, value- or interest-based informal alliances between formal members, such phenomena are non-existent in a transmission-belt party. For the party is a simple executor: not a politician's party but a vassals' party where members with only *de jure* competences have no *de facto* powers that could be united for a common goal in a faction. Conflicts might arise only between members of the adopted political family, and the fights that seem to be between formal members of the party are, in fact, linked to the internal matters of the informal patronal network.

The wealth of the oligarchs and poligarchs is not party wealth either. They have personal allegiance to the chief patron, not bureaucratic allegiance to the party leadership. Matters of accumulation are not decided on in formal party bodies, which have no jurisdiction over the money or the companies belonging to the adopted political family.

20. THE PROFESSIONAL STATE BUREAUCRACY of public servants becomes a domain of patronal servants in a patronal autocracy.

The rule of the informal patronal network and the corresponding supremacy of informal norms over formal ones brings about the top-down demolition of the professional bureaucratic administration, as it was described by Max Weber in *Economy and Society*.

The "clearly defined sphere of competence subject to impersonal rules" are loosened; the political appointees handle a great variety of roles in the adopted political family, within the legitimate sphere of administration: front man, governor, commissar, steward, treasurer, etc., expressions that describe the real functions of their roles more accurately in sociological terms, than would the official definitions of the administrative positions. The "rationally established hierarchy" is disrupted; the affiliates of the adopted political family traverse the lower and higher regions of public administration freely. The normative system of "a regular system of appointment on the basis of free contract, and orderly promotion" is disassembled; total political cleansing is carried out, the realignment of the whole professional apparatus by a variety of means, as well as the replacement of the normative system of promotion by discretional decision-making mechanisms. "Technical training as a regular requirement" is relativized; when necessary, peculiar exemptions pave the way for the positions that previously had strict prerequisites in terms of professional training. Allowances and property entitlements added on to "fixed salaries" as we rise through the hierarchy are increasingly in domains well past legal sources of income.

The bureaucracy of patronal servants contrasts to the communist bureaucracy of apparatchiks as well. Beyond the usual difference between formality (communist dictatorship) and informality (patronal autocracy), we should also note that an apparatchik follows the line which the party dictates, and they are loyal to the party as an organization. As Hungarian historian Miklós Szabó often noted in his lectures, "the good communist firmly fluctuates with the party." In turn, the patronal servant proves their goodness, and loyalty to the (chief) patron, by stepping over the formal (legal) rules on the patron's order. It is not just organizational loyalty being replaced by personal loyalty: making the patronal servant commit illegal acts, which are persecuted only if the chief patron wants them to, creates the informal subordination the patron-client network of the mafia state depends on. While in a liberal democracy a bureaucrat is fired if he commits a crime, in a patronal autocracy he is fired if he fails to commit the crime he is ordered to commit, and thus fails to be compromisable in the case of disloyalty.

21.

THE OPERATION AND COORDINATION OF THE INFORMAL NETWORK necessitates the involvement of two types of informal actors: the patron's hand, and corruption brokers. Although in a patronal autocracy everyone is subject ultimately to the will of the chief patron, he cannot be everywhere. Rather, the co-ordination of the political-economic network of clients is coordinated through informal trustees. The "patron's hand," referred to in Russian as *smotryasciy* (literally "watcher"), acts on behalf of the chief patron, overseeing and instructing the various state and non-state entities belonging to the adopted political family. "In Putin's sistema," sociologists Alena Ledeneva and Claudia Baez-Camargo write, "state institutions are controlled through his 'core contacts', 'curators' and highly personalized monitoring and reporting practices within Putin's networks. Such control practices penetrate also non-state companies, which are likely to be informally supervised by 'parachuters' — people appointed over the heads of their formal bosses and personally connected to the political leadership." ("Where Does Informality Stop and Corruption Begin?," 2017, 63).

On the other hand, the corruption broker connects participants of a corrupt transaction as a mediator, or legitimizes the illegitimate business deal as a judicial expert. Two main types may be distinguished by their function and *de jure* position. First, there are the so-called gatekeepers, who are corruption brokers within the public administration employed to ensure the bureaucratic background and protection of illegitimate deals. In non-patronal, classical corruption, they are the official of the bureaucracy as posited by Max Weber, who is led astray by an occasional commission. With the establishment of the patronal autocracy, however, not only the appointment of the official in charge but orders for continued activity as a corruption broker also come from above. Gatekeepers thus include heads of law enforcement bodies, members of tender boards, judges etc.

The other significant type of corruption broker is the corruption designer, whose function is to find and provide the appropriate legal-institutional *(de jure)* form to the *(de facto)* corrupt intentions. Corruption designers can be individuals, like in cases of corruption brokers managing (international) laundromat schemes, or firms, the main function of which is to facilitate the process of transferring governmental monies to private hands. In the latter case, the function is fulfilled by law firms, tender writing companies, project management companies etc.

22. INFORMAL PATRONALISM IS DIFFERENT FROM INFORMALITY IN COMMUNIST DICTATORSHIPS because it grants power to those outside the formal hierarchy. In communist dictatorships, informal relations existed between the members of the nomenklatura in the form of personal relations, informal oral commands, and handshake agreements. Yet such relations were formed inside the formal network, that is, between *de jure* members of the nomenklatura and respecting the bureaucratic hierarchy of the party. The classical literature of "Kremlinology," while studying leader-

ship conflict and the differences in the level of power between those in positions of power that are formally on an identical level, cannot disregard the fact that even the very question of informal power makes sense only within a formalized party structure. For without being a member of the political committee, no one can exercise real power and influence decision-making, and being removed from this political committee is concomitant with the loss of prerogatives of power.

In contrast, informal patronalism overrules formal institutions. Informal relations do not presuppose the formal rank of the actor and may enable someone with no political position to have political power. Informal ties are formed between those with as well as without formal power, and the resultant network extends beyond the boundaries of the formal institutional setting. An adopted political family involves various kinds of poligarchs, oligarchs, and front men, permeating a wide range of institutions in the political sphere (from parliamentary factions through secret service to judicial bodies), the economic sphere (from corporations through foundations to giant financial and industrial conglomerates), and the communal sphere (from *de facto* governmental NGOs, or GONGOs, to the client church). In some cases, formal party membership overlaps with the belonging to the adopted political family, but it is far from necessary. Informal patronal networks use formal institutions to the extent they are needed, but otherwise informality replaces formality as the primary determinant of power, law, and elite behavior. Table 4 summarizes the main differences between communist informality and informal patronalism.

Table 4: Informality in communist dictatorship and patronal autocracy.

Informality…	
in a communist dictatorship (bureaucratic patronal regime)	in a patronal autocracy (informal patronal regime)
informality exists around formal institutions (relations formed between formal members of the politburo)	informality overrules formal institutions (relations between actors with and without formal positions)
no informal power positions (those who have power must have a formal position in the party)	informal power positions (those without formal party or state positions may also have power)
de jure positions entail *de facto* power (members of the politburo are decision-makers)	*de jure* positions may not entail *de facto* power (members of the cabinet may be political front men)

23. **INFORMAL PATRONALISM IS DIFFERENT FROM INFORMALITY IN LIBERAL DEMOCRACIES** because it deprives formal bodies of their *de facto* decision-making role. In liberal democracies, informality may appear on the level of elites in the form of informal agreements, concluded prior to formal (e.g., parliamentary) debates between political actors. However, when politicians agree outside the formal bodies, the point is secrecy, that is, to keep the real motives and bargains from the public. But those who make the decisions *de facto* and *de jure* are the same: the same people who have formal right to decide make the informal deals as well.

In contrast, formal decision-making bodies in patronal autocracies become transmission-belt organizations, deprived of real power in favor of the adopted political family. One set of informally connected people make the decisions, some with *de jure* political power but reaching beyond their formal competences (like a president/prime minister chief patron) and some without *de jure* political power (like inner-circle oligarchs), while others who represent and vote on these decisions in the formal, transparent institutional realm do not do so autonomously, in accordance with their formal authorization.

In a patronal autocracy, it is the informal position that matters: those who are close to the chief patron have decision-making power, with or without formal authority, whereas those inside the party but outside the chief patron's closest circle are not decision-makers, and they are not "politicians" either. While they look like politicians, they indeed are political front men: clients who, just like economic front men, cannot use their formal power autonomously, according to their own will. In their case, the omertà, the code of silence applies even to their rare public appearances, and neither public opinion, nor the politicians of the opposition consider them political actors of authority, who could be held accountable. The people filling most of the functions of public authority in a patronal autocracy can practically be considered the chief patron's political front men, positioned at various levels. Their role is to channel the decisions made outside the legally defined institutions into the legitimate sphere of political action. They constitute the public display of informal governance, and bridge the gap between the formal and informal spheres with their formal position and status. Table 5 summarizes the main differences between informality in liberal democracies and patronal autocracies.

Table 5: Informality in liberal democracy and patronal autocracy.

| Informality… ||
in a liberal democracy (non-patronal regime)	in a patronal autocracy (informal patronal regime)
informality does not deprive formal bodies of their de facto decision-making role (informal deals are made between de jure decision-makers)	formal decision-making bodies become transmission-belt organizations (informally made decisions are being executed by the de jure decision-makers)
informality exists for the sake of secrecy, without overruling formal constraints and roles	informality exists to overrule formal constraints and roles
informal norms exist as the routinization of a cultured "best practice" (informal norms are not coercively imposed)	informality manifests in informal patron-client relations of the adopted political family (informal orders are coercively enforced by the chief patron through the instruments of public authority)

24. **INFORMAL PATRONALISM IS DIFFERENT FROM CRONYISM because it is not a voluntary cooperation of equal parties.** "Crony capitalism" is a catchword for corrupt systems like the post-communist ones, denoting a regime where the leading political elite gives discretional favors to their friends and family members. But the term "friend" or "crony," in the context of corrupt transactions, assumes parties or partners of equal rank (even if acting in different roles) and implies voluntary transactions—occasional, though repeatable—that can be terminated or continued by either party at their convenience, without one party coercing the other into continuing the relationship. There is free entry into the relationship, and there is free exit from it as well. In contrast, there is no free entry to the patronal network, only adoption, being given access, or forced surrender; and no free exit either, only exclusion.

Within the patronal network, people are in a hierarchy composed of vertical chains of command with a strong element of unconditionality and inequality in power. The chief patron can dismiss an oligarch; an oligarch cannot dismiss the chief patron. In a patron-client relation, one of the participants—the client—is a vassal (i.e., subordinate) of the other—the patron, and the head of the network, the chief patron decides on the distribution of wealth and status among the clients.

In a patronal democracy like Ukraine, no patronal network has complete power over the state, and the oligarchs have more options and means to exercise control over political actors (Proposition 40). In a patronal autocracy like Russia, however, it is no longer an open question as to who the leader is, who depends on whom, who gives orders and who executes them. The chief patron is evidently "the boss," and there is no *de facto* elite accountability from the side of the oligarchs. In contrast, cronyism is not a patron-client but more of a "client-client relation" with equal parties who use their informal connection for corrupt transactions only occasionally, on a case-by-case basis and not as part of a corrupt network of regular transactions of (bribe or protection) monies. Permanent chains of vassalage are characteristic of patronal networks, where the patron at the top of the network becomes the central organizer of corruption, or using public resources for private gains (Proposition 86).

Dissolving Axiom #3: From Constitutional State to the Mafia State

25.

DIFFERENT GROUPS OF STATE TYPES CAN BE DEFINED by the motivation of the ruling elite: societal interest, ideology implementation, and elite interest. The state is the institution by which the ruling elite exercises the monopoly of legitimate use of violence to extract, manage, and distribute resources within the borders of a certain territory. The mainstream axiom about the state being committed to the public good is but one opportunity: states can run on various dominant principles, based on the goals, basic program, and attitude of the ruling elite toward governance (Table 6). Identifying different principles of state functioning, we can draw the most fundamental line of division between different concepts of state.

First, concepts such as the "welfare state" and the "night-watchman state" are based on the principle of societal interest. This means that the ruling elite aims at using political power to realize values, an ideology, to further the interests of social groups outside the political sphere and the ruling elite itself (e.g., an economic class). "Societal interest" consists of the particular interests of concrete social groups the ruling elite decides to prioritize, whereas which particular interests are to be served by the state is decided in an open, transparent, and formalized process of public deliberation, involving every interested group of the society (Proposition 43). The basic rights and liberties of the whole population are respected: under this principle, ruling elites try to get political power to realize their goals but do not aim at exclusively possessing it. The rulers compete within the boundaries of the constitutional playing field, and debate over public policy issues based on certain ideological, left- or right-wing positions. If the element of exclusive possession of political power appears, we move from the principle of societal interest to the principle of ideology implementation. This is the case in the party state of a communist dictatorship, where the self-defined societal interest is replaced by a kind of postulated interest, defined by the ideology-driven party state itself.

The third principle in our framework is the principle of elite interest, which consists of the twin motives of power monopolization and personal-wealth accumulation. The ruling elite tries to exclusively possess political power through the extension of formal and informal influence over the political sphere, ensuring unchallengeability (breaking the autonomy and power of competing actors), and this unconstrained power is used to enrich the top of the ruling elite and those in lower levels of its personal (patron-client) network. State concepts from "kleptocracy" through "neopatrimonialism" to the "mafia state" all belong in this group of elite-interest based states, as we discuss below. The key point here is that, due to the stubborn structures resulting in patrimonialization and informal patronal networks (Proposition 10), post-communist countries can be best approached by state concepts based on the principle of elite interest. Post-communist regimes are not "welfare states" in the Western sense, nor "party states" in the old, communist sense: most of them are organized and operated, to varying degrees, by the logic of informal patronalism.

Table 6: Ideal type principles of state functioning (with state concepts as examples).

	Ideology (aiming at using political power to realize values on social level)	**Power monopolization** (aiming at exclusively possessing political power)	**Personal-wealth accumulation** (aiming at using political power for personal enrichment)
Principle of societal interest (e.g., welfare state in a liberal democracy)	X	–	–
Principle of ideology implementation (e.g., party state in a communist dictatorship)	X	X	–
Principle of elite interest (e.g., mafia state in a patronal autocracy)	–	X	X

26.

STATES RUNNING ON THE PRINCIPLE OF ELITE INTEREST can be distinguished by four basic dimensions: actor, action targeting state institutions, action targeting property, and legality. While concepts like "kleptocracy" and "clan state" are well-known, they are often used as synonyms, without a clear definition of the regime framework beneath the regime labels and also without a clear logical order between these categories. Such an order can be created along four basic interpretative layers. At each layer, the concepts are interpreted as degrees on the same scale, where consecutive state types also include the characteristics of the states preceding them in the row (Table 7).

The first question is what the nature of the ruling elite is: in this context we can speak of a state where the ruling elite is dominantly informal in nature (network state); where the ruling elite is not only informal but also a patronal network (patronal state); and where this informal patronal network also embodies the characteristics of a patriarchal family (clan state). The second question is how institutions are appropriated: in this context, we can talk about states that the ruling elite treats as their private domain but in a legitimate way (patrimonial or sultanistic state); and those with which they do the same, but in an illegitimate way, feigning the rule of law behind the formal institutional setting of democracy (neopatrimonial or neosultanistic state).

The third question is how property is appropriated: in this context, we can speak of a state that legally over-taxes and distributes the income from it (rent-seeking state); which does the same illegally (kleptocratic state); and which, in addition to the above-mentioned methods, also carries out predation, i.e., forcible takeover of companies and other non-monetary property for loyal members of the ruling elite by state violence (predatory state). Finally, the last question is what the legal status of elite-interest based action is: in this context, we can speak of a state where corruption, although endemic, is nothing more than bribery, and it is carried out occasionally and mainly by actors in the lower levels of government (corrupt state); where corruption extends to government actors and certain laws are enacted to that effect (captured state); and a state operated by the ruling elite itself as a criminal organization (criminal state).

What needs to be seen with respect to these state types is that they are only partial types: they identify the state only from one aspect while not reflecting on the others. But it is precisely their partial nature that allows us to use them simultaneously, or to combine them to describe an elite-interest based state in its entirety.

Table 7: Conceptualization of states subordinated to elite interests.

	The basis for the term used	Alternative terms used for the description of elite interest in post-communist regimes
1.	Actor	network → patronal → clan state
2.	Action (targeting state institutions)	patrimonial / sultanistic → neopatrimonial / neosultanistic state
3.	Action (targeting property)	rent-seeking → kleptocratic → predatory state
4.	Legality	corrupt → captured → criminal state

27. THE MAFIA STATE IS A STATE THAT COMBINES a clan state, a neopatrimonial state, a predatory state, and a criminal state.

Journalists have used the term "mafia state" for states with close ties to organized crime, and/or ones that are particularly aggressive and use brutal, "mafia-like" methods to keep up their rule. In our scholarly discussion, however, the term is defined in a way that a mafia state does not require any of those characteristics. A mafia state is not a symbiosis of state and organized crime but a state which works like a mafia—and not in terms of illicit activities *per se* but in terms of internal culture and rulership.

Historian Eric Hobsbawn writes in *Primitive Rebels* (1965) that the mafia is an adopted family, "the form of artificial kinship, which implied the greatest and most solemn obligations of mutual help on the contracting parties" (55). At the same time, the mafia he describes is the classical mafia—we may say, a form of organized underworld—which exists in a society established along the lines of modern equality of rights. The patriarchal family in this context is a challenger to the state's monopoly of violence, while the attempt to give sanctions to the powers vested in the family head is being thwarted, as far as possible, by the state organs of public authority.

The mafia state—we may say, the organized upperworld—is a project to sanction the authority of the patriarchal head of the family on the level of a country, throughout the bodies of the democratic institutional system, with an invasion of the powers of state and its set of tools. Compared to the classical mafia, the mafia state realizes the same definitive sociological feature in a different context, making the patriarchal family not a challenger of state sovereignty but the possessor of it. What is achieved by the classical mafia by means of threats, blackmail, and—if necessary—violent bloodshed, in the mafia state is achieved through the bloodless coercion of the state, ruled by the adopted political family.

In terms of the patterns of rulership, the exercise of sovereign power by the "Godfather" (the chief patron), the patriarchal family, the household, the estate, and the country are isomorphic concepts. On all these levels, the same cultural patterns of applying power are followed. Just as the patriarchal head of the family is decisive in instances disposing of personal and property matters, also defining status (the status that regulates all aspects of the personal roles and competencies among the "people of his household"), so the head of the adopted political family is leader of the country, where the reinterpreted nation signifies his "household" (*patrimonium*). He does not govern, but disposes over people; he has a share, he dispenses justice, and imparts some of this share and justice on the "people of his household," his nation, according to their status and merit. Furthermore, in the same way that the classical mafia eliminates "private banditry," the mafia state also sets out to end anarchic corruption, and replace it with a centralized and monopolized enforcement of tribute organized from the top. In essence, the mafia state is the business venture of the adopted political family managed through the instruments of public authority: the privatized form a parasite state. To be more precise, the mafia state combines the features and concepts previously associated with political-economic clans, patrimonialism, predation, and criminality (Table 8).

Table 8: Defining the post-communist mafia state.

	The basis for the term used	The term referring to one certain feature of the mafia state	
1.	Actor	clan state	
2.	Action (targeting power)	neopatrimonial / neosultanistic state	mafia state
3.	Action (targeting property)	predatory state	
4.	Legality	criminal state	

28.

THE MAFIA STATE IS DIFFERENT FROM THE CONSTITUTIONAL STATE of a liberal democracy in the amplitude of arbitrariness of state action. On the one hand, these state types belong to different groups: the mafia state is the state *par excellence* of elite interest, while the constitutional state is the state *par excellence* of societal interest. On the other hand, the main difference between them can be captured by the aspect of normativity: whether state action is dominantly normative, and its effects depend on objective and formal criteria equally applying to everyone (impersonal with no double standard), or it is dominantly discretional, and its effects depend on subjective and informal criteria allowing for different treatment of people based on their identity (personal with double standard). In the mafia state, instead of the normative state benefits typical of liberal democracies, personalized rewards and punishments become dominant; and instead of normative regulations, the chief patron's individual decision-making and the instrumental, discretional application of law are decisive.

Although the mafia state maintains a number of normative taxes and benefits, and intervenes in the legal system for reward or punishment only when necessary, state arbitrariness has a much wider range of tools at its disposal than is typical of a constitutional or welfare state. By occupying and politically patronalizing the institutions of public power, the decisions of the leader of the mafia state can move on a much larger "amplitude of arbitrariness" than in the case of the political elite of a liberal democracy. In general, the wider range of institutional competences are under the discretional control of the same person or network, the wider their associated amplitude is (Figure 7). In a captured state, the patronal network may be able to use one local or state institution or some regulatory agency; in a mafia state, the chief patron can use the parliament, the tax office, the chief prosecutor etc. as parts of a single corrupt machinery, carrying out discretional acts in concert.

Figure 7: The amplitude of arbitrariness (correlation between the nature of corruption and state action).

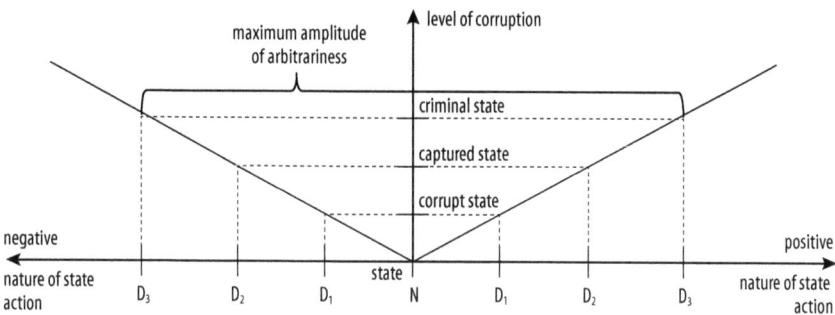

Legend:
N: normative action
D₂: discretional action as structural deviation
D₁: discretional action as non-structural deviation
D₃: discretional action as constitutive element
(Note: the dotted lines are added lines for the sake of clarity.)

29. THE MAFIA STATE IS DIFFERENT FROM THE DEVELOPMENTAL STATE in terms of informality and loyalty-based personal enrichment instead of formality and policy-based capital accumulation. Power concentration and the maximum amplitude of arbitrariness is a common trait in mafia and developmental states. Hence the authors seeing a mafia state often mistake it for a developmental state, arguing it "picks the winners" of market competition just like developmental states like South Korea and Singapore do. However, the motive of personal-wealth accumulation does not appear as a central goal of governmental actors in developmental states. Close economic and family ties between the bureaucrats and the entrepreneurs are possible, but that is not the basis of their support: the state intends to facilitate not the accumulation of wealth of certain people irrespective of their economic performance but the capital formation of certain companies according to an open economic policy, measuring performance in impersonal criteria such as competitiveness in foreign markets (called "export-oriented industrialization," or EOI in the literature). A developmental state also relies on the formal bureaucracy and not the patrimonial logic of informal patronal regimes, whereas the leader's persona or charisma does not play a large role in the system either.

While discretional state intervention naturally creates rents (Proposition 81), their allocation in a developmental state depends on the relative political strength and relations of business groups. In other words, these states feature bottom-up rent-seeking, and not top-down allocation of rents based on loyalty to the chief patron. At the same time, industrial (public) policy goals are never completely disregarded in face of making—perhaps totally uncompetitive—members of the adopted political family rich. This sharply contrasts the practice of patronal autocracies. In Hungary, Lőrinc Mészáros, Viktor Orbán's childhood friend and the former mayor of his home village, was turned from a gas fitter who had amassed in twenty years a modest wealth of ca. 30 million forints (ca. €93 thousand, in 2010) into Hungary's richest man with ca. 479 billion forints (ca. €1.5 billion, in 2021) through domestic public procurement tenders, while he produced virtually nothing for export or the open market. The *de jure* owner of a wide portfolio of political and economic assets, Mészáros is Orbán's economic front man (Proposition 16), which is another phenomenon that distinguishes patronal and developmental regimes. For the head of executive in a developmental state typically does not have economic front men who would accumulate personal wealth from discretional state support.

30.

THE MAFIA STATE IS DIFFERENT FROM THE FAILED STATE of oligarchic anarchy as it appeared in Russia and Ukraine in the 1990s. The stability of the state after the regime change was preserved without any break in the Western-Christian historical region, where the transition was carried out with a more professional bureaucratic apparatus, and in those countries of the Islamic region where the old communist structures themselves—especially the top levels of the party and secret service nomenklatura—turned directly into the "reformed" national centers of power. In the Eastern-Orthodox historical region, however, neither a complete transfer of previous power nor rational-bureaucratic foundations were present. In this region, it depended on the dynamics of competing patron-client networks whether state power could be solidified, and often it took years before a proper state emerged as the local monopolist of legitimate use of violence in the given country.

Vadim Volkov explains in his book *Violent Entrepreneurs* (2002) that, when the new Russian state was unable to protect property rights and enforce contracts, a large number of people and companies turned to the so-called violent entrepreneurs, who moved from the world of organized crime to the suddenly liberated market for defense and attack. The weakness of central control made it impossible for a mafia state to emerge and rearrange ownership rights in a top-down fashion, but it also opened the door to illegal and often violent raidings of companies (called *reiderstvo*) by criminals and individual members of the state bureaucracy (Proposition 82).

In a failed state, predation is a result of the governmental actors not being able to control the state apparatus; members of the latter use their competences as "piranhas," as regional expert Stanislav Markus puts it. In a mafia state, top-level public authority, the chief patron has the power to act both as a predator himself and as a coordinator of predatory actors; the piranhas in such a setting are either servers of the central predator or degrade into cleaner fish, eating food remnants out of the mouth of the shark who tolerates this "theft" if the amount of prey lost to the cleaner fish is miniscule.

Figure 8: Violent actors of different strength by the public/private and illegal/legal dichotomies.

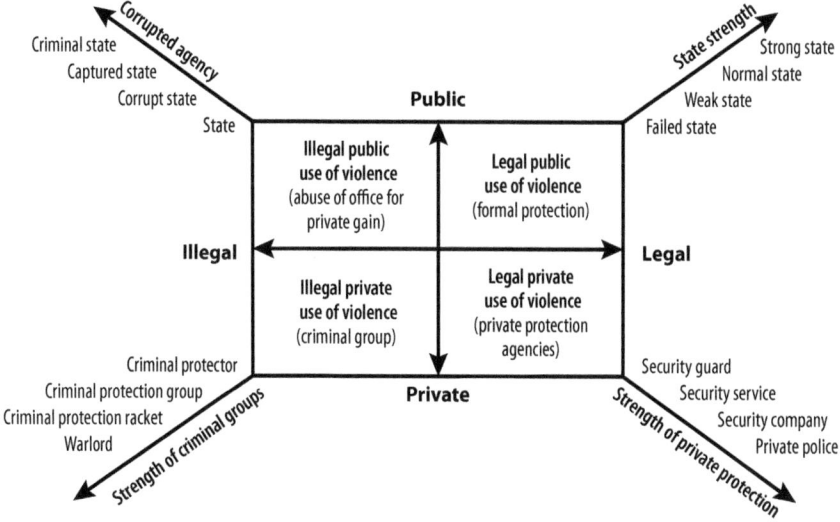

Exploring the continuum between the two opposites, we can distinguish various types of violent actors along the legal-illegal and the public-private axes (Figure 8). Actors in different quarters may coexist in a regime, and they do not work in isolation: they can hire each other, like when a legal state turns to a legal security company, or a criminal state turns to private criminals or criminal groups for certain tasks if its interests so require.

A *Sui Generis* Phenomenon: the Adopted Political Family

31.

SINCE THE IMPERIAL PERIOD, RUSSIA HAS BEEN LED by various kinds of ruling elites: from feudal elite through nomenklatura to the adopted political family. To illustrate differences between ruling elites throughout history, let us take one of the most important and paradigmatic representatives of the post-communist countries: Russia. Throughout its history, we can easily follow the transformation of patronal networks (Table 9). Before the 1917 February Revolution, the tsar wielded most power, and the elite of their patronal network were formed from the service gentry and the feudal estates. The revolutions of 1917 eventually ushered in a new form of patronal network led by the party general secretary and populated largely by the party nomenklatura. In the presidential system that followed the collapse of the communist system and that had stabilized by the end of the 1990s, the elite of the patronal network takes the form of the adopted political family.

The term "ruling elite" is a neutral expression, which in itself neither refers to the organizational makeup, structure, or internal relations within the elite, or even its legitimation. However, when we speak of the ruling elite of a patronal network, this implicitly includes its immediate hierarchical nature. In Russia under the tsars, members of the ruling elite were part of the elite on the basis of birth, by virtue of their status as nobles. The prerogatives of elites were invested in the elite individual. It was possible to lift someone into this circle, to adopt persons into it, but no one could be stripped of their status because of disloyalty. For the disloyal, punishment could mean the loss of life, freedom, or property, but not status. In the case of the communist nomenklatura, the relationship was the reverse: the elite consisted of what might be called an impersonal register of positions of power. Here it was the position, and not the person's status, that was fixed; the person in the position could be changed at the whim of the party general secretary.

Yet the ruling elite of both tsarist and communist patronal networks—whether by virtue of personal status or the register of impersonal positions—had a formalized set of rules for incorporation and expulsion. Not so in the case of the post-communist informal patronal network, developed into a single-pyramid in Russia by Vladimir Putin by 2003 and in which formal and informal roles and positions churn in an opaque, untraceable conglomeration. In the following points, we are going to elaborate on the differences between the historical types of elites, as well as the historical and theoretical concept of the "ruling class."

Table 9: The formal position of the chief patron, the decision making "body" and the type of patronal networks in Russia.

	The formal position of chief patron (as the head of executive power)	The ruling „body" (the decision making center)	Ruling elite according to the type of patronal networks	Type of the patronal state
before 1917	tsar	court	service gentry, feudal "orders"	feudal state
1917-1991	party general secretary	politburo	nomenklatura	party state
after 2003	president	patron's court	adopted political family	mafia state

32. THE ADOPTED POLITICAL FAMILY IS NOT a feudal elite.

An historical analogy, feudal elites and orders are sometimes used to describe the ruling elite in a patronal autocracy. The main parallel the analogy builds on is patronalism: permanent vassalage to a single lord, "master-slave" relations between the king (landlord etc.) and his subjects, as well as the prevalence of nepotism, the importance of the court, and the centrality of personal power in the ruling hierarchy. However, rights and obligations in the feudal rank order were legitimate, formalized in law.

The feudal metaphor is suitable to spotlight the praxis of power, but in the case of feudal forerunners, the real nature of power and its legal status overlapped in a kind of natural harmony, requiring no illegal mechanisms for alignment as it does in post-communist regimes. A king was *de jure* a king as well, not a constitutionally limited president or prime minister; they did not say they had nothing to do with the wealth of their family or barons; nor did they keep their fortune under the name of the stable boy, for they were in no need of economic front men.

In the adopted political family, there is no corporate-type organization, no rank order-type separate positions in relation to the chief patron, and no corporate self-consciousness. Also, the feudal orders stood in some sort of legitimate contractual relationship with their master (the monarch), with rights and obligations limiting both the nobility and the monarch itself. The orders below the king insisted upon, and were ready to protect, their own legally granted rights. In contrast, the adopted political family not only lacks a formal organization and set of binding rules, but the chief patron, being the patriarchal head of the family, has ultimate authority over status within the single-pyramid network as well.

This is related to a key factor: as power is being exercised in illegal ways, the possibility of systemic compromising puts an extra layer of obedience on the network's members toward the chief patron. While people using the feudal analogy trust it brings focus to the regime's central element (i.e., the patron-client relationship), disregarding informality means to lose sight of the fact that the chief patron can blackmail his clients, threatening them to persecute the crimes they have committed. As the workings of the informal network do not coincide with formal laws, it necessarily results in constant violations of lawfulness, and the chief patron has the opportunity to activate the (politically selective) law enforcement in the cases of disloyalty (Propositions 59-60). This leads us to the final point, which we have already mentioned: "law enforcement" in the case of a disloyal member of the feudal elite could mean the loss of life, freedom, or property, but not status as a nobleman. In a patronal autocracy, disinherited members of the adopted politi- cal family lose their status, first in the informal and second, as a consequence, in the formal realm.

33. The adopted political family is not a class. In the West, the fall of feudalism and the emergence of bourgeois social order meant the formation of a class society: a social stratification created by capitalism where both the community of interests within groups and the difference of interest between groups are dynamized by the division of labor and the capitalist mode of production.

Class is a fundamentally economic phenomenon, but it is often used in the case of post-communist ruling elites, underlining their exceptional wealth and the fact that key economic actors ("capitalists") are among the regime's foremost beneficiaries.

But the adopted political family does not emerge within a capitalist society of legal equality, and does not reach its exceptional position as a result of the impersonal forces of market competition. The adopted political family is not a fundamentally economic phenomenon: it is a phenomenon of colluding spheres of social action, and the wealth of its members stems from an instrumentalized legal system, under which the normative status of legal equality is undermined by discretional state intervention and laws arbitrarily tailored to individuals and businesses (Proposition 57).

Adopted political families cross class lines. Their basis of organization is not the members' shared position in the production hierarchy that would create a community of interest among them on the impersonal basis of status. The members of the adopted political family have no class consciousness or identity either; indeed, they can be rather heterogeneous in terms of culture and lifestyle. The cohesive force of the adopted political family is personal loyalty. It is not a horizontal alliance of capital owners but a patronal network, characterized by vertical, hierarchical connections between its members. Those who show no personal loyalty are regularly attacked by the chief patron, even if they are wealthy capitalists themselves.

In other words, similar class status in terms of productive property does not necessarily mean membership in the patronal ruling elite. The relevant cleavages are political and personal, not economic: the targets of the adopted political family include those with no patronal allegiance, who are out-of-circle or disloyal. At the same time, the oligarchs and front men of the adopted family are not "capitalists" in the Western sense as they cannot use their capital without the chief patron's permission (Proposition 16).

34. THE ADOPTED POLITICAL FAMILY IS NOT a nomenklatura.

The ruling elite of the communist regimes fitted into the formal hierarchy of the communist parties, while the positions in the state or public authority were filled according to a strict order imposed by the nomenklatura. But individuals, rather than families belonged to the nomenklatura—on ideological grounds. In their cases dynastic characteristics rarely and only exceptionally appeared, in fact loyalty would have to be demonstrated by turning traitor to family ties (in the classical Stalinist formations). To an adopted political family, families (of blood-related or adopted members) are adopted, through forming with one of its members kinship or quasi-kinship relation, sealed by businesses in common.

The communist nomenklatura did not organizationally follow the logic of the adopted political family in the way it organizes itself in the mafia state; it was not built on patriarchal patterns of informal chains of command, and therefore it did not extend the network of political and bureaucratic administration beyond its formal institutions. The personal privileges of nomenklatura members also manifested themselves in limited consumer advantages and that only bore significance in a shortage economy. As private ownership was only moderately tolerated at best in communist systems, the members of the nomenklatura could only enjoy higher incomes or extra consumption, such as using the state's facilities (cars, real estates, resorts etc.). There was no significant accumulation of wealth, in sharp contrast to the members of the adopted political family.

Finally, as the power of the members of the nomenklatura was purely of a political—and not mixed, political and economic—source and nature, economic privileges as well as political power were limited to the period in office. This is corollary to that, in the nomenklatura, the bureaucratic structure is primary: the range of privileges was tied strictly to positions, and not to persons (Proposition 17). In contrast, the members of the adopted political family have the opportunity to keep their wealth after leaving formal office, and only a break in their informal position results in the revoking of their privileged status. Finally, the adopted political family does not ensure social control through a double-structure of connecting horizontals in different levels of party committees (as it was the case in a communist dictatorship), but through societal patronalization and the changing patterns of existential vulnerability (Propositions 94-95).

35. **The adopted political family is a *sui generis* phenomenon of post-communist regimes.** We use "sui generis" in the sense that the adopted political family is a unique, new phenomenon in the region, which is more different from the above-described (historical) types of ruling elite than it is similar to them.

To sum it up, the informal patronal network in post-communist systems can be characterized as an adopted political family, because: different networks of extended personal acquaintance are organized into a single adopted political family; not only individuals, but families are incorporated; it is informal, without formal membership; it extends over formal institutions; it is based on patronal, and not organizational loyalty (there is no free entrance into or free exit from it); position within the adopted political family does not converge necessarily with formal administrative positions; its power is based on the merger of political and economic "resources"; it follows the cultural patterns of rule of the patriarchal family (patriarchal domination). The adopted political family is also a criminal network, the norms of which are not formalized and therefore enforced against the structure of formal institutions. Therefore the adopted political family needs to neutralize control mechanisms such as the chief prosecutor's office (Proposition 60).

The expression "adopted political family" is a summary of its key features, to be understood as follows: "adopted" refers to the structure of the network in general and to the kinds of links (kinship and quasi-kinship ones) it uses in particular; "political" refers to the elite's function within the polity, namely that it strives for political positions and coercive (state) power over every sphere of social action; "family" refers to the cultural pattern of patriarchal families, particularly patriarchal domination by the chief patron. The adopted political family involves the kinds of actors we have described above and associated with patronal regimes, from oligarchs to poligarchs, from front men to vassals' parties. The informal patronal network of these actors is what we call the adopted political family, which embodies a collusion of political, economic, and communal spheres.

36.

ADOPTED POLITICAL FAMILIES IN THE POST-COMMUNIST REGION differ in their genesis: that is, the kind of social group that comprises the core of the network. If one talks about post-communist ruling elites, and wants to reflect on the anthropological aspect of linkage alone, they can use the word "clan" instead of the multi-faceted "adopted political family" (just like one can say, with respect to a patronal autocracy, "clan state" instead of "mafia state" if their primary focus is the nature of the ruling elite; Propositions 26-27).

The clans of pre-modern society were, just like dynastic houses in feudal times, organized on the basis of bloodlines, but they also took in outsiders as they expanded on a personal, family basis. In post-communist clans, kinship relations are supplemented by quasi-kinship relations as the network (or its core of founders) itself is continuously complemented by families not connected to other members on the basis of bloodlines.

The fundament upon which post-communist clans are built can be various: besides ethnicity, we can observe nomenklatura-, party-, fraternity-, and criminality-based clans as well (Table 10). For instance, in the post-communist regimes of Central Asia, while it is the top positions of the communist party and the secret service that switched into informal patronal networks, these post-Soviet republics bear the signs of strong ethnic divisiveness (Proposition 106). In Ukraine, clans show a peculiar regional character, while they were also connected at their genesis with organized crime.

Somewhere between the ideal typical nomenklatura-based and fraternity-based clans is the adopted political family of Vladimir Putin in Russia. There, the patron's court is grounded in the relationships that developed (1) on the lower levels of the former party and secret service nomenklatura and (2) between people who were born in Leningrad and graduated from its university (like Putin himself). Finally, in Hungary we can see the rise of a fraternity-based clan. For it was the former alternative liberal party Fidesz, founded originally as a youth organization in the late 1980s, that changed directly into a patronal network, grounded in early friendships from student fraternities at university.

Table 10: A typology of post-communist clans.

	The recruiting basis of the clan	Identity of the core membership	Typical example (country)
Ethnicity-based clan	common ethnicity, ancestry, language, culture, and/or nation	common ethnic identity	Kazakhstan, Uzbekistan, Kyrgyzstan
Nomenklatura-based clan	common pre-regime-change history (in the nomenklatura)	nomenklatura membership	Russia
Party-based clan	common post-regime change history (in a newly formed party)	party membership	Romania, Bulgaria
Fraternity-based clan	small, very close and tightly knit community of friend or colleagues	fraternity and close friendship	Hungary
Criminality-based clan	criminal group or syndicate	criminal-group belonging	Ukraine

37. CULTURALLY, THE HEAD OF THE ADOPTED POLITICAL FAMILY

fulfills the role of *pater familias*. The cultural models of the chief patron and the features of his rule differ vastly from the model of communist dictators. He rarely shows his power in parades or party congresses, and the manifestations of his rule bear the characteristics of relations within the patriarchal family. If we were to place it in historical-logical order, we would find that the role of the head of the adopted political family begins with the archaic patriarchal head, followed by the Roman *pater familias*, and the chief patron of patronal autocracies. What is common in the concept of the roles can best be described through the role of the *pater familias*.

The Roman family unit, as a household community subject to the initially unbridled power of the *pater familias* enjoyed a rather high degree of autonomy from the state. As legal historian András Földi explains, "the scope of public law, the *ius publicum*, that is, the power of the magistrates in a sense came to a stop (in principle and in general) at the border of the private estates, on the doorstep of the private houses, from where the rules of private law, *ius privatum* were instated, ensuring absolute power to the head of the family." ("A római család jogi rendje" [The Legal Order of the Roman Family], 1997). This power extended to all matters of life, individuals, property and activity. The "existence of the family is the sum of those who stand beneath the power of the head of the family," from the head of the family down, through the wife, as well as the children by blood and adopted children, and other relatives living in the household, down to the servants and menials of various statuses. The Latin word *familia*, where the English "family" comes from, also comes from *famulus*, meaning "servant, slave."

In patronal autocracies, the patriarchal head of the adopted political family extends his entitlements over persons, property and activities by illegitimate and illegal means to a national level, by the means of a monopoly on the enforcement of state power. The family, the household, the estate and the country belong to the same cultural pattern for the head of the political family. His actions, although he formally "governs" the country, cannot be expressed appropriately by this verb, just like the *pater familias* did not "govern" his family. Indeed, he disposed over them, their property and status. Accordingly, the proper verb for describing the ruling action of the chief patron is "to dispose over," concerning all spheres of social action.

38. MEMBERS OF THE ADOPTED POLITICAL FAMILY **enjoy shelter provision; disloyal members or outsiders may be subject to integrity breaking.** The main form of shelter-provision is what the Russians call "krysha" (roof): the informal, discretional protection of the members' freedom and property from legal and illegal threats. Simply put, members of the organized upperworld enjoy impunity: protection from law enforcement and the various punishments imposed by formal control mechanisms.

As long as their krysha is intact, a client need have no scruples to violate formal laws or commit outright crimes. Naturally, they cannot do anything they want; the chief patron gives precise authorization, defining the allowed extent and scope of corruption and the territory (a region, a city, a ministry etc.) to which one's corrupt activities are confined. These limits are also zealously monitored. But as long as they play by the rules, the client can be sure that the institutions which have *de jure* obligation to counteract them, like police or prosecution, will be *de facto* neutralized, disabled or biased in their favor upon the chief patron's top-down (informal) orders.

Krysha is a key element of patronal autocracies from two respects: (1) it means the disabling of control mechanisms in favor of informal norms, and thus it is tantamount to the supremacy of informal rules over formal ones; (2) the prospect of removal of krysha from above one's head grants the possibility of discretional punishment and, therefore, blackmailing potential for the chief patron.

On the other hand, those who are disloyal, pose a risk, or seem like enticing prey in the economic sphere, must face different forms of integrity breaking. It may be moral (character killing through negative campaigns, employing the prosecutor's office in the campaign staff as well), existential (referring to wealth or more generally the living conditions of a person), or physical (abuse of the target person by the police or other violent actors like criminal groups). Each of these categories of integrity breaking has different levels: threat, which refers to (verbal) messages about potential attack if the target does not obey the adopted political family ("an offer you can't refuse"); harassment, which refers to "warning shots" which do not permanently damage the target but clearly signal the chief patron's hostility; and attack, which refers to the full-scale use of the legal as well as illegal means, potentially leading to the loss of wealth, freedom, or life.

39.

Amoral familism coupled with the enforced discipline of loyalty characterizes the internal culture of the adopted political family. The sin above all sins in the adopted political family, which is always avenged, is disloyalty. Loyalty is the condition of both adoption and being party to a share of the proceeds.

Those who want to leave the system, or turn against it, may be penalized for things they could never be penalized for in a liberal democracy, and the way they are penalized could never be pulled off in a democratic setting. As a result of the establishment of the patron-client system, discretional tools—that would never be accessible with functioning checks and balances and separated powers—become available to enforce silence and obedience. The victims coerced under threat of their existences are silent—as familiar from criminology—for if they would speak, it would only visit more troubles upon them. There are no peaceful means—by individual volition—of stepping out of the system: once adopted, the member is either discharged by the head of the political family, or if deserting, they will be chased down. No matter what formal position they were appointed by the chief patron, they know the consequences of opposition and of quitting.

On the other hand, while disloyalty counts as a sin, members of the political family who commit some other offence, whether against the law or decency, can avoid punishment as long as their krysha is intact. If public opinion pursues the offender more vociferously, or the case meets with an exceptionally serious international response, it may come to a sacrifice of the one responsible. Yet these individuals can still be assured of one thing: the chief patron will always be there for them. At most, the family will create a new existence for them—just like in witness-protection programs—somewhere else, removing them from public view. Only, however, if the individual is loyal. This gives the regime its strength: they do not serve their own people up to "alien powers." And for those who know the disadvantages of confrontation and the protection that adherence means, not only the possibility of confrontation is lost, but its rationale as well.

It is no coincidence that Edward C. Banfield's category "amoral familism," describing the poverty-ridden conditions of a Southern Italy woven through-and-through with mafia culture, can also be used describe the rules of conduct determining the behavior of the adopted political family (*Moral Basis of a Backward Society*, 1967). Almost unlimited solidarity with family members is complemented by an almost complete lack of solidarity with those outside the adopted family, manifesting in a culture and attitude of neglecting.

40.

OLIGARCHS CAN DECIDE between insider belonging and outsider autonomy if there are multiple adopted political families in the regime. Oligarchs are key members of the adopted political family, who may have been there already at the beginning of the network's history, or joined later when they wanted to benefit from an established network's access to political and economic resources (Table 11). Among them, the oligarchs with the most influence in the adopted political family are the inner circle oligarchs. They did not have significant wealth to begin with, and actually managed to secure their startup capital from positions weaving through politics. They are followed in the chain of influence by adopted oligarchs, who accumulated their wealth outside the network, often in the period of oligarchic anarchy as a result of the chaotic, spontaneous privatizations of former (communist) state property. Their admission into a political family only stabilizes their position and protects them in the world of politically motivated, violent redistributions of wealth.

The most vulnerable type of oligarch within the adopted political family is the patron-bred oligarch, who gained wealth after the patronal network was developed and they were adopted. There are various ideal typical subtypes of patron-bred oligarchs, such as: the one who is connected to the adopted political family as a relative (wife, husband, son-in-law etc.); the one who had been a member of the adopted political family primarily in the political sphere and left that for the economic sphere (former ministers etc.); or the one who became wealthy as an economic front man.

The common point in the inner circle, adopted, and patron-bred oligarchs is that they are members of an adopted political family; in contrast, another path is represented by the autonomous oligarchs, who do not commit themselves permanently to any patronal pyramid, and they do not want to create their own political force either. While attempting to establish corrupt business relations with actors in the political sphere, they try to keep their integrity. In a sense, what they develop are not strictly patronal-client but rather client-client relations, which means voluntary (albeit informal) business deals with every patronal network on a more occasional basis, retaining the opportunity of free entry and exit. This, however, is only possible in a patronal democracy: if the regime is a multi-pyramid system, and no patronal network manages to monopolize all political power. Otherwise a single-pyramid patronal network emerges, and the space for independent movement virtually evaporates.

Table 11: A typology of oligarchs in patronal regimes (in descending order according to distance from the chief patron in a patronal autocracy).

	Initial source of wealth	Patronal connections	To which feature the category refers to	Presence in patronal regimes
Inner circle oligarch	Patronal network	Embedded	Being founder of a patronal network	Patronal democracy + autocracy
Adopted oligarch	Private sector / patronal network (different from present)	Embedded	Having been accepted as member of an already existing network	Patronal democracy + autocracy
Patron-bred oligarch	Patronal network	Embedded	Being fostered by a patron	Patronal democracy + autocracy
Surrendered oligarch	Private sector / patronal network (different from dominant)	Embedded	Having been subjugated by the chief patron	Patronal autocracy
Fellow-traveler oligarch	Private sector	Not embedded	Maintaining constrained autonomy from the single-pyramid network	Patronal autocracy
Recalcitrant oligarch	Private sector / patronal network (different from dominant)	Not embedded	Being undecided as to what attitude he should have toward the chief patron	Patronal autocracy (temporarily)
Autonomous oligarch	Private sector	Not embedded	Having no patronal allegiance (maintaining equally good relations to every network)	Patronal democracy
Rival oligarch	Private sector / patronal network (different from dominant)	Not embedded	Resisting domination attempt of the single-pyramid network	Patronal autocracy (temporarily)
Liquidated oligarch	Private sector / patronal network (different from dominant)	n.a.	Being removed from the game (alive or dead)	Patronal autocracy
Renegade oligarch	Private sector / patronal network	Not embedded (previously embedded)	Betraying and turning against his adopted political family	Patronal democracy + autocracy

41.

OLIGARCHS CAN NO LONGER HAVE an autonomous existence when there is only one, dominant adopted political family. Drawing upon its monopoly of power, a single-pyramid patronal network destroys the relative autonomy of the oligarchs and aims to integrate them into its own chain of command. Autonomous oligarchs have three possibilities if a patronal democracy—where they established their oligarchic position—turns into a patronal autocracy (Figure 9). First, they can be positive toward the chief patron, accepting the new state of affairs and asking for adoption. In this case, the autonomous oligarch becomes an adopted oligarch. Second, they can be negative, not accepting the new state of affairs and actively fighting the patronal network's domination attempt. This gives rise to the type of the rival oligarch.

Should the single-pyramid prevail, oligarchic rivalry can lead to either forced removal from the regime, or forced surrender. In the former case, we speak about liquidated oligarchs: they are meted out direct state coercion if they have their own political ambitions (as in the "Khodorkovsky model"), while those who have no such ambitions and only support alternative political forces can count on more peaceful forms of expulsion (the "Berezovsky model"). In the latter case, we speak about surrendered oligarchs. Those who previously "played in the rival team" are also surrendered into the adopted political family; since they are struggling to survive economically, with a lot to lose but no protected bargaining position with the regime, they are compelled to find their place in the chain of command under the chief patron. They enjoy privileges, but pay their protection monies to the political family as required, meeting all expectations.

Finally, besides positive and negative attitudes toward the chief patron's domination attempt, the oligarch can try and remain neutral. While the strategy of autonomous oligarchs—keeping equal distance from the competing patronal networks—is no longer tenable, client-client relation to the adopted political family may be possible if the chief patron is unable to surrender the oligarch. This leads us to the rare and specific type of the fellow-traveler oligarch. Fellow-traveler oligarchs are not beholden for their wealth to any competing patronal network: their network reaches back to the period before or during the regime change, or they first became major entrepreneurs and then turned oligarchs to survive and prosper in a patronal environment. While still autonomous, the favors of fellow-traveler oligarchs were courted by different political sides for support, and they were further reinforced by this mutual dependence. In a patronal autocracy, they are pacified by the chief patron, who offers them benefits in exchange for staying out of patronal politics. Yet the lack of subjugation makes fellow-traveler oligarchs a source of danger: the chief patron will

A *Sui Generis* Phenomenon: the Adopted Political Family • 59

always try to find ways to force them into submission, marginalize them, or take over their assets if possible.

Figure 9: Possible trajectories of autonomous oligarchs in a single-pyramid patronal network.

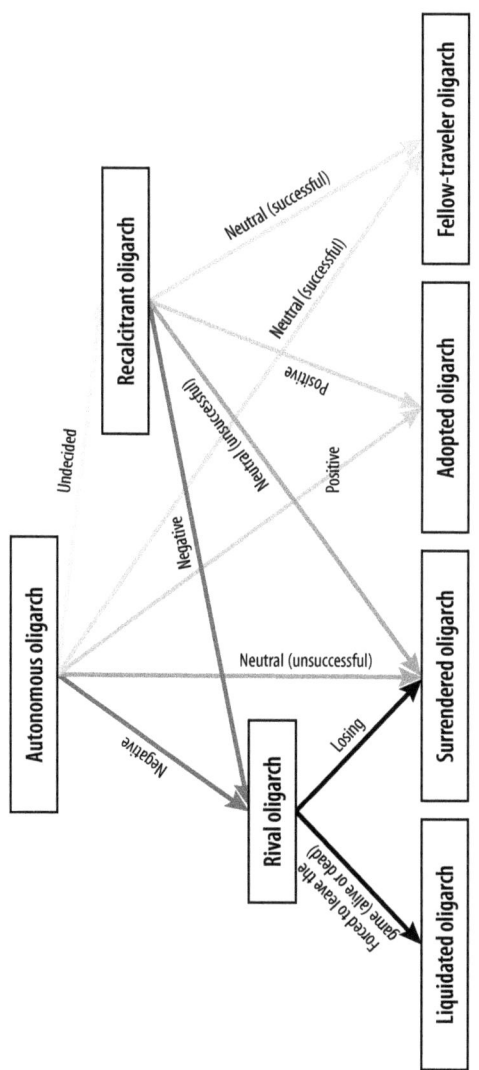

The Formal Institutional Setting: Changing Patterns of Legitimacy

42.

CIVIL LEGITIMACY HAS BEEN THE BASIS of modern states, which have developed different interpretations of it fitting to their nature of rule. The state's legitimacy has rested upon the notion of popular sovereignty since the Age of Enlightenment. Earlier, leaders could rely on so-called numinous legitimacy (divine authority) which implied no notion of the people: the state was not legitimized on the grounds that it serves either the popular will or the common good but that domination follows from sanctity. In modern times, states rely on civil legitimacy, meaning the leading political elite always claims it is a representative of the popular will and/or (therefore) it serves the common good, that is, the interest of the people.

Civil legitimacy prevails in all three polar type regimes—moreover, all three call themselves some sort of "democracy," referring to the fact that they indeed realize a form of the people's rule. Liberal democracy is either named as such or as a "constitutional democracy;" patronal autocracy is called "sovereign democracy" or "illiberal democracy;" and communist dictatorship is called a "people's democracy." However, as the differences of these terms already imply, in the three polar type regimes civil legitimacy is interpreted in different ways, with different narrative panels and in the context of different ideological frameworks. And the different narratives legitimize different forms of state decision-making. Table 12 sums up three narratives: constitutionalism, populism, and Marxism-Leninism, which provide the framework of civil legitimacy in liberal democracy, patronal autocracy, and communist dictatorship, respectively.

The general difference between the three legitimacy frameworks lies in which actor or process they delegate the right to interpret the common good. Though it might seem self-evident sometimes, "common good" can hardly be defined in an objective way.

Rather, each legitimacy framework points to certain people (or a person) who shall have right to define the common good, that is, the popular interest, and the state is legitimized by the fact that the goals of its actions are set, directly or indirectly, by the legitimate interpreter.

Table 12: Ideologies of civil legitimacy in the three polar type regimes (constitutionalism, populism, Marxism-Leninism).

Constitutionalism (in liberal democracy)	Populism (in patronal autocracy)	Marxism-Leninism (in communist dictatorship)
universalistic protection of human dignity represented by the citizens	particularistic protection of the nation represented by the adopted political family	particularistic protection of the working class represented by the party
individualist	collectivist	collectivist
universalist on humanistic base	nationalist on clan base (amoral familism)	internationalist on class base
unlimited moral obligation	limited moral obligation	limited moral obligation
pluralism	anti-pluralism (majoritarianism)	anti-pluralism
→ PUBLIC DELIBERATION of the interpretation of the common good: ensuring a variety of competitive processes and channels for the expression and realization of interests and values (the people are citizens)	→ PATRONAL APPROPRIATION of the interpretation of the common good: ensuring ultimate authority of the adopted political family in state decision-making without legitimate opposition or criticism (the people are servants)	→ BUREAUCRATIC APPROPRIATION of the interpretation of the common good: ensuring ultimate authority of the party in state decision-making without legitimate opposition or criticism (the people are subjects)

43.

In a liberal democracy, civil legitimacy is interpreted in the framework of constitutionalism, which legitimizes public deliberation of the interpretation of the common good. Grounded in liberal political philosophy, the starting point of constitutionalism is the individual citizen and the respect for their human dignity, which implies that they have to be treated as free people who have a say in how their life is run. Accordingly, a constitutional state (Proposition 28) is obliged to respect the human dignity of everyone, for every adult the state deals with—typically those who happen to be in its territory—are beings worthy of respect for their human dignity (universalist on humanistic base); to defend the rights of every person, meaning the state should not exclude certain people or groups but treat every human equally (unlimited moral obligation); and to ensure a public realm where no one's interest or opinion is suppressed, for if every adult individual is equally respected, that means everyone's views, values and interests are equally legitimate and representable (pluralism).

The type of institutional setting this framework legitimizes is public deliberation: the question of how political power shall be used is decided in the conversation and competition of the variety of values and interests of the people as legitimate alternatives. The process of public deliberation can be divided into five consecutive but overlapping phases: (1) discussing, where every citizen has a chance to express their views on political matters and confront them with the views of other citizens in peaceful debate, where other opinions are treated as legitimate and hence freely representable; (2) associating, where citizens decide voluntarily to form autonomous and relatively independent associations and organizations like interest groups and parties, representing their interests in competition with other citizens; (3) electing, where values and interests come to be represented among decision-makers as a result of a peaceful, fairly conducted contest; (4) lawmaking, where laws and regulations are made by the elected representatives on the basis of majority rule, deciding on the use of political power; (5) enforcing, where political power is actually used, and the laws and regulations are implemented and the state makes the people follow them.

The public deliberation process is also cyclical to ensure the accountability of the rulers, who are not protected in their position by virtue of incumbency. As Adam Przeworski put it, liberal democracy is characterized by institutionalized uncertainty: institutions help the changing will of the people manifest in the composition of the rulers.

44.

In a patronal autocracy, civil legitimacy is interpreted in the framework of populism, which legitimizes patronal appropriation of the interpretation of the common good. Unlike populism in the West, populism in post-communist patronal autocracies is not a bottom-up phenomenon that would challenge the establishment and elevate the populist leader into power but it is used in a top-down fashion, from a ruling position to legitimize the chief patron's rule. The starting point of populism is not the individual but a collective: populists say they represent "the people," "the nation," and "the national interest." What follows from this in the populist narrative is that anyone who is against the populist is also against the people and the nation, and therefore not simply morally despicable but illegitimate.

Declaring itself the only legitimate representative of the people, populism wrecks the logic of public deliberation: as the populist leader fends off every criticism and idea dissimilar to their own as "anti-nation," discussing the use of political power becomes impossible as different values and interests cannot be represented legitimately. It is important to see that opposition in general is declared illegitimate, both now and in the future. Therefore, when the people become dissatisfied with their leaders and want to support someone else, they too automatically become illegitimate. Populism, in fact, deprives the people themselves of the chance to change their minds legitimately, turning against the legitimate populist. The process of public deliberation, even if it formally remains cyclical, essentially freezes: the people, no matter how wisely and rightfully they elected the leaders to advocate their interests, will have no other choice but to accept the way the populist leaders use political power. State decision-making is practically displaced from the hands of the people, and the populist becomes the only legitimate interpreter of the common good.

Populism is not an ideology but an ideological instrument: an argumentative tool which anyone with or without an initial ideology can use to justify their actions. This is what makes it the interpretation of civil legitimacy that fits to a patronal autocracy. Unconstrained power that the chief patron has both within the adopted political family and the nation cannot be legitimized by constitutionalism where power is limited by public deliberation, competing factions, and the constitution. But in populism, no challenge is legitimate toward the chief patron, the only legitimate interpreter of the common good who, in turn, can legitimately disregard formal, constitutional rules which would constrain the realization of the "common good" he defines. Populism means the legitimization of unaccountability: in the place of public deliberation, patronal appropriation of the interpretation of the common good by the chief patron and the adopted political family.

45. **Populism is a legitimacy challenge, advocating a shift from legal-rational legitimacy to substantive-rational legitimacy.** Max Weber distinguished three "pure types" of legitimate domination: legal, traditional, and charismatic, which differ in the reason the people accept domination as legitimate. In legal legitimacy, the people argue that "because it is the law"; in traditional, the argument is "because it is the custom." In charismatic legitimacy, the argument is "because he is the most exceptional one." Noticing the exceptional role of the chief patron in legitimacy, it is commonplace to speak about charismatic legitimacy of patronal regimes. But a deeper analysis of populism suggests a different pattern, one that goes beyond the classic Weberian triad.

The essence of legal (rational) legitimacy is that people see the legal settlement of things as an end in itself. Elected leaders are legitimized not by their person or their actions, but by the fact that they have been elected: that they have come to power by climbing the ranks of formal, legal institutions. The essence of populism, however, is that the maintenance of law and formal institutions is not an end in itself, but can be considered legitimate if and only if they serve the realization of the "common good." The "national interest," as the populist defines it, is the bedrock of legitimacy; whatever that stands in the way of its realization may be disregarded, be it a law or a social group, an organization, or a political actor.

This means the replacement of legal-rational legitimacy with substantive-rational legitimacy (Table 13). In the case of the former, the carrier of legitimacy is the impersonal institutional order; in the case of the latter, it is a certain person, the populist. Legal-rational legitimacy means that everyone's interest may be legitimate; substantive-rational legitimacy means that the only legitimate interest is what the populist declares to be the common good, and everyone in opposition to it and him are *eo ipso* illegitimate. Thus, under legal-rational legitimacy, the leaders can be subordinated to something like the rule of law, while under substantive-rational legitimacy, the law can only be a servant of the populist leader who appropriated the interpretation of the common good. In the context of legal-rational legitimacy, a deliberative process of interest reconciliation of multiple actors is considered ideal; in the context of substantive-rational legitimacy, a declarative process that asserts the interests of the leader and suppresses other interests becomes ideal.

Table 13: Legal-rational legitimacy and substantive-rational legitimacy.

	Legal-rational legitimacy (constitutionalism)	Substantive-rational legitimacy (populism)
Carrier of legitimacy	impersonal institutions (manifested in formal rules)	personal actors (manifested in an informal organization)
Status of ruling elite	subordinated to law	served by law
Resultant process	deliberative: interest reconciliation of multiple actors (taking various interests into account)	declarative: interest enforcement of a single actor (suppressing other interests)

46.

A PATRONAL AUTOCRACY FORMALLY MAINTAINS the institutions of public deliberation but neutralizes them, placing them on a new legitimacy basis. In a communist dictatorship, the institutions of public deliberation are under doctrinarian repression and control. The rule of the party state is totalitarian: all the actors in every sphere of social action are compelled to fit in the party line and those who contradict the central will are punished accordingly.

In contrast, the institutions of public deliberation in a patronal autocracy are pragmatically neutralized and used. The adopted political family represses only what poses a threat to the stability of its monopoly of political power, not everything that opposes it. It is not doctrinarian: everyone is left alone, meaning they can exercise their rights and can participate in activities related to democratic public deliberation (free speech, running in elections etc.) as far as it does not threaten the autocratic rule. Moreover, such processes become part of the healthy functioning of the system. This has been recognized by hybridologists (Propositions 2-3) who speak about a democratic "façade," a Potemkin institutional system that has been emptied of its function of giving citizens a say in how their life is run. Also, they rightly add that the democratic façade makes sharp distancing from the regime harder, and allows the rulers to avoid overt oppression that would be very costly, both in terms of potential popular support and economic development.

On the other hand, it needs to be realized that the institutional façade is not even nominally democratic: it is placed on a new legitimacy basis, changing from legal-rational legitimacy (which is the basis for establishing the Western-type institutional setting) to substantive-rational legitimacy. In a communist dictatorship, the repression of public deliberation by the communist party can be derived from an ideology, Marxism-Leninism. From populism, the neutralizing actions of the chief patron cannot be derived, hence it is not the "ideology" of neutralization. The populist chief patron is not ideology-driven but ideology-applying (Proposition 98), and thus the relationship is reversed: neutralization cannot be derived from populism, but it is justified by it.

The chief patron uses populism as an instrument; with it, he can always argue about the institutional *status quo* that it is in the nation's interest to change it, while the way of changing it—formally maintaining the institutions but eliminating their regime-disrupting potential—is decided by the chief patron alone on a pragmatic basis (Proposition 99). This is where the often-noted "anti-elitism" of populism comes in: the populist's attack on the institutions of public deliberation is legitimized by using the people's anti-establishment ressentiment. While it appears as anti-elitism on the demand side, it is indeed "anti-deliberationism" on the supply side (Proposition 103). The populist challenges the legitimacy of legal-rational institutions to break them down, to his liking, on a substantive basis.

47.

IN THE DISCUSSING PHASE OF PUBLIC DELIBERATION, the mafia state creates a dominated sphere of communication with neutralized media rights. In a liberal democracy, the essence of discussing is that every citizen has a chance to express their views on political matters and engage peacefully with the views of other citizens. This means the upholding of four media rights, as defined by Miklós Haraszti ("Illiberal State Censorship," 2019): the right to know, which is the right to obtain information in political matters (especially information of public interest); the right to speak, which is the right to share information and one's opinion; the right to choose, which is the right to access a diverse and plural media landscape; and the right to connect, which is the right to engage in free communication and information-sharing with people at home and abroad via internet (Table 14).

In a patronal autocracy, the right to know is hindered by classifying information or creating rules that otherwise make state functioning less transparent. Regarding the right to speak, a patronal autocracy limits not content but outreach. In a process that may be called "ghettoization," the adopted political family traps critical voices in small circles where those who were already staunch opponents of the government merely converse amongst themselves, leaving a limited viability for a change in the proportion of loyal versus critical voices in the larger audience. This is once again an example for the mafia state not being doctrinarian: while a culture of self-censorship might evolve, there is no top-down censorship like in a communist dictatorship. The regime is not afraid of words, it can handle criticism—so long as it does not have outreach.

The right to choose is limited by patronal media: state media is biased, while private media is either bought up by the adopted political family or crowded out, taken over, or ghettoized. Finally, while patronal autocracies like Russia make attempts to restrict the right to connect, the general difficulty of regulating the online space has led to the application of noisemaking: muddling up communication by the broadcast of numerous contradictory narratives, combining truthful and fake news alike.

On the one hand, noisemaking creates an atmosphere of general confusion and distrust. The centrally organized and industrialized use of armies of trolls to spread these narratives in the social media disrupt discussion and contaminate it with fake news (Proposition 104). On the other hand, it also means that many different viewpoints are introduced into the public discussion with the sole purpose of perturbation. This makes public deliberation practically impossible as opposition narratives blend into the noise of the chaotic sphere of communication, wherein the people cannot decide among the cacophony of narratives which are to be taken seriously.

Table 14: Open, closed, and dominated spheres of communication.

	Right to know (obtaining information)	*Right to speak (sharing information)*	*Right to choose (diversity of sources of information)*	*Right to connect (online information)*
Open sphere of communication (liberal democracy: media rights are upheld)	allowing access to information of public interest	free speech (the state moderates content)	impartial state media free private (opposition) media	free internet access
Closed sphere of communication (communist dictatorship: media rights are suppressed)	denying access to information of public interest	censored speech (the state limits content)	directed state media banned private (opposition) media	restricted internet access
Dominated sphere of communication (patronal autocracy: media rights are neutralized)	hindering access to information of public interest	free speech (the state limits reach)	biased state media crowded out and ghettoized private (opposition) media	regulated internet access

48. IN THE ASSOCIATING PHASE OF PUBLIC DELIBERATION, first, **the mafia state neutralizes real opposition parties and creates fake ones.** Opposition parties are among the most important pillars of a liberal democracy, guaranteeing the altering of administrations. In a patronal autocracy, the mafia state tries to neutralize them: allow them to exist and win votes and seats but deny them victory (Table 15).

First, we can speak about marginalized parties. This type is not dependent on the chief patron, but is forced into a marginalized position without prospects by being financially incapacitated and through the centralization of power, restricted media access, discrimination against activists, criminalization, and politically selective law enforcement.

Second, the domesticated party is a party that is formally in opposition but informally, in the trap of deals and blackmail, it acts out the role of an opposition incapable of ever winning against the dominant party. Nevertheless, its leading cadres may be well served by this in the form of some financial and political career opportunities.

Third, the absorbed party is co-opted, perhaps while in opposition, and made an ally or even a coalition partner to the ruling (transmission-belt) party (Proposition 19). But co-optation in this case is a "deadly embrace" as the regime eventually neutralizes the party by emptying it in terms of popular support.

Fourth, the liquidated party is an opposition party that was threatening for the mafia state and was banned or liquidated through the imprisonment or perhaps even murder of its leaders, after unsuccessful attempts to force it into a domesticated position. A special kind of liquidated party is one that is not allowed to be formed in the first place: this may be called an "aborted party" (such as Russia of the Future, the unregistered opposition party of Alexei Navalny).

The last type of *de jure* opposition party cannot be said to be "neutralized" as it has never represented actual opposition. The fake parties fulfil a double function. On the one hand, in regimes where brushing the opposition parties off the party structure has been too successful, the central power itself launches "opposition" parties and candidates under its control, fitting well into the democratic scene. This has been the case in Turkmenistan since 2007, where a fake opposition emerged in form of fake parties as well as fake presidential candidates, all being vocal supporters of chief patron Gurbanguly Berdimuhamedow.

On the other hand, a chief patron may decide to launch fake parties, directly or indirectly, to divide and therefore reduce the winning chances of the opposition. The appearance of these parties can disorient voters and fragment the government-critical votes; in Hungary, this was instrumental in keeping the supermajority of Fidesz in the 2014 elections. The stability of a political landscape of neutralized and fake parties is not a given: formerly domesticated or marginalized parties may try to break out of their position (like the Communist Party in Russia), and protest sentiments against both the government and the opposition can boost anti-establishment formations. Should such movements be serious, the mafia state can be expected to intervene, and introduce further measures to ensure the neutralized state of the political playing field.

Table 15: Opposition parties with different formal and *de facto* status in a patronal autocracy.

	Formal status	De facto status	Function
Marginalized party	Opposition	Neutralized opposition (without winning chances)	Pretense of competition (with minimal oversight and gains)
Domesticated party	Opposition	Neutralized opposition (subordinated to the chief patron)	Pretense of competition
Absorbed party	Opposition (former coalition partner)	Neutralized opposition (emptied by the chief patron)	Pretense of competition
Liquidated party	Opposition	Neutralized opposition (liquidated by the chief patron)	n.a.
Fake party	Opposition	Virtual opposition (created by the chief patron)	Pretense of competition / obstruction of real opposition

IN THE ASSOCIATING PHASE OF PUBLIC DELIBERATION, second, **49.** **the mafia state upholds a dominant-party system with competitive fringe or fake opposition.** With a few exceptions like China, most of the post-communist countries have developed multi-party systems. The most important question about these is whether they are composed of patronal or non-patronal parties: that is, whether the competition of parties is indeed a competition of patron-client networks. In a patronal democracy, a number of patron's parties, with informal networks of relatively equal size, compete; in a patronal autocracy, the party system features a dominant patron's party with opposition parties confined to a competitive fringe.

"Competitive fringe" is a term adopted from economics: in the model of dominant firm with competitive fringe, the concept is used to describe a high number of relatively small firms, each having a minor fraction of the market compared to the market leader who controls the industry and to whom the competitive fringe adjusts. Similarly, the dominant patron's party is opposed by several relatively small parties, and the dominant party effectively determines the rules and content of the competition.

A second parallel to the economic model comes from the fact that the dominant firm is not a monopolist: it has competitive advantage but must work on maintaining it, preventing potential entrants from the competitive fringe to take over. The dominant party has, as a client of the adopted political family, much more (formal and informal) resources than the opposition, but it still needs to take into account what the opposition does. The adopted political family may need to weaken real opposition further, and/or adjust its policy decisions so the opposition cannot capitalize on them (Proposition 115).

The third parallel is that there is usually competition between the competitive-fringe firms, and the competition there may be more intense than it is toward the dominant firm. In a dominant-party system with competitive fringe, while some opposition parties might still try to genuinely fight the leading political elite, they are likely to realize that winning is not an option—but maximizing seats and votes, and thus, access to state resources at each other's expense is. As a result, opposition parties "run for the silver medal instead of the gold one" as they try to lay their hands on as much access to public resources as possible. However, a dominant-party system can also be accompanied by a purely fake opposition. In that case, the real opposition has been eliminated and the remaining "rivals" of the dominant party are actually the creations of the adopted political family.

50.

IN THE ASSOCIATING PHASE OF PUBLIC DELIBERATION, third, the mafia state employs GONGOs and TRANSBOs in the communal sphere while suppressing NGOs. The main collective actors of the sphere of communal action are the non-profit organizations (NGOs), which represent a special type of association. An NGO is, ideal typically, "single issue": it works for one cause or represents one viewpoint in a certain issue, not regarding the financial or political hardships it may face. At the same time, NGOs are bottom-up organizations, functioning *de jure* and *de facto* independently from the state.

The term "GONGO" (government-organized NGO), on the other hand, attempts to capture a *contradictio in adjecto*: that these organizations formally position themselves as NGOs whereas they are actually state organizations, founded and fostered (informally) by the ruling elite and it serves the existing power. As mafia states are pragmatic and do not ban (all) opposition groups, NGOs which do not challenge the power and applied ideology of the ruling elite can exist in a patronal autocracy. The NGOs that do pose a challenge, especially human rights and anti-corruption watchdogs, are subject to neutralization by the authorities, whereas GONGOs enjoy privileged status in terms of regulations and funding.

The mafia state employs a multistep domestication methodology. First, it centralizes funding and its control; second, it deploys the media by conducting negative campaigns against the opposition-oriented NGOs, or the ones that advocate the ethos of curbing the state's dominance in general. As a last step, it may employ coercive means in order to enforce the chief patron's will (Proposition 82).

Beyond NGOs and GONGOs, we need to mention TRANSBOs, or transmission-belt organizations which are established *de jure* by the state. Originating in communist dictatorship, TRANSBOs like labor unions, popular front-like organizations, communist youth organizations, cultural associations, women's organization, and so on were founded by and enrolled into the nomenklatura of the state party to transmit its will and the proposed communal lifestyles to the dictatorships' subjects. In a patronal autocracy, the party itself becomes a transmission-belt organization (Proposition 19), while various TRANSBOs in the cultural, scientific, sport etc. fields are established by the state to fulfill three main roles: corrupt pay-offices, sources of public money and sinecure for beneficiaries of the adopted political family; places of recruitment, or adoption to the political family; and bastions of symbolic politics, supplying and publicly supporting the ideological legitimation of the regime (Proposition 99).

51.

IN THE ASSOCIATING PHASE OF PUBLIC DELIBERATION, fourth, the mafia state organizes pro-government, loyalty-demonstrating rallies while demobilizing protests. In a liberal democracy where public deliberation equally accommodates both supportive and critical voices, the state treats protests in the same way as rallies: that is, as events of association. As we are moving toward more repressive systems, a gap appears between these two types. Protests are decreasingly tolerated, while rallies become more and more prominent.

On the repressive end of the scale, communist dictatorships do not tolerate protests, while pro-government rallies take the form of parades, flamboyant state celebrations where the people are obliged to swarm the streets and hail the system and its leaders. A patronal autocracy is on the middle of the scale, with both protests and pro-government rallies being prominent. The latter, like the pro-government rallies of Nashi in Russia and the so-called Peace Marches in Hungary, are different from communist parades, which were mainly enforced ritual actions. They act as an event where the chief patron can demonstrate popular support and the marchers can demonstrate their loyalty. On the other hand, such events can typically access more financial resources and face a more benevolent state apparatus than (anti-government) protests, which can not only access fewer resources, but also contend with the repression of the state.

The mafia state takes advantage of the problem of conflicting rights, such as the fact that exercising freedom of assembly may require shutting down traffic—restricting freedom of movement—or it may disturb people living in the streets the protesters occupy—constituting a danger to public order. While a constitutional state engages in balancing rights, trying to create a system where no of basic right is completely suppressed by another, the mafia state engages in "non-balancing rights:" the state uses the less threatening right as an excuse to suppress the more threatening one. On the other hand, the mafia state may employ a range of techniques to demobilize protesters from simple ignoring through "buying off" protesting social groups to negative signaling, which means making people believe they can lose their jobs or similar access to resources if they protest.

In general, two types of protests can be distinguished: policy-questioning and legitimacy-questioning ones. In the case of the former, certain groups (students, teachers, pensioners etc.) express their grievances separately, focusing only on certain policies regarding their own group. These can be dismantled by the mafia state with partial promises or simple ignoring, waiting for them to run out of steam. However, the legitimacy-questioning protests go beyond the professional critique of a particular field as well as the political logic of the regime itself: they embody the regime-critique paradigm instead of the government-critique paradigm (Proposition 74).

52. In the electing phase of public deliberation, first, the mafia state organizes loyalty-structuring and floor-monopolizing campaigns. In liberal democracies, elections represent a situation of free choice (Table 16). Marketing campaigns involve a market-like competition, following the prevalence of free supply—citizens are free to form, join, and support conflicting parties—and free demand—citizens are free to learn about the available alternatives through access to alternative sources of information. At the same time, the *ad hoc* organization (of the party) that directs a campaign is independent of the executive and judicial organs of the state, even—or especially—in the case of the governing party's campaign. This is an institutional guarantee of the citizens' freedom of choice as well as that the campaigns, even those with conflicting goals, can compete freely on the political market.

In sharp contrast, the mafia state organizes loyalty-structuring, floor-monopolizing campaigns in which not only patronal media but state organs are also involved. While the uneven playing field is often noticed, the role of the Prosecutor's Office in criminalizing opponents during elections is wrapped in embarrassed silence even by international observers. The Prosecutor's Office leaks information that vilifies the opponents to patronal media carefully in keeping with the campaign schedule, while sometimes qualifying the cases as state secret so the accused is not allowed to even defend themselves in public. In certain cases, public opinion is preconditioned with a detention, house arrest or a photograph of the accused being led through court. The scoops are well timed: their public presentation follows the timetable of the most varied campaigns. In the end, the Prosecutor's Office can also disqualify political opponents, removing them from the competition altogether.

Selective law enforcement adjusted to campaign objectives appears in communist dictatorships as well, but campaign has a different meaning in a communist setting. There, rights-suspending campaigns exist as a coercive mechanism, representing no choice, used by high-level nomenklaturists who turn the state apparatus into "movement-mode." This means that lower-level nomenklaturists and/or certain groups of the population are assigned to fulfill a centrally determined goal that could not be demanded legally or the fulfillment of which could not be insured with the routine legal operation of the apparatus. Such campaigns may be economic as well as political; in the latter case, they often involve show trials and vigilance campaigns (Proposition 62). Non-compliance with campaigns brings direct sanctions, which can be extra-legal or "social" (public humiliation) as well as legal. This is naturally in contrast with liberal democracies, whereas in patronal autocracies sanction of not voting for the ruling party appears primarily for certain social groups highly dependent on state and patronal subsidies.

Table 16: Campaigns in the three polar type regimes.

Marketing campaign (in liberal democracy)	Loyalty-structuring campaign (in patronal autocracy)	Rights-suspending campaign (in communist dictatorship)
free choice	unfree choice	no choice
bottom-up (non-state conducted)	top-down (mafia state conducted)	top-down (party state conducted)
periodic	occasional/permanent	occasional/periodic
competitive campaign (for convincing the people)	floor-monopolizing campaign (for crowding others out)	managing campaign (for coercing a state goal)
no sanction for refusal	no or indirect sanction for refusal	direct sanction for refusal

53. IN THE ELECTING PHASE OF PUBLIC DELIBERATION, second, the mafia state holds manipulated elections.

As the government and the opposition have perfectly equal conditions in no country in terms of the resources and media access of electoral competitors, it would be difficult to draw the clear line between a "relatively even" and a "seriously or undemocratically uneven" playing field. But there are two aspects which allow for a clear typology of elections in post-communist regimes (Table 17). First, the legality of campaign funding: in fair elections, the ruling party uses the monies legally allocated to them for the purpose of campaigning, while unfair elections make use of illegal channels of party financing. In Russia, tens of millions of dollars in government bonds were diverted to Yeltsin's 1996 re-election campaign, making the election unfair.

However, although minor changes in the electoral law were instituted a few months before the election, the adoption of the electoral system back then was consensual. This is the aspect distinguishing unfair and those manipulated elections where the electoral law is changed and adopted one-sidedly by the incumbents. In the Putin and Orbán regimes, the use of state and governmental media for campaigning constitutes illegal campaign funding, whereas the electoral law was substantially revised by the incumbents alone, involving gerrymandering and the introduction of several majoritarian elements to strengthen the current position of the ruling party.

Based on the research of Henry E. Hale in his seminal *Patronal Politics* (2015), the functions of manipulated elections can be grouped as follows. First, in the case of manipulated elections, a profane, electoral act becomes a sacred demonstration of loyalty. The "elections" are a show of subservience on the part of patronal networks and their members, an occasion for the leaders to mobilize supporters.

Second, elections provide a useful mechanism of the controlled renewing of formal, political positions of the patronal network. This involves the co-optation of other networks, distribution of monies, or it facilitates power-sharing among the important elite groups as well.

Third, regimes that do not allow regular elections face crises and revolutions, but these tend to be highly unpredictable for the ruler. This risk gives leaders an interest in channeling public challenges through more predictable mechanisms, i.e., (manipulated) elections. In so doing, chief patrons structure the political struggle according to ground rules that they themselves design, that enable them to prepare long in advance, and that reduce the chances of losing power.

Finally, chief patrons derive legitimation even from manipulated elections. The issue is not simply that the populist can more effectively speak in the name of the nation after an electoral victory; such victories tell everyone that the officially winning chief patron in fact does possess the raw power to manipulate elections and orchestrate a win. This creates incentives for social actors to coordinate around the winners' networks, reinforcing the single-pyramid arrangement.

Table 17: Types of elections.

	Adoption of electoral system	Legality of the leaders' campaign funding	Access to nation-wide TVs for the real opposition	Neutrality of public institutions
Fair elections	Consensual	Legal	Open	Neutral
Unfair elections	Consensual	Legal + illegal	↓ Restricted	↓ Biased
Manipulated elections	One-sided	Legal + illegal	↓	↓
Uncontested elections	One-sided	Legal + illegal	Closed	Hand-guided

54.

WHAT IS AT STAKE FOR THE CHIEF PATRON in the elections is not simply to stay in power but to avoid loss of personal freedom. In a liberal democracy, losing an election means the loss of governing power and ability to realize policies. But a party, having been removed from power, does not get excluded from the political arena. Former rulers go to opposition, where they can go on participating in the process of public deliberation in its next cycle. Democratic rulers commit nothing illegal in power, or at least they do not have krysha (Proposition 38) eliminating any possibility of prosecution against them for the time of their rule. In short, they do not need to face a reactivated prosecution once they are ousted from power.

In a patronal autocracy, the rulers commit crimes according to the existing criminal code by the very nature of the system, heading an informal patronal network that accumulates personal wealth with deactivated control mechanisms. Running the state as a criminal organization, the chief patron risks persecution and going into prison if he loses.

In his study entitled "Accountable for What?" (2013), Spanish political scientist Abel Escribà-Folch found that in so-called personalist regimes (of which patronal autocracy would be a subtype) the political career of post-WWII autocrats ended in exile, jail, or death 63% of the time—more often than military dictators (51%) and nearly twice as often as monarchs (37%). We may mention three notable examples from the post-communist region: Viktor Yanukovich, former Ukrainian chief patron who was overthrown in the Euromaidan revolution and has been in exile in Russia since, while a Ukrainian court sentenced him in absentia to thirteen years' imprisonment for high treason; Nikola Gruevski, former Macedonian chief patron who was forced to resign and was sentenced to two years in prison on corruption charges, although he has managed to escape with the help of the Macedonian and Hungarian secret services; and Vladimir Plahotniuc, former Moldovan chief patron who fled the country with his patron's court in face of strong international pressure.

The point of these cases is that electoral victory is a matter of "life or death" for the chief patron, not a matter of staying in power or temporarily losing influence over public policy (as in liberal democracy). This is one important reason why chief patrons manipulate elections and try to make sure they stay in power, not only to fulfill their patronal policy goals in general.

55.

REFERENDA ARE USED BY CHIEF PATRONS in patronal autocracies to consolidate their power while denying the opposition to use this type of vote. Referenda represent a shortcut of the public deliberation process. While elections are embodiments of representative democracy, referenda are a form of direct democracy where the people vote directly on issues, laws or people in a binary "yes or no" format. The structured institutions of mediation of the popular will do not play a role—a feature that is part and parcel of populism as well (Propositions 44-45). Indeed, what referenda realize is precisely a direct link between the people and the head of executive, who is told in the referendum what the majority wants. But just as we have seen that populism, while referring to the people and civil legitimacy, indeed leads to removal of state decision-making from the hands of the people and the populist decides instead what is in the "national" or "in the people's interest," patronal referenda are also means of patronal appropriation of the interpretation of the common good.

Referenda in patronal autocracies are used to reinforce the chief patron in his position of sole interpreter of the common good and to remove limits on his power (or, in the populist narrative, to allow him to step over unnecessary legal constraints to the realization of the goals of "the people": substantive-rational legitimacy). Among several examples, we may mention the referenda in Belarus (2004), Azerbaijan (2009), and Russia (2020), which changed or abolished constitutional term limits for the president-chief patron, and the referenda in Hungary (2016, 2022), which were campaign events that used the themes of "illegal migration" and "LGBTQ propaganda," respectively, to position chief patron Orbán as the defender of the nation, mobilizing supporters and demobilizing opponents.

Other examples can be found in Central Asian post-communist countries, which all fit in the general tendency to enhance the power of the presidency and reduce democratic provisions. On the other hand, no opposition referenda have been held in patronal autocracies yet. Referendum as a means of public deliberation is neutralized: the reference to direct popular will becomes a means of excluding deliberated popular will.

Legislation and the Legal System: From the Rule of Law to the Law of Rule

56.

IN THE LAWMAKING PHASE OF PUBLIC DELIBERATION, first, the mafia state's legislative aims are patronal policies, which have no public policy objectives, only public policy consequences. In a patronal autocracy, public interest is permanently and not incidentally subordinated to private goals, determining political decisions fundamentally in a systematic way. As elite interest, or the twin motives of power concentration and personal-wealth accumulation become the dominant principle of state functioning (Proposition 25) public policy objectives as reasons for political decisions are relegated to the background.

Once we have identified a regime as a patronal autocracy, the fields which would be regarded as fields of public policy in a liberal democracy (like education, social policy, or cultural policy) should be observed through "regime-specific glasses," presuming elite interest and considering the interests of the adopted political family. This approach not only harmonizes with the analytical framework we have chosen for the regime but also offers an understanding and predictive power that we would not achieve if we drew our assumption of motivation from formal policy considerations rather than how the system works. Thus, instead of registering policy "mistakes" that do not consistently serve officially declared purposes, we get an accurate description of decisions that serve the motives of power and wealth.

Naturally, the chief patron needs to recognize and adapt to the current opportunities and political climate, and these influence the content of policies in the sense that actually which actors and institutions are targeted, and when an attempt to break their autonomy is initiated. But the underlying motivation remains the same: decisions that look like policies, "restructuring" or "reform" are, in fact, decisions of patronalization and patrimonialization. Under the given circumstances, the chief patron always tries to build patron-client relations, exploit the political climate, and extend his power in general so he can treat the state and the society as his private domain (Propositions 26-27). Thus, instead of public policies, we should speak about patronal policies.

Patronal policies have no public policy motives, only public policy consequences. Effects like growing inequality, impoverishment of lower social strata, or decreasing performance in education are only the corollaries or "side effects" of the realization of the central motives of the adopted political family (Proposition 114).

57. IN THE LAWMAKING PHASE OF PUBLIC DELIBERATION, second, the mafia state formulates instrumental, discretional law in the form of custom-tailored lexes. As state decisions are pragmatically customized to the needs of the adopted political family where both wealth and power are concerned, autocratic and discretional action takes the place of formal and legal processes in the established political institutional system without checks and balances.

The instrumentalization of the legal system is made possible by the legitimacy basis of substantive-rational legitimacy (Proposition 45). While the legal-rational legitimacy of liberal democracies is a constraint to politicians, placing them under the rule of law, substantive-rational legitimacy is an enabling device of the chief patron that degrades law into a secondary, instrumental position to the adopted political family.

Legislation is no longer a field of legal and normative rules that are applicable to all and can be called to account, but the adopted political family's "tailor shop for fitted garments," where laws are tailored to fit the needs of the family. This is in contrast to communist dictatorships: there, the instrumentalization of law is reached via sub-statutory acts, which overrule existing legal norms on a case-by-case basis. Communist constitutions also openly declared substantive-rational legitimacy, becoming enabling laws themselves by calling the communist party the "vanguard," "leading force," or "guide" of the people.

In a patronal autocracy, the constitution declares legal-rational legitimacy, not the actual substantive-rational, whereas legal arbitrariness is reached via custom-tailored lexes. The legislation is used to create laws tailored to individuals, groups, political friends and foes. This is performed with the precision of a surgeon based on the case-by-case authorizations given by the head of the political family, offering reward or punishment, privilege or discrimination (Table 18). Targeting takes place in a covert way: while the law itself appears to be normative, the criteria for its application are compiled in a way that only the target falls under its scope. This practice is called technicization in corruption literature, but it is elevated on the rank of central politics in patronal autocracies. The corpus of statutes is constantly adjusted to the continuously changing whims of the adopted political family. The legislation is, therefore, of paramount importance, for mass *ad hoc* procedures are required to formulate and create the appropriate lexes.

Table 18: Types of custom-tailored lexes, with general examples for rewarding and punishing policies.

Type of target	Patronal policy objective	General example for... rewarding policy	General example for... punishing policy
Political actor	Disposition over the fulfillment of public offices	lifting conflicts of interest requirements to ensure that the front men of the adopted political family can be appointed to public positions	the arbitrary removal of persons from public offices enabled by legislation
Political actor (institution)	Disposition over the remuneration of political actors	growing remunerations or support for political front men of the adopted political family, or the civil and political organization, municipal governments dominated by them	decrease in the remunerations or support of political opponents of the regime in public positions and critical civil or political organizations, municipal governments
Political actor (institution)	Disposition over the competences of political actors	extension of the competencies of the institutions under political front men, after they are appointed	narrowing competencies of institutions, or municipal and professional bodies monitoring government
Economic actor	Disposition over profitability of economic actors	ensuring positions of advantage to loyal business ventures	removal of businesses not integrated into the adopted political family from the market, or ensuring their takeover
Political / economic / communal actor	Achieving political benefit	making actors non-convictable (even retroactively) who the courts would convict but the adopted political family does not want them to	making actors convictable (even retroactively) who the courts did not convict but the people want them to

58. In the lawmaking phase of public deliberation, third, the mafia state passes laws in a transmission-belt legislation.

Since the decisions that determine the future of society are brought outside of the formalized bodies, the parliament in a patronal autocracy only serves to give the stamp of approval for the autocratic decisions. The parliament ceases to be the control of the executive, and becomes another transmission belt of the adopted political family.

In liberal democracies, the members of parliament are politicians: autonomous actors who can use their formal political power at their will. While they may be bound by party discipline, politicians are allowed to debate, to hold a minority opinion, and even to submit a legislative bill on their own right. In other words, there exists public deliberation within the governing party: there is (1) discussing, as far as the members can voice their opinions and try to convince others; (2) associating, as far as factions and platforms can be formed vis-à-vis the party leadership; (3) electing, as far as the party leaders (and sometimes even the party's candidates) are chosen by the members after intra-party campaigns; (4) lawmaking, as far as the party creates its own internal rules and regulations which the members (including the leadership) are expected to follow; and (5) enforcing, as far as a violation of the party's internal rules is followed by disciplinary action. Therefore, MPs are not simple executors of the will of their party's leaders but can shape, or at least have an effect on, policy decisions.

In contrast, governing MPs in a transmission-belt legislature are dominantly political front men: simple executors with no autonomy and virtually no say in shaping policy. Transmission-belt legislatures are only required to "keep the books" on decisions taken elsewhere, in the realm of informal institutions. What matters is the extent of the majority of the adopted political family's parliamentary faction. The main difference between patronal democracies and autocracies stems from this fact: the ruling adopted political family in a patronal democracy does not have supermajority, or the power to one-sidedly change constitutional rules.

Supermajority is the prerequisite for instituting and stabilizing the single-pyramid patronal network of a patronal autocracy.

While to the everyday working of a mafia state—including the instrumental use of law and passing custom-tailored lexes whenever they are needed—an absolute majority is sufficient, chief patrons usually strive to keep supermajority in elections, to be able to change anything in the legal system if the need arises.

59. IN THE ENFORCING PHASE OF PUBLIC DELIBERATION, first, the mafia state replaces equality before the law with inequality after the law. With some playing with words, we can differentiate the period before a law is applied—when it has been formulated and adopted but not yet used in a legal case—and the period as it is applied. "Equality before the law" refers to the former period, to whether people are legally entitled to the same protection of rights, and whether the word of the law includes discrimination; "equality after the law" refers to the latter period, and asks whether legally granted rights and the promulgated laws are equally enforced or not.

In liberal democracy, the rule of law prevails, which rests on the principles of equality before and after the law. In a mafia state, rule of law is replaced by the law of rule: equality before the law is accompanied by inequality after the law (Table 19). *De jure*, on the level of formal institutions each law equally applies to everyone, meaning they should be enforced against everyone who falls under their scope; *de facto*, politically selective law enforcement along informal commands prevails, treating friends and foes, surrendered and non-surrendered economic actors, political allies and rivals in different ways. Political status, patronal dependence, and loyalty constitute the basis of the informal norms that guide law enforcement in a patronal autocracy.

The chief patron can always decide between non-enforcement of law and custom-tailoring the law which then can be enforced; and he can be expected to choose the one which impairs the regime's democratic façade less and conceals the real (patronal policy) motives of the adopted political family more. However, this applies only to cases of high salience. The case is not that every law is instrumental and every legal procedure is hand-guided; everyday people can be sure that their rights will be respected, and there will be no interference from the top in more mundane cases. But the people's rights have a conditional character: they are enforced only as far as they do not interfere with the plans of the chief patron, or until he does not want to interfere to punish or reward. The actions of the chief patron move on a wide amplitude of arbitrariness (Proposition 28), ranging from no interference to outright shelter provision and integrity breaking (Proposition 38).

Table 19: The status of law in the three polar type regimes.

	Before the law	*After the law*
Rule of law (as in liberal democracy)	Equality	Equality
Law of rule (as in patronal autocracy)	Equality	Inequality
Lawlessness (as in communist dictatorship)	Inequality	Inequality

60.

IN THE ENFORCING PHASE OF PUBLIC DELIBERATION, second, **the mafia state neutralizes the judicial branch to provide impunity for its clients.** Often it is not necessary to directly control judges to make them act by informal norms. Officials may learn what needs to be done through the unambiguous signals generated by the various direct interventions of the chief patron in other parts of the society. As a result of this chilling effect, informal rules are gradually becoming the norm. But the adopted political family can make sure its will is being served in the judiciary if it takes more concrete steps to neutralize it.

We may list three ways of neutralization, which can be combined and used in unison as well. First, the simplest—but also least subtle—way for the chief patron is to break the autonomy of the judiciary. By this method, he or a political front man he institutes as a supervisor of the judges will intervene in legal cases, relocate court cases arbitrarily, restrict the competences of the courts, or informally envisage negative repercussions against "wrongfully unbiased" judges.

Second, a patronal autocracy can decide to replace politically sensitive judicial cases from ordinary courts to the hands of newly instituted administrative courts. This method of neutralization has been applied by several patronal autocracies, including Armenia, Azerbaijan, Belarus, Kazakhstan, and Uzbekistan. Administrative courts in patronal autocracy are packed with patronal servants (Proposition 20) and/or instituted with a special legal framework that limits normative adjudication. Such courts exist parallel to the normal judicial system and remove complaints against the state from the system of guarantees that formally exist in normal courts. In these special courts, there is no genuine debate, the judges only examine compliance to specific laws concerning the state institution in question, whereas the complainant might have some chance of winning if he complains about formalities (missed deadlines etc.).

The third option of neutralization of the judicial branch is subordinating prosecution to the adopted political family's informal interests. If this way is chosen, there is almost no need to deal with the courts because criminal cases do not reach that level of the legal process, as the prosecution does not start criminal investigations against the adopted political family in the first place. Moreover, in post-Soviet countries prosecution has been historically strong in the legal system, making it a particularly important weapon in the hands of chief patrons. Hence, hand-guided prosecution is not simply neutralized but can also be used to attack or blackmail the enemies of the adopted political family. Thus, prosecution in patronal autocracies can easily become a principal means of politically selective law enforcement.

61. **I**N THE ENFORCING PHASE OF PUBLIC DELIBERATION, third, the mafia state weaponizes kompromat and charges opponents with common criminal, rather than political, offenses.** Kompromat is not particular to patronal autocracies; it exists in communist dictatorships and even in patronal democracies. In general, kompromat is a piece of information—a real fact—that a political actor can be blackmailed with, either because (a) it would reveal their criminality or (b) it is a part of their personal life they do not want to publicize (evidence of extravagant spending habits, sexual behavior etc.). In contrast to show-trial "evidence," kompromat is not fabricated but collected. Kompromat has been abundant in post-communist countries: first, transition and privatization were done in a rather shaky legal environment, and with many abuses on the part of those who became important economic and/or political actors; later, the functioning of patronal systems with predatory institutions and low-quality public services gave rise to a wide sector of shadow economy, which is a fertile medium for kompromat.

Being a valuable asset, markets for kompromat developed in these countries with entrepreneurs (often criminals or former secret service people) specializing in collecting kompromat, and selling pieces of information to interested parties. In patronal democracies and also the nascent oligarchic anarchies (Proposition 30), competing patronal networks and oligarchs use kompromat in their fights ("kompromat wars"), whereas oligarchs can also use it to blackmail politicians in bottom-up state capture.

But for a competitive kompromat market to exist there are two conditions: media pluralism, for a piece of information can potentially damage a person's reputation only if it can be publicized; and a non-hand guided prosecution and judiciary, for otherwise no matter what kompromat one might have, nobody will be convicted unless the one who hand-guides approves. This explains why the establishment of single-pyramid patronal network brings the end of a competitive kompromat market. In a patronal autocracy, the chief patron becomes the foremost user of kompromat. It not only helps him keep his clients in check, whose krysha protects them from prosecution but the evidence of their criminality exists in the chief patron's hands.

Kompromat helps bridge the discrepancy between the equality before and the inequality after the law. In communist dictatorships, political opponents could be sent to jail as opposition activities were legally banned, and the category of political prisoner existed accordingly (typically separated spatially, as a distinct "class," from ordinary criminals in penitentiary institutions). But in a patronal autocracy, the system is formally a democracy, and the basic rights and liberties of people are formally upheld. Therefore, the adopted political family must transform political opponents into common criminals to jail them. Kompromat is collected and used by the adopted political family for this purpose particularly, where the chief patron can activate prosecution discretionally and hand over (through front men) the evidence, on the basis of which political opponents can be convicted.

IN THE ENFORCING PHASE OF PUBLIC DELIBERATION, fourth, **62.** the mafia state stages, for unyielding opponents in whose case no kompromat is available, show trials with fabricated evidence. A kompromat trial in a patronal autocracy goes by the following structure: a crime is committed; prosecution launches the legal process and investigation on the basis of political decision; judges compare existing law with kompromat, that is, real facts that the chief patron collects and uses for blackmail and punishing disloyal actors when necessary; the court makes a decision (typically about guilt) based on assessment of kompromat. In contrast, the structure of a show trial is the following: the crime is not committed; prosecution launches the legal process and investigation on the basis of political decision; judges compare existing law with fabricated evidence, that is, fictitious data and accusations made up by the rulers to frame the number one scapegoat as guilty; the court makes a decision (about guilt) based on the predefined political verdict.

Show trials have been central to the practice of communist dictatorships. There, the "show" element referred to both campaign objectives (Proposition 52) and the presence of fabricated evidence, whereas the process involved waves of cleansing the nomenklatura personnel as well. In a patronal autocracy, political interference in court trials for campaign objectives (such as in the case of the Russian feminist protest punk rock band Pussy Riot) does not necessarily mean the application of fabricated evidence. For that appears only when the trial is an attempt to neutralize an unyielding opponent, for whom no incriminating kompromat is available. Unable to neutralize them in other ways or co-opt them in the adopted political family, the chief patron may stage a show trial, although such practice has appeared only in more consolidated autocracies like Belarus and Russia.

Just as in the case of kompromat, the fabricated evidence a chief patron uses always refers to common criminal offenses such as embezzlement and drug trafficking; this is in contrast to the communist practice, where show trials centered on political crimes such as high treason. Finally, an important show-element of the communist show trials was the accused themselves pleading guilty, confessing they sinned against the state party and communist principles. This sharply contrasts patronal autocracies, where the accused typically does not plead guilty and uses the opportunity to express strong criticism of the regime instead (like in the case of opposition politician Alexei Navalny in Putin's Russia).

63.

IN THE ENFORCING PHASE OF PUBLIC DELIBERATION, fifth, the mafia state employs outsourced as well as insourced state coercion to enforce its will. A constitutional state may use state coercion only against criminals, enforcing the laws that have been created by elected representatives of the people. Its arsenal embodying the monopoly of the legitimate use of violence is composed of formal, legal institutions such as law enforcement agencies (police, SWAT etc.), revenue agencies (tax office etc.), and secret services.

A mafia state also relies on these institutions, but it changes their characteristic function and supplements them with new means (Table 20). We may illustrate the changing of function on the example of secret services. In a liberal democracy, we speak about a state's secret service; in a communist dictatorship, it is the party's secret service, committed to the defense of the interests of the party state. In a patronal autocracy, the secret service is subordinated the chief patron, serving his interests by his informal commands, conducting surveillance of formal and informal opposition (parties, NGOs, even individuals). There has also been precedent for the creation of a new, parallel agency from loyal men of the chief patron, such as in the case of the National Guard of the Russian Federation, headed by Putin's personal bodyguard, and the Counter Terrorism Center (TEK) in Hungary, directed by Orbán's former personal bodyguard.

The use of violence through institutions formally belonging to the state, which may be dubbed as white coercion, is supplemented by authorized legal use of violence, or grey coercion, as well as illegal use of violence, or black coercion, in a patronal autocracy. However, the mafia state may consider the use of physical violence only as a last resort. The chief patron is pragmatic; as he is interested in keeping a façade of non-repression, he moves on to more violent, less democratic means only when the normal, democratic-looking means are no longer sufficient. This is the key principle for the neutralization of the public deliberation process: between free competition and the liquidation of opponents, or the lack of repression in liberal democracies and the mass terror in communist dictatorships, there exists a wide range of tools of political and economic impediment from blackmail and co-optation through the fining or disqualification of opposition actors to changing the rules of competition altogether. Only when these means seem unsatisfactory may the chief patron employ physical violence to extort and liquidate specific targets or opponents of the adopted political family. The scale for such targets might range from opposition politicians through rival oligarchs to unyielding journalists.

Table 20: Institutions of state coercion and their functions. White background refers to insourced state coercion while grey, outsourced state coercion.

	Type of organization	Characteristic state function in…	
		Liberal democracy	Patronal autocracy
White coercion (default legal use of violence)	Law enforcement agency (police, SWAT etc.)	Normative law enforcement through (threats of) violence	Extortion through selective law enforcement, protection of the adopted political family
	Revenue agency (tax office, accounting office etc.)	Collection of normatively imposed levies	Extortion through selective inspection and penalties
	Intelligence agency (secret service etc.)	Surveillance and neutralizing national security threats	Surveillance of formal and informal opposition (parties, NGOs, individuals)
Grey coercion (authorized legal use of violence)	Auxiliary police (self-defense organization etc.)	Part-time reserves of national police force	Helping law enforcement agencies in serving the adopted political family
	Private protection agencies (secret service, private police etc.)	Protection of people and objects of public importance	Protection of people and objects of patronal importance
Black coercion (illegal of use violence)	Fan clubs (ultras, skinheads etc.)	n.a.	Neutralizing protests and other opposition-related activities
	Paramilitary group (militias etc.)	n.a.	Intimidation, violent resolution of mass opposition activities
	Organized underworld (criminal groups, classical mafia etc.)	n.a.	Extortion and liquidation of specific targets or opponents of the adopted political family

Defensive Mechanisms: Stability and Erosion of Democracies and Autocracies

64.

DEMOCRACIES AND AUTOCRACIES ARE STABLE, self-sustaining systems as far as they have defensive mechanisms against erosion. Self-sustaining systems may fall as a result of exogenous shocks like wars or worldwide depressions, but their endogenous components, i.e., the internal processes that make up the system, do not break it down. As Hungarian philosopher János Kis explains ("Demokrácia vagy autokrácia?" [Democracy or autocracy?], 2016), a regime is stable in the event of the constellation of three criteria: (1) the regime's components are compatible, that is, the activity of one institution does not preclude the others from performing the tasks that are assigned to them; (2) the regime's components are mutually supportive, that is, an institution, while performing its own task, also creates favorable conditions for the smooth running of other components, thus increasing the self-sustaining capacity of the whole system and contributing to the prevention of unwanted fluctuations in the regime; (3) the regime has effective defensive mechanisms, which prevent or contain destructive tendencies so they do not lead to the destruction of the regime's essence.

Defensive mechanisms are most important when they are under attack, and in post-communist systems this has happened either when actors attempted to transform liberal democracy into an autocracy—like in the case of Hungary, where the attempt was successful—or when a patronal democracy is being transformed into a patronal autocracy—like in the case of Ukraine, where the attempts have been unsuccessful. In each case, the essence of the respective regimes has been threatened.

In a liberal democracy, this essence of the regime is the universal protection of human rights and the people's equal right to have a say in how their life is governed: these are embodied in limited political power and public deliberation, respectively. In a patronal democracy, the essence of the regime is the competition of patronal networks: the plurality of informal power pyramids of roughly equal size existing in a dynamic equilibrium, with each network always trying to become dominant but unable to do so. The differences between the two regimes necessitate different kinds of defensive mechanisms, which we are going to explore below.

Autocracies also require defensive mechanisms—not to maintain pluralism but to prevent it, protecting the unconstrained, monopolistic rule of the chief patron. The chief patron is not a simple thief but a stationary bandit, to use the expression of economist Mancur Olson (*Power and Prosperity*, 2000). Looting not some momentarily chosen target but his own homeland, the chief patron cannot simply take what he wants today but must think about tomorrow as well. He needs to achieve sustainability and, hence, institute defensive mechanisms to ensure his regime's survival (Proposition 115).

65. **THE SEPARATION OF BRANCHES OF POWER is a defensive mechanism in liberal democracies, limiting political power to avoid autocratic tendencies.** Limiting political power stems from the constitutionalist principle of human rights: the state's use of violence must not be used to carry out rights violations. On the contrary, the *raison d'être* of a constitutional state is precisely to prevent rights violations, and although it can be democratically enabled to fulfill other (public policy) functions, even the people—typically the majority—are prohibited from initiating centrally-led infringement of the basic rights and liberties of others—typically the minority.

Beyond simple prohibition, the effective defense against the tyranny of a branch of power, particularly the executive, is the separation of powers. Advocated most famously by Montesquieu, the basic idea of the separation of powers is to prevent every state function being exercised by the same person or a single elite group. Institutions are set up in a way that not every political actor is either dependent or answerable to the executive head, whereas, when an autocratic tendency starts, the other branches are legally empowered to contain it (through veto rights, impeachment procedures, votes of no confidence etc.). Being capable of preventing some of each other's actions, the separated branches can work as checks and balances of each other and of autocratic actors.

Power in a constitutional state is separated horizontally as well as vertically. Besides narrowing the power of the executive by taking away some of its competences and giving them to separate branches (horizontal separation), power is also shared between the central government and local governments (vertical separation). On the municipal, county or other sub-national level, the presence of local governments acts as a check and balance on the central government, which does not have full authority over the lives of citizens as some of that authority is passed on to the people's elected local representatives.

There is a great variety in how local governments are organized and how many levels of federalism there are—indeed, it is more of a country-specific rather than a regime-specific question (Proposition 105). But the principle of subsidiarity holds that social and political problems should be dealt with at the most immediate level consistent with their solution. Hence, the competences of local governments ideal typically include substantial legislative, judicial and executive powers regarding local issues (public schooling, land management, local investment projects etc.). Over these issues, the authority of central government is constrained and therefore alternative "islands of liberty" can exist and regulate the lives of local citizens with substantial autonomy.

66. **PUBLIC DELIBERATION is a defensive mechanism in liberal democracies, granting the people effective influence on how their life is governed.** Treating citizens as free people who have a say in how their life is governed is another key principle of constitutionalism, the overarching legitimacy framework of liberal democracy (Proposition 43). The guarantee for this principle is public deliberation: by its process, the people can evaluate the performance of the current government and the various alternatives to it (discussing phase, with an open sphere of communication); have the alternatives to the government manifested in demonstrations and political parties (associating phase, with the free exercise of the right of association without state interference); choose an alternative in a race where the decisive factor is who they prefer, not who the manipulated electoral system or the illegal access to campaign funds benefits (electing phase, with fair elections); have the type of policy they voted for embodied in laws (lawmaking, with decision-maker legislature); and have the laws created by their representatives enforced, so their life is indeed governed in the way they have chosen (enforcing phase, with equality after the law).

It can be seen from this overview that the presence of elections alone does not mean the people have a say how their life is governed. Claiming otherwise has been identified as "the fallacy of electoralism" by scholars, reflecting on elections that the incumbents can manipulate to produce the result they want. The people's right to choose how their life is run necessitates knowing the alternatives, and also that the alternatives have a chance in winning the election, forming the government, and creating laws that will regulate the people's life as they want it to be regulated. And as this right should be guaranteed for every citizen in every time period, the process of public deliberation must be cyclical. The people's will must be able to remove the incumbent who, in turn, must not be able to manipulate electoral competition in face of losing popularity. For that would mean that he keeps himself in power in spite of the people changing their mind about how their life should be governed.

In short, the separation of branches of power prevents autocratic tendencies by limiting the scope of rule, both horizontally and vertically, whereas the cyclicality of public deliberation prevents autocrats from everlasting rule by ensuring removability and accountability. These two institutional settings ensure dynamics that are inimical to autocracy and favorable to limited, democratic rule.

67. FACTIONALISM AND THE FOUR AUTONOMIES OF CIVIL SOCIETY

are the sociological guarantees for the functioning of liberal democracy's defensive mechanisms. Even if powers are *de jure* separated, and the basic (political) rights to engage in public deliberation are legally protected, ensuring *de facto* separation and protection has an underlying condition: the independence of the people operating these institutions. An American Founding Father, James Madison famously argued that a constitutional system can be self-sustaining only if the members of each institution have as little dependence as possible on other institutions, for this is what allows them to act freely and ensures that they are not coerced into supporting the other institutions. In Madison's words, the maxim of effective checks and balances goes as follows: "Ambition must be made to counteract ambition." To impede autocratic tendencies or "the turbulency and weakness of unruly passions," factionalism is required, meaning the competition of independent groups with different interests involved in the procedure of state-decision making. Since no faction is interested in another faction's single rule, they have a clear incentive to fight autocratic tendencies and their involvement in the state decision-making process; independence from the autocratic actor enables them to do so.

Madison's argument for factionalism regarded public institutions, that is, the separation of branches of power, but it can be well be extended to the private sphere, as well as to the entire process of public deliberation. This leads us to the autonomy of civil society, defined broadly as the autonomy of four groups: the autonomy of media, which allows them to broadcast critical opinions without the fear of repercussions from the state; the autonomy of entrepreneurs, which makes it possible to support whichever political actor they want, whereas for the opposition it facilitates to gather the financial resources needed for effective functioning; the autonomy of NGOs, which enables independent watchdog functions to investigate the workings of public institutions; and the autonomy of citizens, which means that they cannot be coerced or intimidated by financial means, particularly in expressing their opinion (discussing) and choosing their leaders (electing).

The four autonomies of civil society are a sociological guarantee against autocracy. For it is the ground from which alternative centers of power can grow. With autonomous civil groups, democracy is protected, and autocratic tendencies may be fought off; without them, there is no social basis for an effective opposition to arise.

68.

THE EROSION OF LIBERAL DEMOCRACY HAS THREE STAGES: autocratic attempt, autocratic breakthrough, and autocratic consolidation. A party system in a liberal democracy may be divided by deep cleavages, and the parties may conduct fiery debates on policy issues in which they hold opposing ideological, right or left, positions. But they do so within the framework of liberal democracy: they question each other's policy, not their legitimacy, and they accept the legal-rational legitimacy of the system, adhering to the constitutional rules of the political arena. These two features are not shared by populists, who declare themselves to be the only legitimate representatives of the people in the framework of substantive-rational legitimacy (Proposition 45).

Populists in power bring the erosion of liberal democracy, which can be divided into three stages (Table 21). First, an autocratic attempt involves a series of formal institutional changes initiated by the populist and aiming at the systemic transformation of a democracy to an autocracy. Populists use their democratic mandate to connect the branches of power: to strengthen the power of the executive, to narrow the competences of other branches and local governments, and/or to replace their leading members with personal loyalists (patronal servants; Proposition 20). Court packing, replacement of the heads of civil courts, takeover of prosecution with a patronal servant, weakening of local governments, rewriting electoral rules one-sidedly, and changing the constitution to expand the competencies of the executive all belong to the arsenal of a populist carrying out an autocratic attempt.

The success of an autocratic attempt depends on mainly one factor: whether the populist gets the monopoly of political power, usually by winning the elections with supermajority. If this happens, the populist carries out a constitutional coup. Unlike a military coup, a constitutional coup maintains legal continuity, and the populist does not *de jure* eliminate the separation of powers. But they connect the branches through their competences of appointment in a single vertical of vassalage, gaining neopatrimonial control over the state (Proposition 26). Thus, the populist disables the first defensive mechanism of liberal democracy, i.e., the separation of powers. This is the point where we can speak, after an autocratic attempt, about an autocratic breakthrough.

The third and final step is autocratic consolidation. This may happen only if the populist can disable the second defensive mechanism as well: if they use the power of the state to subjugate the four autonomies of civil society, undermining effective opposition and the public deliberation process.

Table 21: Different levels of autocratic change.

	The leading political elite successfully disables...	
	First defensive mechanism (separation of branches of power)	Second defensive mechanism (autonomy of civil society)
Autocratic attempt	–	–
Autocratic breakthrough	X	–
Autocratic consolidation	X	X

69.

DIVIDED EXECUTIVE POWER AND PROPORTIONATE ELECTORAL SYSTEM **are defensive mechanisms in patronal democracies, maintaining the competition of patronal networks.** In liberal democratic systems, autocratic tendencies or the emergence of a populist, patronal challenger is an anomaly. In patronal democracies, patronal challenge is the norm. The stubborn structures of pre-communist and communist times have thrived in the post-communist era, especially in countries that carried a strong patronal legacy (Proposition 10). Competing patronal networks emerged with oligarchs and poligarchs entering the political playing field in the guise of patron's parties. This creates what we called a multi-pyramid patronal network, where party competition is the façade appearance of the competition of patronal networks.

As each network aims at breaking down the democratic system, and establishing a single-pyramid patronal network, the survival of patronal democracy depends on the difficulty of achieving the monopoly of political power. This is the point where the formal institutional setting matters, even though the major players are informal patronal networks (Table 22). In a purely presidentialist system, the presidency centralizes executive power in the hands of a single actor, and there are no similarly strong positions in the regime in terms of political power. In contrast, in divided-executive systems where the president and the prime minister both have executive powers and they are elected in different elections, cohabitation is possible: the two executive positions can be filled by patrons from different patronal networks.

Cohabitation offers more institutional possibilities for competing patronal networks to keep each other in check, in contrast to the purely presidentialist setup. Also, as Hale explains, such systems do not have a clear signaling effect: in a presidential system, it is clear that the president's patronal network is the dominant one, and societal actors start to coordinate around it; in a divided-executive system, the question of dominance stays unanswered. It is no coincidence that when a patronal network strives for a dominant role in a regime characterized by such divided executive power it usually attempts to switch to a purely presidential system. And similarly, when such attempts fail, the other patronal networks fight for the reintroduction of divided executive power. Events proceeded like this in Eastern-Orthodox countries like Ukraine, Moldova, and Romania.

Table 22: Formal constitutions and patronalism in post-communist countries since the mid-1990s (modified from *Patronal Politics* by Henry E. Hale).

Degree of Patronalism	Type of Executive Power		
	Presidentialism	Divided Executive	Parliamentarism
High	Azerbaijan*, Belarus*, Georgia*, Kazakhstan*, Kyrgyzstan (until 2010*), Moldova (until 2000*), Russia*, Tajikistan*, Turkmenistan*, Ukraine* (1991-2006; 2010-2014), Uzbekistan*	Armenia*, Ukraine (2006-10*; 2014-*), Kyrgyzstan (2010-*), Moldova (2016-*), Romania*	Albania, Bulgaria*, Hungary (2010-), North Macedonia*, Moldova (2000-2016)
Moderate			Estonia, Hungary (1998-2010), Latvia, Lithuania*, Serbia*, Slovakia*
Low		Croatia (until 2000*), Poland*	Croatia (2001-*), Czech Republic (2012-*), Hungary (until 1998), Slovenia*

* Countries having direct presidential elections.

On the other hand, in patronal democracies with a parliamentarist constitution, the attainment of the monopoly of political power can be prevented by a proportionate electoral system. For it makes reaching supermajority highly unlikely, or at least more difficult than majoritarian systems do. Some patronal democracies remain stable because of mainly one institutional constraint. For example, a divided executive has been an effective constraint in Bulgaria, where patronal democracy prevails and no single-pyramid has been established yet. Whereas in the parliamentary regimes of Albania and Slovakia proportionate electoral systems have been instrumental in preventing and breaking autocratic attempts. Proportionate electoral systems have contributed to the stability of semi-presidential regimes like Romania as well, where the powers of the president have been counterbalanced by those of the proportionally elected parliament.

70. COLOR REVOLUTIONS are defensive mechanisms in patronal democracies, restoring the competition of patronal networks (and not instituting liberal democracy).

The so-called color revolutions in the post-communist region are not classical revolutions. For classical revolutions that took place in the West in the 18-19th centuries were against feudal systems, where monarchs relied on numinous legitimacy, and the revolutions set out to change this pattern of legitimation to another pattern, that of civil legitimacy. The "lawful revolutions" of the regime changes in Central Europe in 1989 achieved, peacefully, the replacement of substantive-rational legitimacy of the party state with legal-rational legitimacy of a democratic system. In contrast, color revolutions do not want to switch from one coherent legitimacy pattern to another but aim at preserving the initial, coherent legitimacy pattern of democracy by overthrowing a corrupt autocrat.

As such, color revolutions in countries like Armenia, Kyrgyzstan, and Ukraine have been a source of optimism in Western circles. Placing events on the democracy-dictatorship axis, a popular revolt replacing a repressive system meant a step towards the democratic pole, or a Western-type liberal democracy for them. But color revolutions would rarely bring the expected results; rather, they usually meant a fall back to the ordinary affairs of patronal democracy. Indeed, color revolutions are a defensive mechanism: a societal defense to break autocratic attempts and push the regime back to the dynamic equilibrium of competing patronal networks.

The typical process of successful color revolutions goes by the following steps: (1) the ruling patronal network creates a breakdown of the public deliberation process, typically electoral fraud, to cement its position; (2) the breakdown triggers mass legitimacy-questioning protests, aiming at rerunning the elections or at recognizing the victory of the opposition (and the resignation of the current government); (3) legitimacy-questioning protests get supported by external actors such as foreign NGOs, foundations, governments or international alliances; (4) both the formal and informal support of the government melts in the domestic and the international political arena, until their room for maneuver shrinks to the point that they cannot operate and the leaders are forced to meet the demands of the revolutionaries.

The reason why these revolutions do not lead to liberal democracy is that they are not accompanied by anti-patronal transformations. Although revolutionary movements march under the slogans of democracy, transparency, and anti-corruption, behind the democratic endeavor of the masses one can find, as organizing force and political as well as financial resource, the discontent of the to-be suppressed patronal networks. It is true that, without popular discontent stemming from a breakdown of public deliberation, patronal networks are less able to counter autocratic tendencies. But the opposite is also true: without the resources of the competing patronal networks, popular discontent cannot stop the ruling autocrat from breaking "fair," democratic (patronal) competition.

71. Autocratic consolidation is a defensive mechanism in patronal autocracies, protecting the single-pyramid patronal network against pressures from the outside.

Turning to the defensive mechanisms of patronal autocracies, we may start with the ones that defend against pressures from outside the adopted political family. "Outside" refers not to exogenous shocks like wars or economic crises but such opposition pressures as electoral blocs and color revolutions. In some cases, like Armenia, the chief patron successfully achieves an autocratic breakthrough and establishes a single-pyramid system, but he is eventually overthrown because he is unable to achieve autocratic consolidation. For autocratic consolidation, the autonomy of civil society must be neutralized: without this, the regime remains vulnerable, because the still existing autonomies may be used to form an effective opposition.

The most important autonomy to break is that of the media, which explains why a crackdown on the press, using the formal power of the state and informally connected actors, is among the first acts of a chief patron regarding civil society. Second, the autonomy of entrepreneurs needs to be broken: the chief patron can make entrepreneurs interested in sustaining the system by making them clients, while opposition-inclined entrepreneurs and oligarchs can be deprived of their financial resources or forced to funnel monies and property to the adopted political family instead. Third, neutralizing NGOs and starting GONGOs is important both to ease watchdog control and for propaganda purposes, and it is done by the multistep domestication methodology explained above (Proposition 50). Finally, the autonomy of the citizens is broken *en masse* through societal patronalization (Proposition 94). Using Albert O. Hirschman's voice-exit-loyalty triad, we can say that patronal autocracies try to turn potential voice into coerced loyalty, while it also lets people exit from the regime (which actually contributes to stability by the "voluntary exile" of dissatisfied people).

In the end, the consolidated system is maintained by the discretional use of the instruments of public authority, neutralizing public deliberation by the following means: (1) creation of a dominated sphere of communication, neutralizing the opposition in the discussing phase; (2) non-balancing of rights and the institutionalization of a dominant-party system, neutralizing opposition associations and movements; (3) holding loyalty-structuring campaigns and manipulated elections, turning the voters' free choice into unfree choice; (4) creating instrumental law and custom-tailored lexes attacking opposition figures in the political, economic and communal spheres alike; and (5) using politically selective law enforcement against opponents and in favor of the adopted political family. This sums up how a consolidated patronal autocracy can defend itself from pressures from the outside, without mass terror or the *de jure* elimination of pluralism in politics.

72.

The separation of resources of power is a defensive mechanism in patronal autocracies, protecting the chief patron against threats from the inside. Within the adopted political family, competition of high-ranking members is not disruptive until it is not a challenge to the chief patron but only concerns the distribution of privileges among the respective members. Indeed, the orchestrated and controlled competition below the level of top leadership can contribute to stability, and it may be fostered by the chief patron himself. But the chief patron must be able to fight off those who would wish to replace him.

Discretional punishments, or the same arsenal of public authority that is used against external pressures can be applied against disloyal actors; moreover, the clients must expect that the chief patron is not only willing but able to punish disloyalty, which means he must be merciless and leave no disloyalty unpunished. However, there are also preventive measures against the emergence of an effective internal opposition.

While the chief patron eliminates the separation of branches of power within the state, he separates the resources of power within the adopted political family. This is the most important preventive measure of stability: the chief patron does not allow anyone but himself to dispose over the kinds of political and economic resources that would be necessary to challenge him and/or to build an autonomous patronal network independently (Table 23).

The poligarchs below the chief patron in the patronal pyramid, while having some informal economic power, can keep either executive power or party background. In democratic parties, these roles are typically not split: those in the executive are also important members of their party; they can voice their critical opinions; or even act against the party leader if they disagree with him. However, a transmission-belt party is a vassals' party precisely because such mechanisms of intra-party democracy are eliminated (Proposition 58). Poligarchs with party background fulfil roles like party director or whip, but they are not involved in the executive decision-making ideal typically. Oligarchs in a single-pyramid patronal network are also "single-profile": while they have implicit political (executive or party) power, they cannot have nation-level economic and media power simultaneously. Finally, political and economic front men have no *de facto* power: they have formal positions, but they cannot exercise the powers vested in them autonomously (Propositions 16, 19).

The separation of resources of power also means that actors with different resources cannot form informal alliances bypassing the patronal hierarchy. If such attempts are made, the chief patron can be expected to intervene, preventing the formation of an alternative center of power within the adopted political family.

Table 23: Ideal typical separation of resources of power within the adopted political family.

	Executive power	Party power (party background)	Nation-level economic power	Nation-level media power
Chief patron	+	+	+	+
Poligarch (1)	+	–	+ –	–
Poligarch (2)	–	+	+ –	–
Oligarch (1)	+ –	–	+	–
Oligarch (2)	+ –	–	–	+
Political front man	–	–	–	–
Economic front man	–	–	–	–

Legend: "+": the actor has the power, "-": the actor does not have power; "+ -": the actor has power but only in a limited manner.

73. Patronal autocracies face the problem of succession, which carries great revolutionary potential for the chief patron's opponents. While chief patrons cement their position for eternity, they are not immortal. Even if the regime is protected against threats from the outside and the inside, the chief patron eventually retires, dies, or otherwise becomes unable to fulfil his position. This raises the problem of succession if the regime is to survive.

The problem stems precisely from the essence of the system: that the chief patron has centralized all power and cracked down on competing patronal networks. In a single-pyramid system, the position of the chief patron carries a unique concentration of political power that sub-patrons do not match. As a result, it is not obvious who should come after the chief patron: there is not a second-most powerful patronal network and sub-chief but a set of actors roughly equal in size.

One solution to this problem may be identified as gradual succession by making the presidency a divisible good. This solution was attempted by Kazakhstan's Nursultan Nazarbayev, who resigned after three decades of presidency in 2019. The 78-year-old chief patron gave the presidency to one of his loyal clients while retaining political power in the form of veto rights (he supervises program documents with the president and the government). Another solution for the outgoing chief patron is to name his successor, like Heidar Aliev did with his son, Ilham in Azerbaijan. Seemingly simpler, this solution is more uncertain than the previous one because the appointed heir must win the trust and loyalty of the clients whose loyalty was to a person (his predecessor), not to his office.

On the other hand, even before the chief patron leaves, the expectation of departure spurs defection which can undermine his capacity to mete out discretional rewards and punishments. Hale describes this as the "lame-duck syndrome," when the perception of the dissipating power of the chief patron becomes a self-fulfilling prophecy.

Such situations that produce lame ducks present the best opportunities to change a patronal autocracy to democracy. If a competition among the clients for the top position develops, the single-pyramid network may divide up into multiple patronal networks. They all want to become dominant, but none of them is interested in being suppressed by a competing network: the logic of patronal democracy emerges. Naturally, if the regime has a presidentialist constitution, systemic reproduction with a new chief patron is more likely after the internal fighting plays out. But if the chief patron has been a prime minister in a parliamentarist system, there is a greater chance to break the self-reproducing capacity of patronal autocracy.

74. THE GOVERNMENT CANNOT BE REMOVED through elections in consolidated autocracies, but an autocratic attempt or breakthrough may still be reversed by electoral change.

According to János Kornai's concept of autocracy, which we used in the definition of our six-regime typology (Proposition 12), a primary feature of the system is that "the government cannot be removed through a peaceful and civilized procedure." The ideal type regime of patronal autocracy, on the lowest pole of the triangle, fulfills this criterion, for the ideal type is defined as a consolidated system. But real-life patronal autocracies may function by the logic of a single-pyramid patronal network without achieving autocratic consolidation as well. In such cases, the regime may be defeated by electoral means. Speaking in more general terms, autocratic change can be reversed by elections after an autocratic attempt or breakthrough before consolidation (Figure 10).

Considering opposition strategy, a crucial point of returning from autocratic breakthrough is to switch from the government-critique paradigm to the regime-critique paradigm. In liberal democracies, the opposition usually remains within the boundaries of the government-critique paradigm, whereby it: attacks the government, not the regime as a whole; debates public policy, as if it followed from the declared ideological goals; forms strategy on the basis of competition of parties, without cooperation in opposition or nationwide movement; largely preserves distance between political parties and NGOs and entrepreneurs, supporting certain public policies rather than certain political forces.

Scholars often argue that attacking the government instead of the regime is a sign of democratic consolidation, for it indicates that democracy is "the only game in town" for the regime's actors. But when an opposition faces an autocracy, it is crucial that they do not believe the regime to be the only game in town.

The regime-critique paradigm means that the opposition: attacks the autocratic regime, not the government *per se*; criticizes not the declared ideological goals of the policies but the way they serve power concentration and personal-wealth accumulation; forms strategy on the basis of cooperation in opposition and a nationwide movement, along the regime-level cleavage of "democratic opposition" vs. "autocratic system"; gets NGOs and entrepreneurs to side with opposition against the leading political elite that sets out to destroy democracy.

The regime-critique paradigm can signal to the people that the opposition is ready and capable of winning, breaking the perception about the irreplaceability of the system—a perception that is otherwise a crucial element of autocratic consolidation.

Figure 10: Ideal type comebacks from different levels of autocratic change.

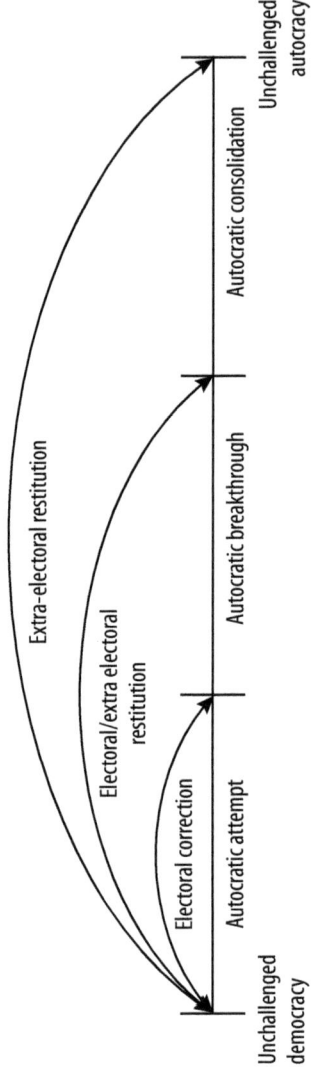

Relational Economics: Corruption, Predation, and the Redistribution of Markets

75.

QUESTIONING THE AXIOM that the state is an actor pursuing the common good, we can introduce relational economics as a challenger of the mainstream neoclassical synthesis. In the beginning of our exposition, we argued that three axioms of mainstream hybridology need to be dissolved to understand post-communist regimes. These were: the axiom of the separation of spheres of social action, the axiom of the coincidence of *de jure* and *de facto* positions, and the axiom of the state pursuing the common good (Proposition 5).

Dissolving axioms has been central to economic science as well since the second half of the 20th century. The starting point of economists was the "orthodox" neoclassical synthesis, and by questioning the axiomatic assumptions of its models they introduced a number of new, so-called heterodox schools of economic thought (Figure 11). Behavioral economics questioned views on the rationality of market participants; institutional economics pointed out that the market is not necessarily dominated by the simple mechanisms of supply and demand, or voluntary exchanges dictated by individual preferences.

If we want to understand how the economies of the post-communist region work, we have to give up a third axiom—one that is virtually same as the third axiom we gave up. This axiom holds that the state is benevolent, an institution for correcting market failures, and by asking for its intervention we can achieve an outcome that the free market alone did not create. But, if the state intervenes, it may not do what economists think it should: the actual form of state intervention depends on the individual or group interests of the members of the ruling elite, as well as the relations between state actors and private actors. Based on this insight, we arrive at relational economics.

Relational economics is not a mere neologism for the schools of economic thought critical of state functioning (such as public choice). First, relational economics is not concerned with the economic analysis of political processes—it is concerned with political analysis of economic processes. Relational economics is a branch of political economy that marries comparative regime theory and economic analysis: the former describes the formal and informal relations of public and private actors in the six ideal-type regimes, while the latter is guided by this description in analyzing economic functioning. Second, relational economics includes established theories of rent-seeking, regulatory capture, predatory state, and corruption, but it also identifies a common starting point for them. Thus, it constitutes the overarching framework where theories developed for Western economies can be expanded for post-communist regimes.

Figure 11: Three challengers of the neoclassical synthesis questioning 1-1 of its basic axioms.

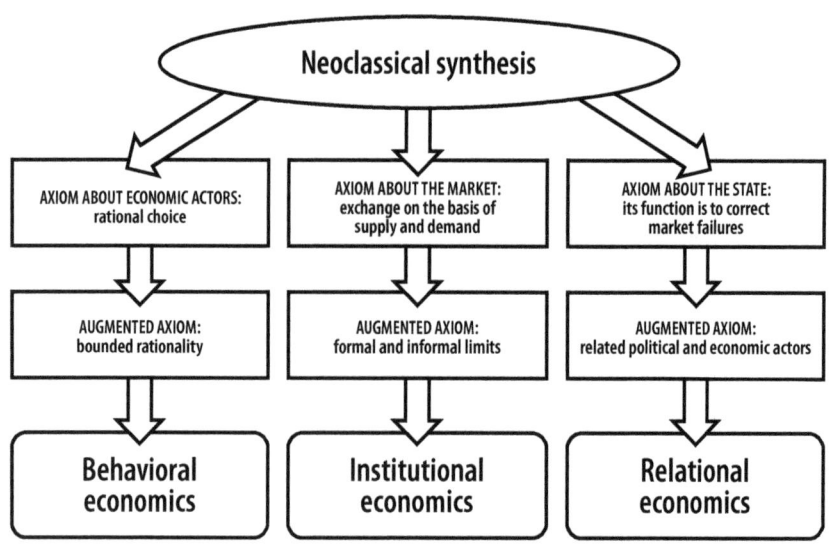

76. Relations between political and economic actors range from formal and voluntary relations (lobbying) to informal and coercive relations (patronalism). In a liberal market economy, public decision-makers interact with private economic actors through conciliation forums and lobbying. Although economists,

especially those observing large corporate lobbies in the United States, often talk about the "collusion" of the political and economic spheres, in reality, this kind of cooperation does eliminate the separation of spheres of social action (Proposition 6).

In a lobbying relation, the politician seeks political benefits (e.g., campaign support) and the major entrepreneur seeks economic benefits (e.g., favorable regulations). They want to strengthen their positions at the top of the hierarchy in their own sphere of social action: they have separate political and economic objectives, and the benefits they attain also serve the reinforcement of their formal positions in their own, separated sphere. The politician does not become an entrepreneur, and the entrepreneur does not become a politician. The relation is formed within the formal institutional setting, where lobbying itself is formalized and therefore more transparent than informal relations; and the two parties enter into a business deal with each other on a voluntary basis, as autonomous parties. They come together and form a horizontal, rather than a vertical or vassal-type, relation, and each party can exit the relation freely if they see a more beneficial offer.

This form of lobbying represents the beginning of a scale, from which we can start exploring other types of relations which do represent a collusion of spheres. First, the parties involved are situated in formally separated spheres that can be informally connected. Second, if the relation between the two elites is informal, it can be voluntary as well as coercive. In the case of voluntary transactions, the economics of the relationship is not unlike the situation in lobbying: both parties need to offer something of value to the other to make them voluntarily relate. In this case, the relation can be described as horizontal and non-patronal, where no party can force the other one into the exchange (free entry) or force them to continue to make the exchange (free exit).

In the case of coercive transactions, the economics of the relationship is considerably different. For then it is the cost-benefit calculation of the coercer that decides whether the relation comes into being. In this case, the relation can be described as vertical and patronal, where one party can force the other one into the exchange (unfree entry) and force them to continue to make the exchange (unfree exit). If participants are related informally as well as coercively, the members of the economic elite become part of the political elite (oligarchs, Proposition 14) and the members of the political elite become part of the economic elite (poligarchs, Proposition 15).

77. BOTTOM-UP CORRUPTION PATTERNS, initiated from the side of the private to the public sphere, include free-market corruption and bottom-up state capture.

Different corruption patterns can be modelled by dividing corrupt actors into three layers: private actors, public administrators, and governmental actors; and by three types of roles: demander, supplier, and the server, who is a subordinate in the corrupt machinery (Figure 12). In the case of free-market corruption, private interests hold an illegitimate sway in state and local government decisions concerning the allocation of resources, procurements, concessions, and entitlements. As a result, illegal barter deals are concluded between discrete private actors and non-elite, everyday administrators of state bureaucracy (office clerks, policemen etc.).

Free-market corruption consists of a series of individual phenomena: an official responsible for a decision accepts or requests financial or other benefits for handling a case in a manner advantageous to the private actor. A state may be considered "corrupt" if there is a high occurrence of such incidents, or if civil administrative or business matters can only be managed through bribes (Proposition 26). It is this case when free-market corruption is countrywide, instead of remaining only local. However, even if the pattern appears countrywide, these actions of free-market corruption are occasional: they happen case-by-case when one decides, voluntarily, to take part in a corrupt transaction, and they are not organized as a group function on either side.

The term "free market" in the name of this pattern partly refers to its competitive nature. Corrupt opportunities are not restricted to a specific group of people: anyone with the right amount of money or power can enter such corrupt relationships. And where both corrupt supply and demand are numerous, private actors can compete in the amount of bribe they offer, and the public actors, in the amount they ask.

In the case of bottom-up state capture, the actors' cooperation becomes more complex not only on the side of corruption supply but also on the side of corruption demand, given that the corruption partners from the private sector are oligarchs (whose economic activity is otherwise legal; oligarchic state capture) or crime bosses of the organized underworld (whose economic activity is otherwise illegal; criminal state capture). Here, corruption vertically reaches the higher levels of the public sphere, and permanently subordinates political actors to the economic elite. Under bottom-up state capture, the legislation is systematically subjugated to private interests, and members of the political elite, and the public administrators as well, become the systemic, and not merely occasional parts of the machinery of corruption, channeling of public goods and services to the oligarchs or crime bosses.

Figure 12: Schematic depiction of free-market corruption and bottom-up state capture.

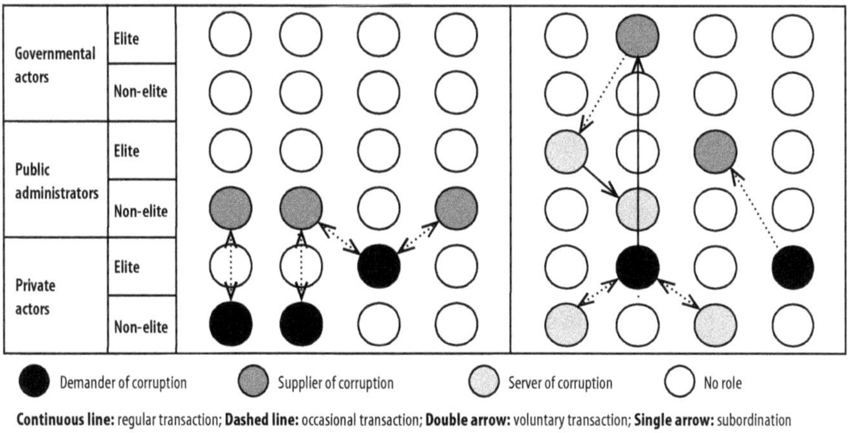

● Demander of corruption   ◐ Supplier of corruption   ◒ Server of corruption   ○ No role

Continuous line: regular transaction; Dashed line: occasional transaction; Double arrow: voluntary transaction; Single arrow: subordination

78. **TOP-DOWN CORRUPTION PATTERNS, initiated from the side of the public to the private sphere, include top-down state capture and the criminal state pattern.** Top-down state capture can be initiated by a single actor—such as a mayor of a municipal government—or by a group of actors—such as a party. As a part of public administration is turned into a racket by its leaders, the hierarchy of their domain is filled up with their clients, resulting in patronalization. The captured part of the state apparatus begins to be operated by the informal patronal network, systemically working by informal rules over formal ones.

However, in top-down state capture, no patron possesses unconstrained political power in the entire polity (Figure 13). This limits every patron's amplitude of arbitrariness: they can rule over only a certain part of the state, limited to its formal competences, but cannot dispose over a wider range of state institutions (Proposition 28). First, this makes linked actions of corruption, where the cooperation of several state bodies would be necessary, less attainable. Second, the patron's position is dependent on political turns. An opposition victory can easily remove them, making it practically impossible to sustain their patronal network any further. Finally, the lack of a power monopoly means the patron cannot disable institutional checks. Constitutional limits on power concentration as well as effective law enforcement have the ability to contain informal networks and prevent the patron from wielding exclusive political power and making the entire state their private domain.

When the monopoly of political power is gained, we speak about a criminal state pattern. We add the word "pattern" to criminal state, a concept we introduced earlier (Propositions 26-27), to underline that this state of affairs does not necessarily encompass the entire state. On the contrary, there are local cases, when the elite governmental actor is a mayor, and he patronalizes a whole local government, turning it into a geographically limited patronal racket: practically a "state in the state." Such cases happen in non-criminal states as well, like patronal democracy or market-exploiting dictatorship (Proposition 90). But in patronal autocracies, the criminal state pattern characterizes the central government.

The criminal state is built by the development of a single-pyramid patronal network. In it, actors of the public administration are deprived of their autonomy to make corrupt offers to private actors or to accept bribes in exchange for favorable treatment. Instead, they are subordinated to the chief patron's will and treat favorably those who are designated from above, i.e., the clients of the chief patron. The building of the single-pyramid network extends to the private sector as well, breaking the autonomy of the oligarchs (Proposition 41), whereas a network of subcontractors and suppliers extends this patron-client relationship to the lower reaches of the private sector as well.

Figure 13: Schematic depiction of top-down state capture and the criminal state pattern.

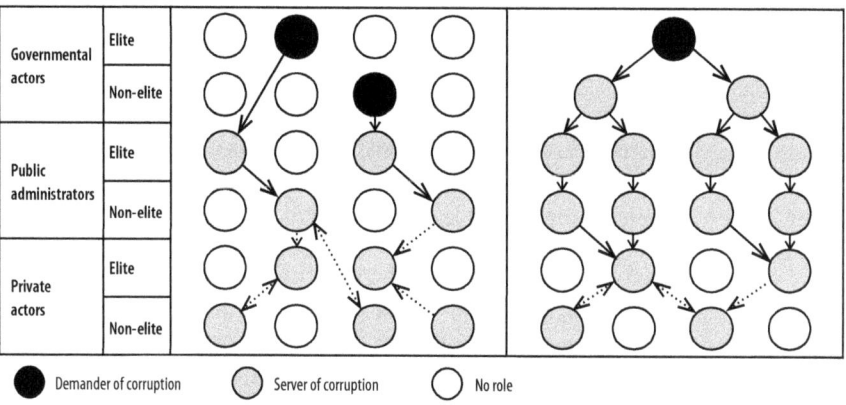

Continuous line: regular transaction; Dashed line: occasional transaction; Double arrow: voluntary transaction; Single arrow: subordination

Note: In the criminal state pattern, all governmental actors are subordinated to the chief patron. We decided not to represent every governmental actor with circles for the sake of clarity.

79. COUNTRY-WIDE CORRUPTION PATTERNS may be either endemic or systemic, and may feature either autonomous actors or permanent chains of vassalage. In corruption literature, "systemic" is used synonymously with "endemic" in situations when corruption is integrated as an essential aspect of the political, social, and economic system. But this understanding obscures the difference between cases when corruption is widespread and cases when corruption is made a system by an organizer from the top.

For example, the former case can be socially accepted forms of free-market corruption, such as "gratitude money" in most of post-communist countries in Eastern Europe (doctors and nurses in state healthcare are regularly given extra money, without which one can barely get decent service). These transactions are scattered, made occasionally, and they are face-to-face, with each pair of actors making corrupt transactions without being part of a corruption network. It is crucial to distinguish such cases from state enterprise collusion, bottom-up and top-down state capture, and the criminal state pattern (Table 24). For in those types, corruption is systematized by someone, that is, organized as a group function or network with permanent relations and a complex corruption scheme.

Thus, it is worth making the following differentiation: (1) corruption is endemic if it becomes a social norm (that is, an informal understanding that governs the behavior of social actors) without the organizing action of a central will and resulting in a large number of occasional transactions between various people; (2) corruption is systemic if it is developed into a scheme (that is, a corrupt machinery of permanent relations) due to the organizing action of a central will and resulting in regular transactions between certain people.

Closely related to this are the dimensions of autonomy—which refers to the free entry of the participants into corruption—and dependency—which refers to the exit options of corrupt participants. When corrupt transactions are occasional, autonomy of actors is retained, and no chains of dependency are formed. In cases of regular transactions, there is a higher chance of dependency, especially because the more illegal acts are committed, the more the parties can blackmail each other, forcing them to continue to make corrupt exchanges. Also, coercive collusion immediately implies dependency, for there even the entry of one of the participants was involuntary.

Table 24: Main characteristics of the six corruption patterns (with coercive corruption patterns in grey).

	Nature of corruption	Entry of corrupt parties	Distribution of corrupt transactions	Direction of corrupt action	Economic nature of corruption	Regularity and scope of corrupt actions	Medium of corrupt exchange
Free-market corruption	Petty corruption	Voluntary	Non-centralized	Horizontal	Competitive	Occasional and partial	Bribe money
Cronyism		Voluntary	Non-centralized	Horizontal	Competitive	Occasional / permanent and partial	Bribe money
State organization collusion		Voluntary	Non-centralized	Vertical (top-down)	Oligopolistic / locally monopolistic	Occasional and partial	Bribe money
Bottom-up state capture		Coercive	Moderately centralized	Vertical (bottom-up)	Oligopolistic / locally monopolistic	Occasional / permanent and partial	Bribe money
Top-down state capture		Coercive	Partially centralized	Vertical (top-down)	Oligopolistic / locally monopolistic	Permanent and partial (vassal chains)	Protection money
Criminal state pattern	Grand corruption	Coercive	Centralized	Vertical (top-down)	Monopolistic	Permanent and general (vassal chains)	Protection money

As for autonomy, the partial nature of state captures allows some participants to retain a relative autonomy, a bargaining position and a competitive edge. But in a criminal state, the chief patron is the monopolist of autonomy: he is the only one who *de facto* answers to nobody in the regime, and he can delegate partial autonomy, with limited authorization, to sub-patrons in the patron-client network. The sub-patrons are both patrons and clients: clients to the chief patron but patrons to the lower-level clients in the adopted political family.

80. **THE TYPE OF ECONOMY under the criminal state pattern of corruption, operating by the logic of informal patronal networks, is called a relational economy.** In his renowned essay "The Economy as Instituted Process," Karl Polanyi distinguishes three forms of integration of the economy: reciprocity, redistribution, and exchange. As he explains, reciprocity "denotes movements between correlative points of symmetrical groupings; redistribution designated appropriational movements toward a center and out of it again; exchange refers here to vice-versa movements taking place as between 'hands' under a market system." Polanyi adds that, while one mechanism is always dominant in an economy, the other mechanisms are not eliminated but continue to coexist with it. In a similar vein, János Kornai speaks in *The Socialist System* about different coordination mechanisms, particularly the ones related to the main dichotomy of the discipline of comparative economic systems: socialism and capitalism.

Inspired by Polanyi and Kornai, we can construct a typology of economic systems distinguished by their dominant mechanisms (Table 25). First, the dominant mechanism of a market economy is regulated market coordination. In Kornai's words (*The Socialist System*, 1992), market coordination is "a lateral, horizontal linkage" where individuals "rank equally in legal terms," and take on the role of sellers and buyers (90–94). Their voluntary decisions of buying and selling constitute profits and losses, providing a scheme of incentives for the coordination of the activities of enterprising people. However, when describing economies of the modern day we cannot disregard the fact that they are "regulated" by a central authority, and liberal democracies today feature mixed economies as a norm.

The dominant mechanisms in the two other types of economies are types of redistribution in the Polanyian sense. In a planned economy, the dominant mechanism is bureaucratic resource-redistribution. In the socialist system, the whole sphere of market action is merged with the sphere of political action in a single bureaucratic entity, coordinated through central planning. In this formalized and normative system, the nomenklatura determines both the ownership structure and the production structure with physical targets (meaning, in the central plan, production targets are expressed in exact numbers of natural units and quantities).

In contrast, patronal autocracies only determine the ownership structure: the chief patron is not the planner and manager of production, but the redistributor of markets and rent-seeking opportunities. Accordingly, we speak about relational market-redistribution, whereas the economy is not a planned economy but a relational economy. The systemic corruption pattern of the criminal state permeates the economy, adjusting its operation to the logic of informal patronal networks. In other words, while staying capitalist in the sense of the dominance of *de jure* private property, the chief patron makes the system patronally embedded: economically patronalized and subordinated to the interests of the adopted political family.

Table 25: Market economy, relational economy, planned economy.

Capitalism		Socialism
Market economy	**Relational economy**	**Planned economy**
Politically disembedded economy	Patronally embedded economy	Bureaucratically embedded economy
Regulated market coordination	Relational market-redistribution	Bureaucratic resource-redistribution
• regulated • impersonal • normative • dominance of competitive markets	• non-formalized • personal • discretional • dominance of relational markets	• formalized • impersonal • normative • dominance of administrative markets
Invisible hand of the impersonal market forces	Visible hand of the patron interfering with market forces	Central planning of the nomenklatura bypassing market forces
Horizontal	Vertical	Vertical

81.

IN A RELATIONAL ECONOMY, RENTS ARE CREATED through discretional state intervention, replacing normatively closed markets with discretionally closed markets. Rent is the profit stemming from the lack of competition. When the state regulates economic functioning in a market or industry, it closes an open market: it outlaws certain kinds of competitors, and allows only those meeting the criteria set by the state (standards of quality and safety, licenses etc.) to compete. This creates barriers to entry, which partially protect incumbents from new entrants, i.e., potential competition. As a result, the incumbents can reduce production and increase prices—in short, can reach higher profits, other things being equal. Rent is the difference between what income would have been in an open market and the actual income, resulting from closing the market to certain participants.

Rents are created also under the regulated market coordination of market economies. The key difference between market and relational economies is that, while market economies close markets normatively, relational economies close markets discretionally (Table 26).

The creation of normatively closed markets is part and parcel of modern market economies, as the state outlaws certain types of products (unlicensed drugs, food etc.), forms of production (which do not meet the labor code, environmental regulations etc.), and forms of pricing (dumping, predatory price cutting, setting wages below the minimum wage etc.). But in such cases, rents are created by state intervention that is (1) normative, meaning it targets economic groups that meet criteria irrespective of who the exact persons belonging to the group are (impersonal with no double standard); (2) legal, meaning state intervention manifests in formal laws, regulations and taxes; (3) lobbied for by interest groups, engaging in a competitive process of rent-seeking.

In contrast, rents in a relational economy are created by state intervention that is (1) discretional, meaning it targets certain people or companies the chief patron chooses to affect (personal with double standard); (2) combines legal and illegal elements, meaning state intervention manifests in formal laws as well as informal practices; (3) received by the adopted political family, as rent-seeking loses its competitive character and rents are being distributed from above by the chief patron.

Four techniques of discretional rent creation may be analytically distinguished: (a) formal discretional treatment, when the state grants competitive advantage to a certain firm by issuing a custom-tailored lex (Proposition 57); (b) informal discretional treatment, when the competitive advantage is given by using informal means, such as politically-selective law enforcement (Proposition 60); (c) monopolization of a market, excluding everyone from an existing market besides the ones to be favored, who receive an outright monopoly grant in a top-down corrupted procedure; and (d) creation of a market, when the state commissions a previously non-existent economic activity from private actors and/or guides artificial demand to the company (discretionally allocated and overpriced public procurements, state contracts etc.).

Table 26: Comparing normatively and discretionally closed markets.

	Normatively closed market	**Discretionally closed market**
Decision about entry or exclusion	normative	discretional
Formality of regulations	formal	formal/informal
Benefits and losses of incumbents	normative (sectoral) and non-excludable (the state cannot limit benefits only to certain participants of a market)	discretional (individual) and excludable (the state limits benefits only to certain participants of a market)
Payment for entry (non-exclusion)	normative fee	personal benefit (bribe money / protection money)
Payment for rent-creation (and maintenance)	political benefits (e.g., campaign contribution) personal benefit (bribe money)	economic benefit (ownership rights) patronal benefit (loyalty)
The nature of rent-seeking	open/competitive (no state-imposed barrier to entry)	closed/non-competitive (state-imposed barrier to entry)

82.

IN A RELATIONAL ECONOMY, PROPERTY RIGHTS have a conditional character, constantly threatened by predation using the means of grey and white raiding. In a market economy, property rights are upheld impersonally. As Nobel laureate economist Douglass C. North and his colleagues explain in *Violence and Social Orders* (2009), economic actors in open-access orders "do not need to participate in politics to maintain their rights, to enforce contracts, or to ensure their survival from expropriation; their right to exist and compete does not depend on maintaining privileges."

In a relational economy, property rights have a conditional character: any actor's property may be taken over on a discretional basis in the case they challenge the interests of the chief patron. Such takeovers are called "reiderstvo" in Russian, derived from the English "raiding." However, it would be misleading to try and apply terms such as "corporate raiding" or "hostile takeover" here in their Western meaning. For hostile takeovers in the West are rarely characterized by the illegal use of public authority, and physical violence is even rarer.

Reiderstvo can be defined as a type of predation that (1) targets productive assets, mainly firms, companies, and enterprises, and (2) always involves illegal practices and the use of coercion for private gain. A typology of reiderstvo is summarized in Table 27, indicating the actors involved as well as the political-economic environment in which various types are prevalent. When stateness is low, which was typical in post-communist oligarchic anarchies (Proposition 30), the typical form of reiderstvo is black raiding. Black raiding is a type of reiderstvo which is carried out by the direct threat or use of physical violence (physical abuse, extortion at gunpoint etc.). The next type is grey raiding, when predators rely on corrupted or captured state authorities. The executors of grey raiding are no longer criminal groups but members of the lower, local levels of organs of public authority. They may do so for their own private gain or be employed by oligarchs to eliminate business rivals. Economist Stanislav Markus offers a list of services and prices offered by corrupt administrators in Russia in the mid-2000s, including inspection of target firm by taxation agency ($4.000), opening of a criminal case against target owners ($50.000), a commercial court verdict against the target firm ($10-100.000) and even arrest of a business competitor through Ministry of Internal Affairs ($100.000).

The final form of reiderstvo is white raiding, where instead of the legal environment being misused, it is adapted and tailored to individuals and single companies in a targeted manner. When property is expropriated by top authorities of the central state, typically at the command of and through coordination with the highest holder of executive power, we speak about centrally-led corporate raiding, which often combines grey and white raiding techniques. This is the type of predation the chief patron engages in, routinely taking over companies to increase the wealth of himself and his adopted political family.

Centrally-led corporate raiding utilizes linked actions of corruption, whereby acts that are unlawful in and of themselves—such as extortion or misappropriation of funds—are combined with acts that are not unlawful in and of themselves—such as motions submitted by independent parliamentary representatives or instigating tax audits. This requires wide amplitude of arbitrariness (Proposition 28), or complete control over the state apparatus: under the chief patron, actors from every formally independent and autonomous branch of power (from the prosecution to the police, from the government to the parliament, from the competition office to the tax office and various regulatory bodies) work in unison as cogs in the predatory machinery of the organized upperworld.

Table 27: Types and certain features of reiderstvo in post-communist regimes.

Strength of the state	Legality of raiding	The initiator or client of the corporate raiding			
		Organized upperworld: chief patron (top level public authority)	Low, middle or high level public authority	Rival entrepreneurs or oligarchs	Organized underworld: criminal groups
Strong state ↓ Failed state	White raiding				
	Gray raiding				
	Black raiding				
Institutional environment and features of the raiding action		Criminal state	Corrupt/Captured state		Failed state
		Single-pyramid power network	Multi-pyramid power network		
		Monopolized	Oligarchic	Competitive	
		Oligarch capture	State capture	n.a.	

83. IN A RELATIONAL ECONOMY, NATIONALIZATION as a means of increasing the wealth of the adopted political family appears in three forms: hot, monopolizing, and cold nationalization. Nationalization, as practiced in the mafia state—expropriation of private property through instruments of public authority—is in its function fundamentally different from both its practice in market economies and the planned economy. In a market economy, though non-economic objectives may also appear among the motivating forces of the state, the operation of the nationalized property nevertheless fits into the rationale of the market. In communist dictatorships, the whole economy is operated in an irrevocable and homogeneous way under the ownership of the state—and the dominance of politics.

In the mafia state, nationalization simultaneously serves to increase the wealth of the adopted political family, to provide regulated remuneration for those built into its chain of command, and to keep society in check. Table 28 lists several methods of nationalization, categorized by the kind of property rights they violate.

First, hot nationalization violates the right to security and protection of property: the obligation of the state to provide the protection of private property rights normatively, to everyone living under its authority. This type includes renationalization (the complete seizure of a formerly privatized company by the state for a longer-lasting period), deprivatization (the expansion of state shareholding among privatized companies), and also transit nationalization. In the latter case, the private company of an actor outside the adopted political family is taken into "temporary state care," and reprivatized to chosen actors at a later date. By the interim phase of (re)nationalization, private fortunes are forced into the ownership orbit of the adopted political family. And transit nationalization has its inverse, transit privatization as well, where a state property is temporarily privatized so that the oligarch or front man who receives it can take money out of it, after which the state buys it back (such as in the case of Stroytransgaz in Russia or Mátra Power Plant in Hungary).

The second category of nationalization is monopolizing nationalization, which violates the right to carry out an economic activity: the obligation of the state not to close the entrance to private markets for those who wish to enter and are in a position to do so, and to not to take away the opportunity from those who have already entered. By monopolizing nationalization, the state does not strip owners of their business directly but monopolizes the economic activity in question, after which it is either centralized or decentralized in the form of concessions.

Finally, cold nationalization violates the right to fair treatment, creating a stifling economic environment for certain economic actors by state intervention. In cold nationalization, the state expropriates the market environs of a given economic sector without directly nationalizing the businesses involved in it. Measures like using state authority to determine prices, instituting discretional taxes or regulating/restricting fields of activity through custom-tailored lexes serve to bleed dry owners of businesses, to prepare for a permanent or transit nationalization of a business, to ensure the subordination of key players in a sector. Cold nationalization does not necessarily turn into permanent nationalization or transit nationalization but opens the way to many potential ways to extract resources from businesses.

Table 28: Nationalization methods (forms of violations of exogenous property rights) in predatory states.

	Violated exogenous right (type of nationalization)	Pre-transfer form of property	Mid-transfer form of property	Post-transfer form of property
Renationalization	Right to security and protection of property (hot nationalization)	Private (formerly privatized) company	–	Public company
Deprivatization		Private shares in private companies	–	Public shares in private companies and state-led holding structures
Bandit nationalization		Private property	Private property under state threat or deception	Public property
Transit nationalization		Private company	Public company	Private company (patronal)
Market raiding	Right to carry out an economic activity (monopolizing nationalization)	Private activity with normative license	–	Private activity with discretional license
Market acquiring nationalization		Private market	–	Public monopoly (franchise)
Competency nationalization		Private activity commissioned by a municipality	–	Private activity commissioned by the central state
Cold nationalization	Right to fair treatment (cold nationalization)	Private company	Private company with stifling economic environment	Private company (patronal)

84.

IN A RELATIONAL ECONOMY, CENTRALLY-LED CORPORATE RAIDING is carried out in three phases: stalking phase, hunting phase, and consuming phase. In a market economy, the dynamics of ownership transfers is dominantly defined by bilateral, voluntary decisions of buyers and sellers. As the character of ownership transfers shifts from voluntary to coercive, buyers become predators and sellers become prey. When actors take up these sociological roles, the dynamics of ownership transfers is predominantly defined by the unilateral, coercive decisions of predators.

When the predator is the chief patron, we speak about centrally-led corporate raiding, the process of which can be divided into three consecutive phases (Figure 14). In the stalking phase, the predatory state is looking for a prey. No intervention has happened yet: the would-be target still operates unmolested. But the predator assesses whether the company is worth taking over or not. On the side of the benefits, he needs to consider political gains, like strengthening the patronal network or weakening a rival one, as well as economic gains. The latter involves not only the company's market value, but the potential shelter-providing effect of state activity (Proposition 38) as well that can be provided after the asset is taken over. On the side of the costs, it considers the mobility of the prey (whether it can leave the predator's reach to escape appropriation), its lack of appropriability (stemming from asset specificity, for example), and the collateral damage the takeover may cause on the political, economic, and social level.

When the prey is selected, predation enters the hunting phase. The hunting phase starts with an irrefusable offer: the first price that is set, one-sidedly, by the predator, and offered to the targeted company's owner for the prey. If the owner does refuse, in spite of the obvious coercive capacity of the predator, the process of integrity breaking starts, at different points of which new offers (with lower and lower price) are made. As a result of various *ad hoc* normative and discretional interventions, the company's value in the eye of the market decreases. If the hunting is successful, the prey asset arrives at the ownership orbit of the adopted political family.

Here we enter the last, consuming phase of predation, when the booty value of the asset is realized as it becomes embedded in the relational economy. We may distinguish four pure types of uses of the booty company, any combinations of which in real world cases are possible: competitive market functioning after one-time boosting (e.g., a single budgetary transfer or change in the normative regulatory framework); rent-collection with appropriate discretional regulatory intervention (e.g., by the state guiding artificial demand to the company); building or solidifying patronal networks with the help of the company (when the company can be used in the political machinery, especially media); redistribution within the adopted political family (if the oligarch who received the booty becomes out-of-favor, their own companies become prey).

Figure 14: Ideal typical dynamics of competitive and relational market value of prey companies.

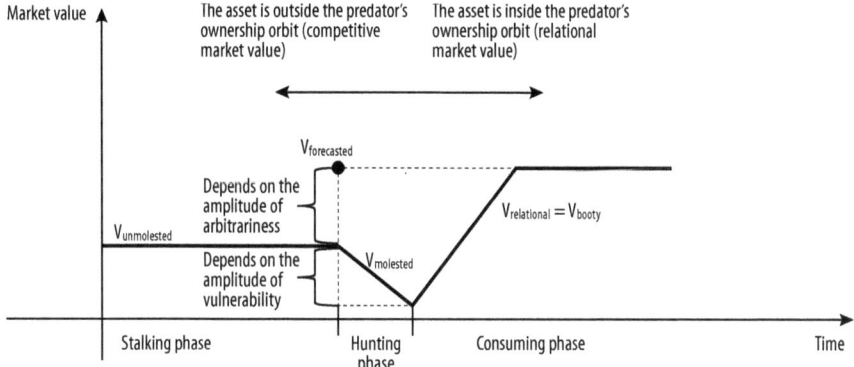

IN A RELATIONAL ECONOMY, ECONOMIC ACTORS MAY ESCAPE APPROPRIATION by having low stalking value, or hiding their assets by the various techniques of double accountancy and financial scheming. Usually, if predation is carried out for economic gain, large companies are chosen, and most of the small and medium-sized enterprises are left alone (as far as predation is concerned) because the cost of appropriation would be higher than the potential benefit. Professor Zoltán Balogh in the 1970s called this, in Marxist language, "uncollectible surplus value," referring to feudal times in Scandinavia where weather conditions made average crop yields so low that the cost of the tax collector apparatus would have been higher than the tax itself.

But even the companies which are not targeted directly change their behavior. Indeed, what matters in a relational economy is not what portion of property is being hunted down, but that anyone's property is a potential target. Predatory activity has a signaling effect, introducing perverse incentives in the not annexed part of the relational economy. Sooner or later, entrepreneurs realize that the primary question of operation in a relational economy is not whether they can stay in fair market competition but whether they become part of the predatory state's food chain. As a result, they get an incentive to allocate their resources not to maximize real production but to minimize stalking value. Large companies may engage in identity splits, or breaking up their company into small or medium-sized units so it can blend into the environment of the SME-sector, hiding it from the stalking eyes of the predator. Others may engage in various methods of double accountancy and financial scheming.

Indicating how widespread such practices are in the post-communist region, Ledeneva in her book *How Russia Really Works?* (2006) cites the post-Soviet saying: "If a company has a profit, it has a bad accountant." In addition to corporate identity split and underreporting profits, she identifies further techniques to avoid predation such as double bookkeeping (i.e., one set of books for corporate insiders and one for tax services), asset stripping (emptying the company that is expected to be taken over), and financial scheming (using shell companies, offshore companies, and fake contracts to take the profits out of the books).

In a market economy, such techniques are generally condemned as means of trying to evade taxes, or operate outside the regulated environment; in a relational economy, they enable the value-producing economic agents to protect their property and business operations. According to expert estimates, the informal economy accounts for at least half of the gross national product of Russia. Nevertheless, the ubiquity of informal practices also indicate a strong network of vested interests committed to their continued existence, making the development of a Western-type formal institutional system more difficult (even if there was political intention to do so).

86.

A RELATIONAL ECONOMY CANNOT BE DESCRIBED adequately in the "varieties of capitalism" paradigm, only as a variant of political capitalism. Recent literature on post-communist regimes has attempted to capture phenomena associated with the relational economy within the paradigm of "varieties of capitalism." In a minimalist sense, the relational economy is capitalist, considering the dominance of *de jure* private property (Proposition 80). But making this the primary criterion of categorization carries the risk of conflating relational economies, and their *sui generis* features, with Western-type economies, hindering the understanding of their actual nature.

In this sense, describing the relational economy in the "varieties of capitalism" paradigm is just as misleading as describing a patronal autocracy like Russia or Hungary in the "varieties of democracy" paradigm, that is, by a diminished subtype of democracy (Propositions 2-3). On the one hand, the categorization seems justified because—*de jure*, on the formal level—the system features similar institutions to the root concept. On the other hand, the categorization is unjustified because—*de facto*, on the informal level—the system has markedly different characteristics, which are also system-constituting features that overrule the system's formal identity. In a relational economy, *de jure* private property is *de facto* intertwined with political power, as expressed in the concept of power&ownership: there cannot be economic power without political power, or at least a stake in the political hinterland, and political power cannot be without economic power (Proposition 10).

If we are to emphasize the capitalistic nature of such a system, we should rather use the concept of "political capitalism." A Weberian term also prominently used by Randall G. Holcombe (*Political Capitalism*, 2018), political capitalism is an umbrella term for capitalist economic systems which are characterized by collusive corruption of governmental actors in significant enough a number to influence the workings of the economy's dominant economic mechanism (Table 29). The lowest form in our typology is crony capitalism: here, cronies initiate occasional corrupt transactions without patronal chains, resulting in a rent-seeking state with free competition for rents (free entry, free exit; Proposition 24). When corruption is no longer voluntary, but a type of capture, the question is whether it is bottom-up state capture—in which case we speak about oligarchic capitalism—or top-down state capture—in which case we speak about patronal capitalism, which can be best associated with patronal democracy.

Finally, we reach the relational economy when we speak about mafia capitalism. This system is characterized by the intrinsic logic of the accumulation of power and wealth, centralizing both in the hands of the adopted political family by means of mafia culture elevated on the rank of central politics. In this analytical framework, the reality of post-communism can be revealed, and features such as power&ownership, discretional state intervention, predation, and top-down corruption can be situated in their rightful place: as essential elements which define the system, and not as some exotic side effects in a fundamentally Western-type capitalism.

Table 29: Types of political capitalism.

	Dominant form of corruption	Initiating actors	Types of capture(s)	Type of state	Corruption market
Crony capitalism	Cronyism	Cronies	Market capture	Rent-seeking state	Free competition (free entry / free exit)
Oligarchic capitalism	Bottom-up state capture	Oligarchs	Market + state capture	↓ Kleptocratic state	↓
Patronal capitalism	Top-down state capture	Poligarch			
Mafia capitalism	Criminal state	Adopted political family	Market + state + oligarch capture	↓ Predatory state	↓ Monopoly (adoption / casting out)

Market-Exploiting Dictatorship: Coexistence of the Three Economic Mechanisms in China

87. THE ECONOMIES OF THE INTERMEDIARY REGIME TYPES— patronal democracy, conservative autocracy, and market-exploiting dictatorship—are mixtures of the economies of the polar types. In the triangular framework (Proposition 12), liberal democracy, patronal autocracy, and communist dictatorship are polar type regimes, not just because of their empirical importance. They are language-forming poles. These are the regime types that require their own language: a distinct set of concepts that reflects on the respective regime's *sui generis* characteristics. In contrast, the intermediary types—patronal democracy, conservative auto- cracy, and market-exploiting dictatorship—can be captured by mixed languages, constructed from the primary languages of the language-forming poles.

The logic is similar to that of a color wheel: languages of the three polar type regimes are like primary colors (red, yellow, blue) which cannot be mixed from any other one; while the languages of the three intermediary types are like the secondary colors (orange, purple, green) as they can be mixed from the primary languages of their neighboring polar types.

For patronal democracy, we need to combine concepts mainly from liberal democracy (multi-pyramid power network) and patronal autocracy (informal patronalism); for conservative autocracy, we need to combine concepts mainly from liberal democracy (non-patronal economy) and communist dictatorship (bureaucratic patronalism). This logic also applies to their economies: patronal democracy has a "mixed" market economy with a (more or less slight) majority of competitive markets and a (more or less slight) minority of relational markets, whereas conservative autocracy has a "mixed" market economy with a (more or less slight) majority of competitive markets and a (more of less slight) minority of administrative markets.

The situation in market-exploiting dictatorships is more complex. Its language is constructed mainly from its neighboring types, communist dictatorship (bureaucratic patronalism) and patronal autocracy (informal patronalism). But in this case, concepts from private economy and regulated market-coordination need to be mixed into the language, too. The economy of market-exploiting dictatorships, of which the paradigmatic example in the post-communist region is China, shows a dynamic balance of the three economic mechanisms, where it is nearly impossible to tell which market type is dominant in the sense that it would "lead" the other (subordinate) types. In the post-communist region, market-exploiting dictatorships grown out of communist dictatorships, keeping the party state and the lack of political opposition, on the one hand, while setting the economic sphere partially free, on the other.

88.

IN A MARKET-EXPLOITING DICTATORSHIP, BUREAUCRATIC-RESOURCE REDISTRIBUTION **is accompanied by regulated market coordination through the deliberate opening of the production structure.** A comparative analytical model for regimes with party states is offered by Mária Csanádi in her book *Self-Consuming Evolutions* (2006). She identifies ideal typical patterns of the party-state network that are differentiated on the basis of how bargaining power—defined as the capacity to extract, attract and distribute (economic) resources and to resist state interventions—is distributed among the actors (Table 30). In the pattern that she calls "self-exploiting," power is centralized in the hands of the top-level nomenklatura. Central planners coordinate the bureaucratic resource-redistribution process with few feedbacks, given the subjects below them have limited capacity to resist or bargain. We may add that the planned economy is also a closed totalitarian production structure: everyone is allowed to produce only what they are assigned to, and there are no formal markets where products that are produced beyond the plan could be sold and bought at market prices. In short, this is the ideal typical model of the communist planned economy.

The evolution of communist dictatorships to market-exploiting dictatorship means a model change without a regime change: the system remains a dictatorship and the party state retains its hegemony in the sphere of political action. However, while the main features of the party-state network in the self-exploiting pattern were (1) power centralization and (2) the closed totalitarian production structure, the process of transformation means that the party state gives up precisely these two features. In market-exploiting dictatorships, power—in our terms, planning of the bureaucratic resource-redistribution—gets decentralized, and the production structure opens within the framework of the party state system. Hence the country moves from the "self-exploiting" model to a "self-withdrawing" one.

Table 30: Ideal typical patterns of power distribution according to Mária Csanádi's Interactive Party-State (IPS) model.

Traits	Self-exploiting (e.g., North Korean and all initial)	Self-disintegrating (e.g., Hungarian from 1956 onwards)	Self-withdrawing (e.g., Chinese from 1979 onwards)
Distribution of power	centralized extraction and distribution, centralized interlinking threads, few feedbacks	centralized extraction and distribution, centralized (or decentralized) interlinking threads with strong economic feedbacks	partially decentralized extraction and distribution and either centralized or decentralized interlinking threads with economic feedbacks
Bargaining capacities of actors in the network	faint attracting and resisting capacity	selectively strong attracting and resisting capacity	selectively strong attracting and resisting capacity, owing to feedbacks and decentralized alternative resources
Constraints of self-reproduction	rarely hard	occasionally hard	frequently hard
Modes of resource extraction	forced resource redeployment	resource mobilizing (decentralizing) reforms within the network	resource mobilizing and resource creating reforms within and outside the network
Economic development	forced growth of heavy industry to physical boundaries	economic recession and reform escalation within the network	economic growth outside the net, recession within the net and reform escalation outside the network
Legitimacy and retreat	tensions growing, no retreat, abrupt collapse	party legitimacy declining, relative and absolute gradual retreat from political sub-field	party legitimacy kept, relative and absolute gradual retreat from economic sub-field

This process took place in China through a series of gradual reforms: more decision-making power (about production, marketing, investment decisions, staff etc.) was delegated to subnational levels and to state-owned enterprises; cooperatives in agriculture were dissolved, and a household responsibility system was introduced; the scope and quantity of compulsory production was narrowed; a dual price system was introduced, allowing the subjects to sell their over-the-plan products at market prices; the market was "opened up" as entrepreneurship outside the network was allowed, both in the form of FDI and local greenfield investments. This explains how bureaucratic resource-redistribution and regulated market coordination mix and form a dynamic balance.

89.

IN A MARKET-EXPLOITING DICTATORSHIP, REGULATED MARKET-COORDINATION results in investment overheating and the retreat of the party-state network. Regulated market coordination in a market-exploiting dictatorship remains rather sensitive to the dynamics of the original party-state network. This may be illustrated by the investment overheating produced by the new economy (Figure 15). In communist dictatorships, central planners try to accelerate economic growth by expanding investment activity. If the plan overestimates the economy's capacities—often because of plan bargain and false reporting—the network faces a hard production constraint, and the inadequacy of resources forces the party state to stop the expansion, resulting in a pattern of investment cycle.

In market-exploiting dictatorships, investment cycles are both amplified and used for the network's expanded self-reproduction. On the one hand, they are amplified as the competitive markets outside the network try to adapt to the allocation priorities of the network instead of adapting to actual market demand. As a result, the amplitude of investment overheating is expanded. On the other hand, the party state can now not only "step on the breaks" in terms of stopping investments but also taxing the newly legalized emerging markets that are overheating. This means that hard production constraints are softened, and the network is capable of expanded self-reproduction, accompanied by the growth of the equilibrated competitive markets.

This leads us to why the communist party state engages in model change. For the answer is not obvious: as a result of letting competitive markets grow, the party-state network retreats in both absolute and relative terms vis-à-vis the private sector. While it arguably keeps its dominant position in strategic industries, and influences the newly emerging markets, it loses the dominance it had in the totalitarian setting of communist dictatorship. The appearance of a private economy also entails autonomy and individual sovereignty, which pose dangers for the indivisibility of power of the party state.

The reason to still engage in reforms that allow this is the escalation of new resources and economic growth they bring. The more the economy grows, the more resources the party state can extract from it, the higher the people's living standards become, and the state party's legitimacy may be prolonged. This is we call this regime type a "market-exploiting" dictatorship: maintaining the formal monopoly of political power, the party state (partially) sets the sphere of market action free so it can reap its fruits in terms of political legitimacy, economic self-reproduction, and social stability.

Figure 15: Investment cycles in the Chinese market-exploiting dictatorship.

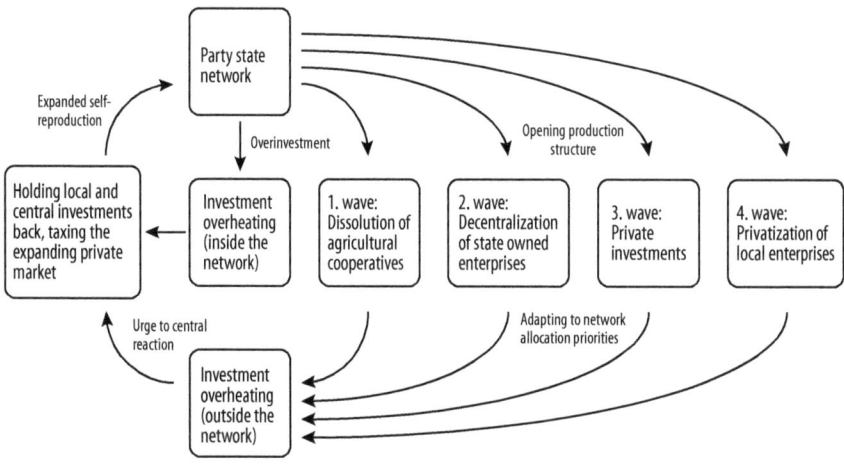

Note: the first wave was a one-time expansion, whereas the other waves continued to expand the private economy parallel to the subsequent waves.

90.

IN A MARKET-EXPLOITING DICTATORSHIP, RELATIONAL MARKET-REDISTRIBUTION emerges as an unintended consequence of decentralization. While the introduction of regulated market coordination is a process launched by the party state deliberately, the appearance of relational market-redistribution is more of an unintended consequence of the model change to market-exploiting dictatorship. The primary reason is that decentralization of power without party competition grants local party leaders a local monopoly of political power. As Chinese corruption expert Jiangnan Zhu explains, "[the] delegation of greater responsibility to lower level governments to optimize economic growth […] inadvertently [leads] to the development of many closed 'local or vertical kingdoms' independent of central oversight and public supervision." ("Corruption Networks in China," 32–33.) On the local level of the bureaucratic patronal hierarchy, centrally assigned resources as well as the tax revenues of locally registered companies are being handled by the local party secretaries, who can easily use this position to develop large patronal networks.

The fact that competitive markets are built upon administrative ones makes market-distribution a discretional power of party secretaries. While competitive markets do start growing outside the party-state network as the production structure is opened up, the party state keeps tight control over most investment projects: the local party leader decides who can enter a newly established market and who cannot. Theoretically, the local governments could bring normative regulations, but in practice the regulations tend to be discretional, and the delegation of economic decision-making powers to the local governments often leads to economic patronalization and patrimonialization. The result of these factors is the annexing of competitive markets via top-down state capture.

The local top patrons may employ kleptocratic means (like when Chinese party cadres demand a share of company profits, practically as protection money, in exchange for providing administrative services) or even predatory means (like systematic theft of public and private assets). Depending on the type of corruption they represent, we can speak about sub-sovereign kleptocratic states or sub-sovereign mafia states as a result. In large mafia states like Russia, sub-sovereign mafia states are local governments realizing in small what the central government does in big, according to informal central authorization (Proposition 108); in large non-mafia states like China, such entities come into being against the intentions of the central leadership, and their relational functioning is disruptive for the reformed party state.

91. **The mafiafication of the party state** appears as a threatening tendency in a market-exploiting dictatorship, and the party leadership must institute defensive mechanisms to protect itself. Going back to the triangular framework, we can see a tendency of patronal autocracy's neighboring regime types to gravitate toward it. In the case of patronal democracies, this gravitation takes the form of autocratic challenge (Proposition 69); in market-exploiting dictatorships, it takes the form of patronal challenge.

In other words, the emergence of sub-sovereign mafia states and informal patronal networks is a problem for the top party leadership not simply because public funds are being misused. The leaders of the regime must bear in mind the bigger picture as well, which is the tendency of "mafiafication" of the party state. Informal patronal networks, even if they start on the level of sub-sovereign government, can grow and capture more parts of the party state as the top patrons go higher and higher in the party-state hierarchy. The growing influence of patronal networks means that power is gradually "grabbed out" from the formal networks of the party state and moved into informal circles, carrying the risk of eventually transforming the state party into a transmission-belt party.

The tendency of mafiafication is a direct threat to the state party; no wonder Chinese scholars claim that the party leadership regards the containment of corruption in China as a matter of life and death for the party. However, while the threat of system-destroying corruption is partially made possible by the lack of party competition, this very same factor explains why the phenomenon can be contained, and why the economy as a whole may not become a relational economy.

In post-communist countries where formally democratic institutions and multi-party systems were established, informal patronal networks could launch autonomous patron's parties and enter the party competition freely, using the parties as interface to the sphere of political action. In market-exploiting dictatorships, those who form the patronal networks are members of the state party, thus the state can penalize an informal patronal network as a violation of party discipline. Already disposing over the monopoly of political power, the top-level nomenklatura of a market-exploiting dictatorship can use nation-level law enforcement to try to crack down on relational markets.

In China, fierce anti-corruption campaigns launched by general party secretary Xi Jinping, while regarded by many as a crackdown on political opponents (and not without reason), mark a fight against the tendency of mafiafication as well. Along with a previously unseen number of officials being arrested, the campaign attempted to root out sub-sovereign mafia states. For example, investigations of corruption no longer require approval of the party committee at the same level, but instead are initiated from above, attacking local top patrons' capacity to disable control mechanisms (Proposition 60).

92.

THE FORMAL INSTITUTIONS OF THE CHINESE PARTY STATE are under a trilateral pressure of informality of Western forms of corruption, post-communist forms of corruption, and *guanxi*. Corruption in China right after the reforms had started did not lead to the tendency of mafiafication immediately. What could be seen initially was the appearance of voluntary forms of corruption, such as free-market corruption and cronyism, which are still present in China to this day. The corruption that had existed within the party state network expanded and took new forms as a private economy was established. As Sebastian Heilmann explains in *China's Political System* (2016), "the Chinese state became an enormous illicit trading floor: company directors, party secretaries, and heads of authorities diverted the means of production and function from the state's economic sector to supply newly created markets; leading political positions and official approvals were exchanged for shares of profits in lucrative private transactions [...]. Major and minor holders of power at every level of the party [...] enriched themselves by taking advantage of the opportunities provided by the still imperfect market and legal order" (228–29).

These types of corruption may be regarded as Western forms, not in the sense that they do not appear in post-communist countries, but because of their moral status. Such forms of corruption are impersonal, business-like deals, and as such, they are illegitimate and morally not accepted. In contrast, patronal forms of corruption in post-communist regimes are also illegitimate but gain more moral acceptance as they represent stealing not for the individual but for the clan—especially in the historical regions where the separation of the spheres of social action is rudimentary (Proposition 7).

In China, both business-like corruption and patronal types are prevalent, putting two layers of pressure of informality on the party state (Table 31). The third layer stems from the age-old social device of *guanxi*. The word literally means "relationship" or "connection," but it is much more than that: it is a dyadic, informal social exchange relationship, a form of reciprocity where people accumulate social capital through mutual help. This social capital can be used to "get things done," gain access to resources or opportunities through personal favors; in this sense, *guanxi* represents a form of corruption. But the Western morality with respect to corruption is meaningless in this context. The illegitimate deals of *guanxi* are not morally condemned, nor simply accepted: they represent a moral obligation.

Table 31: Tensions between formal and informal rules in Chinese politics (from *China's Political System* by Sebastian Heilmann).

Formal rules	Widespread informal rules
Formalized system of cadre recruitment	Party patronage networks and the sale of political positions
Bureaucratic hierarchy and the establishment of universal rules	Domestic lobbies and clientele-based economic regulation
State property rights	Informal privatization and uncontrolled draining of state assets
Equality before the law	Manipulation of the judicial system to benefit party officials and their relatives
Fiscal system with binding allocations of revenue	Revenue retained by local governments and continual negotiations over the division of revenue

The system of *guanxi* grew, under the dictatorship of Mao Zedong, out of pre-existing strong-ties networks like family and friendship of reciprocal favors, and has been an important part of Chinese everyday life ever since. The similar system of *blat* in the Soviet Union, creating a population-wide informal economy of favors amidst the bottlenecks of the planned economy, was replaced by the less democratic and "egalitarian" forms of patronal corruption after the regime change. But the fact that the change from command to market economy in China was more of a gradual process, starting in the late 1970s, contributed to the continuity of social norms between communist and post-communist times.

Clientage Society and the Social Stability of Patronal Autocracy

93.

THE STRENGTH OF WEAK TIES IS REPLACED BY THE STRENGTH OF STRONG TIES as control over resources is concentrated in the hands of patronal networks. In patronal regimes, in place of social configurations that reflect class structure—with autonomous legal standings and advances through market mechanisms—, vassal relationships of the patron-client type ordered into chains of command take over the complete vertical plane of society. The adopted political family is a formation for domination that is organized around the head of the family in a monocentric, hierarchic fashion, through personal and family ties (Proposition 35). There is no free entry to the adopted political family, only adoption, being given access, or forced surrender; and no free exit either, only to be cast out.

The world of democracy that operates on the basis of multitudes of weak personal ties in the sanctuary of institutional guarantees is replaced, as the institutional guarantees fall through, by a world that is based on a few, but strong ties: the impersonal, normative and legal relationships are replaced by personal relationships with discretional rewards and punishments.

In his famous paper entitled "The Strength of Weak Ties" (1973), sociologist Mark Granovetter argues that job search is better helped by weak ties, carrying information from people who we know only little, than strong ties like family or close friendships, which may be with people who we know better but they also frequent the same social circles and therefore have the same information as we do. Indeed, this argument presupposes the separation of spheres of social action: that even if there is a social tie between actors of different spheres, that tie may carry only information but not influence. For if influence entered the picture, for example if a job applicant (i.e., an actor of the economic sphere) uses their family ties (i.e., relationships from the communal sphere) to get the job, information-carrying weak ties devaluate in the face of influence-carrying strong ties.

In patronal regimes, where control over resources is concentrated in the hands of informal patronal networks, access to these resources depends on one's strong, patronal ties. Under such conditions, the development of social networks shifts from scale-free networks, or "rich-gets-richer" patterns, to not scale-free networks, or "winner-takes-all" patterns, to use the expressions of network scientist Albert-László Barabási (Table 32). In his book *Linked* (2002), Barabási analyzes liberal democracies, and describes the principle of preferential attachment, where individual people are more likely to connect to nodes with multiple connections. In societies of patronal regimes, preferential attachment is not based on the number of ties but the range of appropriated resources. In open, competitive systems, new centers in the network may emerge on the basis of market fitness, if people choose to form ties with them rather than their old relationship (free exit). In a patronal autocracy, market fitness is trumped by power fitness: there is a center which prevents the formation of new, independent centers, and with which it is not possible to part ways at any time upon seeing a better offer (no free exit).

Table 32: Networks growing freely (in open access / market economy) and under compulsion (in limited access / command or relational economy).

	Growth	Preferential attachment	Fitness	Network pattern
Open access: free entry and exit (market economy)		Market	Voluntary decision	
		Choosing to connect by the number of ties →	Voluntary choice of new center by market fitness →	Scale-free network (rich-gets-richer)
	Evolving network			
Limited access: unfree entry and exit (command or relational economy)		Choosing to connect by the range of appropriated resources →	Coercive subjugation of competing centers by power fitness →	Not scale-free network (winner-takes-all)
		Patronal	Coercion	

94. SOCIAL STRATIFICATION IN PATRONAL REGIMES follows the logic of clientages, rather than classes, castes, or feudal orders. "Clientage" means not simply patron-client relationship but a basic type of social group that can be used to analyze the social hierarchy of patronal autocracy (Table 33). Usually, upon seeing low levels of social mobility, one is tempted to use historical analogies of "castes" and feudal "orders," or to speak about, using the mainstream language of sociology, a frozen "class" structure.

But a "caste" refers to a formalized social unit, typically legitimized by religion and characterized by hereditary transmission of a style of life (often occupation). Decisions about belonging to a caste do not depend on the arbitrary decision of a member of a higher caste: one cannot be deprived of their caste status, nor be adopted into a higher caste based on loyalty and discretional decision. Similarly, feudal orders or "estates" featured legally defined elite privileges, whereas a monarch could deprive someone of their wealth and freedom, but not their status (Proposition 32).

"Classes" in modern societies are non-formalized groups, just like clientages, but they come into being by the impersonal, dynamic forces of capitalism (Proposition 33). Class membership is defined by one's relation to productive property; in contrast, clientage membership is defined one's relation to the ruling elite, particularly their dependence on the adopted political family's resources. The boundaries of a clientage can be drawn by how dependence is created and maintained: whether it is done through jobs (perhaps in different ways in different sectors), through the vulnerability of entrepreneurial activity, through discretional state benefits etc. In a patronal autocracy, the adopted political family can deny access to these resources in a discretional manner, while also leaving a person no further alternatives. Thus, the adopted political family can make credible existential threats, and clientage status is deprivable.

We may use the metaphor of chokehold, particularly in the sense that, when the attacker's arm encircles the opponent's neck, the former does not necessarily kill the latter but prevents him from moving and controls how much he can breathe. In a clientage society, this corresponds to the elimination of the possibility of autonomous action. If one does not move, that is, acts in a way that it is in line or does not interfere with the goals of the adopted political family, they may never be actually targeted, and can live freely of discretional punishments. But in fact, the arm is always around their neck, and if they try, under the illusion of the lack of repression, to move autonomously as they please, the grip suddenly tightens and repression does appear.

The essence of a chokehold is this: keeping the actor or institution at bay by maintaining a permanent framework of the possibility of repression. While the lack of explicit terror might lead a superficial observer to conclude that the respective regime is indeed free and democratic, the creation of society-wide chains of dependencies means that even around the seemingly free actors' neck there is always the—at the moment, less tightly hold—arm of the patrons of the adopted political family.

Table 33: Types of social groups in various social orders.

	Type of social order	Formality of position	Chances of upward mobility	Deprivability of status
Caste	limited-access	formalized	low	no
Order	limited-access	formalized	moderate	no
Class	open-access	non-formalized	moderate/high	no
Clientage	limited-access	non-formalized	low/moderate	yes

95. MIDDLE, LOWER, AND UPPER CLIENTAGES, rather than classes, can be distinguished when speaking about the layers of a clientage society. While it is customary to speak about the "middle class" or the "upper class" in a liberal democracy, social stratification can be better understood by speaking about middle, lower, and upper clientages in a clientage society.

The upper clientages include the oligarchs, front men, as well as high-income members of the public administration. In a patronal autocracy, virtually everyone on the top of the social hierarchy is connected to the single-pyramid patronal network. This is symptomatically reflected in the list of "most influential people," published annually in several post-communist countries. The lists of influential people prepared in pluralistic societies grounded in the separation of powers will not include people in hierarchical relationship of superiority and inferiority with each other, but autonomous individuals in no relationship of dependence (from politicians to businessmen, media personalities to university professors). By contrast, a decisive majority of those who make it to the list in patronal autocracies can thank the chief patron's beneficence for their influential positions.

The middle clientage is constituted on two main groups, which may be identified, not by their legal but their sociological position, as "service gentry" and "court purveyors." The service gentry involves professional intellectuals, employed in state as well as private institutions; court purveyors are the subcontractors or direct subordinates of the adopted political family's economic units, *de jure* private companies and state holdings. While ideologically referred to as a "national middle class," these groups indeed constitute a level of subordinated vassalage with restricted freedoms in the spheres of political and market action.

Finally, the installation of patron-client relationships in a patronal autocracy may extend to the bottom of the social pyramid as well. The best and most telling example of lower clientage is public workers in Hungary. An earlier institution heavily reformed by the Orbán government, public work is a central employment relief program adapted to the needs of political communication and financed in an unpredictable fashion (for example, it employed nearly twice as many people in the month of the parliamentary elections in 2014 as in the month following it). Those who are employed in this program are not only exposed to the temporary, *ad hoc* nature of this work, along with the fact that they work for half the minimum wage, but they are also burdened by their employment and dismissal being a discretional decision of the local mayor, that cannot be legally questioned.

No wonder the public workers in Orbán's Hungary have no choice but to endure assisting at government party rallies as bio-decorations, participate as counter-demonstrators at anti-government protests, or work on the estates of the local clients. The disciplinary effect of this system can be seen in the election results of small and most vulnerable villages: the more a village was affected by public work, the more its people voted for the ruling party.

96. A CLIENTAGE SOCIETY IS DIFFERENT FROM A NEOLIBERAL SOCIETY, because on the level of social groups neoliberalism atomizes—patronalism vassalizes.

Taking into account the broader context of clientage society reveals why the framework of neoliberalism is misleading when it comes to analyzing social relations in patronal autocracy. The neoliberal ideal is the competitive, profit-and-loss logic of the free market, which it wants to make the basic principle of every type of social relation in every sphere of social action. Restricting the capacity of institutions of social solidarity, neoliberalism promotes pure competition of every social actor, even to the level of atomization. Patronalism, in contrast, promotes the elimination of competition: it vassalizes, rather than atomizes, social groups. The adopted political family sets out to replace free market mechanisms, or the "invisible hand" of market processes with the visible hand of the chief patron (Proposition 80).

We may compare three seemingly identical social consequences of patronal and neoliberal regimes to observe their differences. First, inequalities of wealth and income grow rapidly in both regimes. But neoliberalism results in market inequalities, stemming from the mechanisms of capitalism and the market economy, whereas a clientage society features patronal inequalities, caused and conserved by the mechanisms of informal patronal networks. Those at the top of the social hierarchy get there by the decision of the chief patron; and no one who may have climbed up there through meritocratic channels can retain their position if the chief patron wants to remove them, taking over their assets (Proposition 84). The composition of the ruling elite, the adopted political family is not caused by, but it is the cause of, the patterns of social inequality, association, and distance.

Second, under neoliberalism, the vulnerability of employees vis-à-vis employers increases by the weakening of labor unions and labor rights. This can also happen in a patronal autocracy—but that regime depowers both employers and employees, forcing them into clientage status through patronalization. Although employer discretion is *de jure* widened, the employer, who is either linked to the informal patronal network or tries to avoid crossing its paths, is expected to use their power for political bias, not simply for individual (profit) motive. In the end, we can see not a free employer who can limit the autonomy of their employees but a chief patron who breaks the autonomy of both, directly or indirectly.

Finally, patronal autocracies may have tax policy that would be regarded in a liberal democracy as right-wing conservative, supporting the higher echelons of the middle class. But this can also be understood from the perspective of clientage society. As we mentioned, the chief patron is a stationary bandit: he does not simply steal but does so continuously, therefore he has to ensure his position in power (Proposition 64). Accordingly, he needs the votes of those belonging to non-clientage groups as well, who could escape patronalization: typically either because they are entitled to normative state benefits (pensioners, students etc.) or members of the bourgeoisie, who have enterprising skills, export-oriented companies, and/or already accumulated capital in markets the adopted political family has not annexed. Unable to target them with discretional intervention, the chief patron uses the normative arsenal of the state to win them over. While the votes of those at the bottom of the social hierarchy can be bought for cheap, one-time material gifts, the aforementioned groups (who are also more prone to vote than the poor) can be appeased through tax cuts, perverse redistribution, and the like.

97.

THE SOCIAL STABILITY OF A PATRONAL AUTOCRACY is guaranteed by the vested interest of clientage groups in the *status quo*. Unlike communist dictatorships which relied on the use of mass terror to avoid popular uprising, patronal autocracies use different means of mass political persuasion (Table 34). Among them, we can find ideology, which we will discuss in the next propositions; as well as coercion and co-optation, which are made possible by the creation of clientage society.

The stability of clientages is quite different from that of the political support of autonomous citizens in a liberal democracy. Those who gain positions through the mechanisms of power-based privileges already have something to lose—this is what ties them to the new order. This is especially true in the case of those members of the service gentry who did not attain their positions by merit of expertise, but on account of the unconditional loyalty that was demanded of them. A position, claimed heretofore by merit, became a job delivered—and potentially taken away—by patronal favor. The patronal servant thereby gains a vested interest in upholding the system, as any change would come with an existential risk.

Discipline among those who remain in the filtered system is further increased by a huge gap between their current incomes and what their skills would be worth on the free market. In the circle of court purveyors and the upper clientages, to be a winner or loser of a tender can be measured in fortunes. When the regime is stable, they only worry about potential discretional punishments of the chief patron, which they can avoid with loyalty; if the regime was to collapse, they would need to be afraid of being held accountable for their often illegally obtained contracts and opportunities, which they might fall victim to under a regime of normative law enforcement.

It would be a mistake to underestimate the regime's capacity to cement the cohesion and loyalty of those adopted to the political family. Like the steel structure in reinforced concrete: the social coherence of the will of individuals is not a perceivable dimension for opinion polls, where ideology, program, and existences clearly match up for the members of the clientage.

Beyond material interest and the fear of retaliation, the support of members of clientages for the regime can be genuine as well. In this sense, sheer ideological belief is complemented by the peculiar social psychology of clientage society. In regime-changing countries, whole branches of industry dissolved with the loss of the traditional markets of the Soviet bloc; and after virtually full employment came waves of massive unemployment. Adding to this the suddenly intensifying stress coming from the general uncertainty of market competition, we can conclude that post-communist peoples' general experience of open-access orders was existential anxiety: the notion of uncertainty and the fear from the very real prospect of losing everything.

When in place of such an order a patronal autocracy and a clientage society is established, patronal dependence can grant a feeling of security. While losing their freedom to their patrons, members of clientages must receive certain benefits stably to create dependence and the opportunity of non-violent threats from patrons. These benefits, and the stable nature thereof, creates a calculable environment which gives rise to ontological security: the feeling of personal safety and trust, created by the predictability of everyday routine. And as people are generally risk-averse, even those who are not enraptured followers of the system must see extraordinarily promising prospects to consider supporting a fundamental, regime-level change. A clientage society thereby rests in a social equilibrium of patronalism.

Table 34: Means of mass political persuasion in the three polar type regimes.

		Target group(s)	Form/means of enforcement	Relative importance for mass political persuasion in…		
				Liberal democracy	Patronal autocracy	Communist dictatorship
Coercion	Use of violence	population	White (grey and black) coercion	−	+	+++
	Non-violent threats	transfer recipients	Cutting transfers	−	+++	−
		public employees	Firing from job	−	+++	+
		economic actors	Exclusion from (state) contracts	−	+++	−
Co-optation		population	Clientelism / (targeted) improvement of living standards	++	++	++
Ideology		population	Media	+++	+++	++

Legend: +++: primary means; ++: secondary means; +: tertiary means; −: not used for mass political persuasion.

Populism: an Ideological Instrument for the Political Program of Morally Unconstrained Collective Egoism

98.

PATRONAL ACTORS ARE IDEOLOGY-APPLYING, rather than ideology-driven. Material interests and the social psychology of clientage society are complemented by a third leg of the stability of power: ideology. While crowding out their opponents from the sphere of communication (Proposition 47), the adopted political family uses its own media to spread ideological messages to legitimize the chief patron's rule (Propositions 43-44).

When it comes to analyzing a patronal actors, ideology must not be taken at face value. This is what usually happens in political analyses: when a political actor uses nationalist panels, they are considered a nationalist; when they use right-wing conservative panels, they are considered a conservative etc. Actors are put on the left–right and liberal–conservative axis based on their communicated goals and party manifestos.

Labelling an actor "nationalist" or "conservative" presents ideology as the defining element of the actor, and therefore it seems to presume that they not only communicate the ideology but also take it seriously: that it is the guideline by which they act. This presupposition is justified if the acts of an actor are actually aligned with their communicated ideology. If there is a harmony of words and deeds, we can speak about ideology drivenness.

An example for ideology-driven politics is provided by communist dictatorships. They can be regarded as ideology-driven regimes because their main characteristics (the one-party system and the monopoly of state ownership of the means of production) can be derived from their ideology, Marxism-Leninism (Proposition 42). Jarosław Kaczyński, who has tried to institute a conservative autocracy in Poland and insisted on a strict abortion law in spite of its unpopularity, further illustrates that ideology-driven actors are willing to pay a political price for being firm on certain policies.

And while parties of liberal democracies may make compromises, and they certainly have political tactics, it makes sense to identify them with left and right-wing ideologies as well. For their starting point is an ideology: it is ideological, public policy goals (Proposition 56) which they bring to the table and compromise, design political tactics to, and want to grab power for.

Yet the communicated ideology may not always be the guideline of an actor or the regime he leads. In the case of patronal actors, there is no harmony of words and deeds: their ideology fulfills not the role of a guideline but of a cover. They are neither left, nor right-wing: they are driven by the twin motives of power concentration and wealth accumulation (Proposition 25), and assemble the ideological garb suitable to the anatomy of their autocratic nature from an eclectic assortment of ideological frames. In other words, it is not an ideology that shapes the system by which it rules, but the system that shapes the ideological panels, with huge degrees of freedom and variability. Attempting to explain the driving forces of post-communist patronal actors from nationalism, religious values, or a commitment to state property is as futile an experiment as trying to deduce the nature and operations of the Sicilian mafia from local patriotism, family centeredness, and Christian devotion.

99. ON THE SUPPLY SIDE, VALUE COHERENCE IS REPLACED BY FUNCTIONALITY COHERENCE in the ideological communication of patronal populists.

To analyze the functioning of ideology in patronal regimes, we need to make an analytical distinction between the supply side of the political market—the patronal populists—and the demand side—their voters. As for the former, while the communication of ideology-driven actors shows value coherence, that of ideology-applying actors shows functionality coherence, characterized by a value-free pragmatism.

To be more precise, we can speak about value coherence when the actor's ideology is logically coherent and consistently applied (does not include contradictory positions or double standard). In contrast, functionality coherence means that the actor's ideology is logically incoherent and not applied consistently (i.e., includes contradictory positions or double standards), but the pattern of choosing and varying ideological positions derives coherently from pragmatic considerations, that is, the principle of elite interest in the case of patronal populists (Proposition 25).

In ideology-driven, totalitarian regimes, the state actors serve the same ideology in line with a teleological goal; in an ideology-applying regime, state actors either do not follow any ideology consistently or they follow different ones which are locally functional, resulting in a value-incoherent but functionality-coherent mix of state functioning.

Of course, not all ideological panels readily match the behavioral patterns of patronalism. For example, those ideologies that stress the autonomy and the freedom of the individual are alien to it as the role of the patriarchal family head is easier to reconcile with elements of collectivist ideologies that allow domination over the household. Not all collectivist ideologies can be reconciled with this function either: the class-based and internationalist collectivism of Marxism-Leninism is not suitable for the ideological legitimation of the patriarchal patterns of power. Therefore, a mafia state mostly ends up picking bits and pieces from the ideological inventory of right-wing authoritarian systems.

The overarching framework patronal actors use is populism—a perfect ideological instrument as it entails only the unconstrained rule of the chief patron, not how he uses this power (Propositions 43-44). In general, a patronal populist can label any position as "common good" or "national interest," and therefore make opposition to it illegitimate and anti-nation. In particular, when it comes to justifying concrete acts of power concentration and wealth-accumulation, patronal populists criticize the *status quo* they want to change (they give a "diagnosis") and present their action as the solution (the "therapy"). But the diagnosis and the therapy are logically detached: the function of the former is only to legitimize changing the *status quo*, and delegitimize any criticism of the change as a defense of the *status quo*.

Table 35 contains a summary of such panels used by the Hungarian mafia state: a value-incoherent mix of arguments and actions that coherently serve the functions of concentration of political power and accumulation of personal wealth.

Table 35: Ideological covers fitting to patronal autocracy (from the communication of the Hungarian mafia state).

Motive (guiding principle)	Action	Ideological instrument	Chain of reasoning	Covering ability (logical consequence of the reasoning)
Concentration of political power	Institutional centralization (political patronalization)	Conservatism	National or religious culture must be protected → no one should be permitted to deviate	Control over autonomies marked by the propaganda as deviant → exclusion of alternative lifestyles and critical thinking
		Majoritarianism	Democratic mandate: the rulers represent the public → no non-elected actor, or his pawns, should fetter the volonté générale	Poligarchs get ultimate authority → no opposition and criticism from anyone (including the people) is allowed
	Neutralization of external threats	Nationalism	The rulers are the genuine representatives of the nation and the national interests →national interests should be protected and its enemies should be eliminated	The adopted political family decides what is national → opposition can be excluded from the nation, private/patronal interests become the "national interests"
Accumulation of personal wealth	Illegal favoritism	Statism	Free-market ideology has not led to affluence (but to crisis in 2008) → the state should help the national economy (e.g. by building a "national bourgeoisie")	Discretional favors to inefficient actors become legitimized →market coordination can be replaced by relational market-redistribution
		Anti-liberalism	(Neo)liberal policies have led to the rule of multinationals and high public debt → the state should reverse that via intervention	Discretional taxation and regulation becomes legitimized → the adopted political family can patronize any previously free economic sector
	Illegal predation	Justice-making	The previous elite gained its wealth fraudulently (during privatization) → the state should take the property from the bad and give it to the good	Discretional expropriation of property becomes legitimized → the adopted political family can take the assets of any of its opponents (targets)

100.

ON THE DEMAND SIDE, THE POPULIST VOTERS ALSO FOLLOW THEIR INTERESTS in choosing the ideology that fits best to the aim of preserving their social and economic status. Functional coherence is bilateral: it applies to the supply side of populism as it does to its demand side, the electorate. Many of the populist voters seek and receive an ideological message that provides legitimacy to defending their status from threatening phenomena, processes, and people.

The populists of Western democracies are trying to reach out to the "losers" in the wake of the social shocks caused by immigration and minority identity policies, as well as the economic difficulties and crises associated with globalization. The populists in the post-communist region, too, while partly creating their demand, often reflect on pre-existing social tensions. At the time of the collapse of the Soviet Union, a significant proportion of society expected that, upon adopting a Western-type establishment, the standard of living would also shortly be on a par with the West. Yet the fall of the large monolithic systems of repression was followed by unprecedented new forms of personal day-to-day vulnerability.

First, the people experienced the crisis of economic transformation, pushing large portions of society into existential anxiety. Second, the privatization process was seen unjust, either because of the instances of various forms of power-transformation or simply because most of the population was left out of it, creating a general feeling of having been cheated out of the "common property" (which it never was in fact). Third, oligarchic anarchy and low levels of institutionalization in countries like Ukraine and Russia led to widespread uncertainty in terms of contracts and property rights, especially for entrepreneurs. Economic actors could feel vulnerable as competitors, suppliers, and sometimes even prey to the bureaucracy, local oligarchs, and multinational corporations (Proposition 82). And in general market success or failure have had troublingly little to do with actual performance or consumer service. Finally, inequalities grew in terms of income and wealth, partially as a result of the previous factors but also because of high levels of patronalism (Proposition 96).

These factors have been exploited by patronal populists, who provided a narrative drawing a clear causal relationship between such problems and markets, liberal political elites, and imperialist political and economic actors. In Russia, the people changed words like democrat to *dermokrat* ("shitocrat") and privatization to *prikhvatizatsiya* ("grabitization"). In Orbán's Hungary, "liberal" became a slur, while the elite that had handled the dismantling of state-owned property were accorded the labels of "servants of international capital" and the "supporters of the conversion of communist power."

101. Patronal populists create a collective identity ("us")

with panels like God, nation, and family by the process of value appropriation through redefinition. The populist narrative builds on a Manichean "us and them" opposition, and the discursive construction of these two groups. To construct the "us" group, ideology-applying populists build on existing identities, linked to traditional communities of mutual protection. These identities are engraved in the people's minds as values which, if respected, ensure survival and defense against external threats. The most important of such communities are three: spiritual community (God), ethnic community (nation), and the family. In times of crisis, the people reflexively return to these secure communities, which are therefore functionality-coherent for the people and provide a particularly apt system of values that the populist can build on.

However, to make them functionality-coherent for the populist, too, he does not simply use these identities as they exist but performs value appropriation through redefinition (Figure 16). The populist selects the attractive elements from each traditional-community identity; deselects from them the parts that do not fit into the pattern of patronal domination; and reframes them according to the context of the regime. The selection of "God," for example, is based on the rejection of rationality and enlightened debate, framed in such a way as to give the adopted political family an unquestionable moral position. Meanwhile, the basic religious teachings of solidarity, compassion, and moderation are deselected as they are incompatible with amoral familism (Proposition 39).

The "nation" is an emotionally binding community in the name of which sacrifice can be required; on the other hand, the populist deselect the element of citizenship, as well as the solidarity associated with it. Simply put, some people can be excluded from the nation: not everyone who is a citizen, and therefore part of the nation by its initial definition, is also automatically a national actor, and the moral obligation of the members of the nation toward them is not automatic either. This leads directly to reframing: the nationalism of the mafia state is not directed against other nations, but against those within the nation who are not part of the adopted political family, who are not subordinated to that family as vassals, and the family's opponents.

Finally, in relation to the concept of "family," populists use the secular, progressive tendencies of the West as a deterrent example, and speak in defense of the traditional family model, asserting the social legitimacy of the same pattern of patriarchal rule that is embodied in the role of the chief patron in the country.

Figure 16: The process of value appropriation through redefinition.

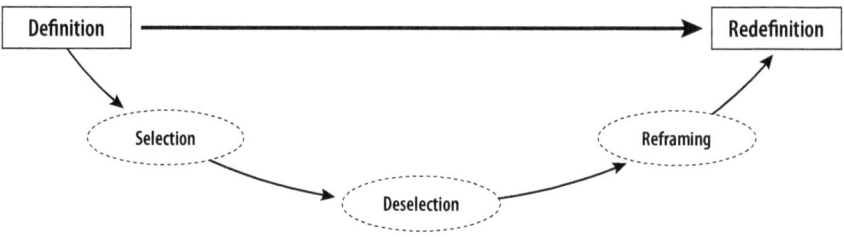

102. Patronal populists select the enemy ("them") in an ideology-applying way, following the political economy of stigmatization. The construction of the "them" group includes techniques of enemy construction and stigmatization. Patronal populists are not anti-Semites: their targets are not "Jews," but they regard anti-Semites as a political target audience. Their problem with banks is not that they are "Jews" but that they are not theirs. They are not racist either—they just want to win over people who have racist inclinations to their camp, too. They do this consciously, pragmatically, without emotional turmoil.

In contrast to ideology-driven extremists such as fascists and xenophobic politicians, ideology-applying populists do not have a stable stigmatized "them" group. They change enemies frequently, according to the current political climate. Ideological stigmatization has a specific "political economy": the enemy is chosen on the basis of which group has the most significant potential for generating hatred and fear, and what capacity of voice and resistance it may have (Table 36).

The fear-generating potential of the "socially disadvantaged," like homeless people, is lower, and they are separated from the majority society primarily by their social status, so they can serve as targets for *ad hoc* hate campaigns at most. However, "LGBT people" are divided from the majority by sexual and cultural cleavages, whereas in the case of "migrants" the people can see ethnic, religious, linguistic, and cultural fault lines. As a result, these groups can be used for a longer period of time due to their high fear-generating potential.

Table 36: Stigmatized groups' criteria to meet the needs of ideology-applying functionality.

	Cleavage dimension (potential for distinguishing 'them' and 'us')						Fear generating potential	Capacity of voice	Ideological panel
	Ethnicity	Religion	Language	Sexual orientation	Cultural tradition	Social status			
Socially disadvantaged / deprived					X	X	X		Lack of solidarity
LGBT people				X	X		XX	XX	Homophobia
Religious minorities		X			X	X	XXX	XXX	Anti-Semitism etc.
Ethnic/racial minorities	X		X		X	X	XXXX	XXX	Racism
Refugees	X	X	X		X	X	XXXXX	X	Xenophobia

In relation to the stigmatized groups, populist often arise conspiracy theories as well. Indeed, conspiracy theories follow logically from populist rhetoric. For in the Manichean worldview, everyone must belong to either side one or the other, whereas in reality the stigmatized groups, especially when they are chosen pragmatically and varied often in line with functionality coherence, constitute a highly heterogeneous set of actors. A group that includes a range of actors from active individuals to passive minorities, from opposition parties and organizations to other nations and international alliances, is necessarily fragmented. If these actors must be together on the side of "them," then there must be a conspiracy between them. A conspiracy theory is a reductive worldview, just as the politically forged identity is a reduction of identity.

103. **THE DEFINITION OF POPULISM in once sentence is this: an ideological instrument for the political program of morally unconstrained collective egoism.** Populism cultivates a sense of victimhood in its voters, who are offered absolution from their own role in their loss of social and economic status through the stigmatization and scapegoating of other social groups. This is what makes voters receptive of populism, which, in turn, triggers a specific line of psychological consequences.

The social psychology of populism can be summed up as follows: (1) victimhood is developed, as the populist defines other social groups, or "them," as an enemy of "us;" (2) victimhood absolves the populist voter from the moral obligation of caring about others, as it is the victim ("us") who deserves empathy and not the non-victims and the victimizers ("them"); (3) salvation leads to moral nihilism, meaning complete indifference with respect to what happens to others; (4) moral nihilism leads to the rejection of solidarity, for the populist voter no longer takes other people's interests into consideration; (5) the rejection of solidarity allows for open selfishness, meaning the voter can feel that they are finally free to help himself instead of others, who can be left alone without breaking any moral obligation; (6) selfishness appears in collective egoism as it is represented by the in-group ("us"), an imagined community that serves as a legitimizing basis for the rejection of solidarity; (7) collective egoism pulls the moral rug out from under public deliberation, as collective mediation and aggregation of various interests (Proposition 43) makes sense only when the interests of other people and groups are to be taken into account (i.e., selfishness is not absolutized in moral nihilism).

Put together, the elements of populism can be summed up in a single sentence: populism is an ideological instrument for the political program of morally unconstrained collective egoism (Figure 17). While various descriptions of populism list its elements mosaically, with smaller or larger overlaps of the scope of the defined elements, this single-sentence definition organizes the supply and demand side elements into a coherent order allowing for a structured analysis. And as the figures shows the elements of the definition can be read in both directions: from left to right, it describes populism from the supply side (the populist who wants to use it as an instrument of substantive-rational legitimacy, attacking public deliberation as the institutional set of legal-rational legitimacy), whereas from right to left it describes populism from the demand side (the people who want to unleash their egoism and have anti-establishment ressentiment, which the populist can capitalize on).

The populist gains unquestionable moral status, exploiting the people's psychological demand for group-belonging and historical need for morally unconstrained selfishness; in turn, the people find an "understanding" actor and collective amidst the difficulties of their lives. Instead of free love, "free hate" prevails: stigmatization and the feeling of victimhood provide the moral ground for doing away with moral constraints.

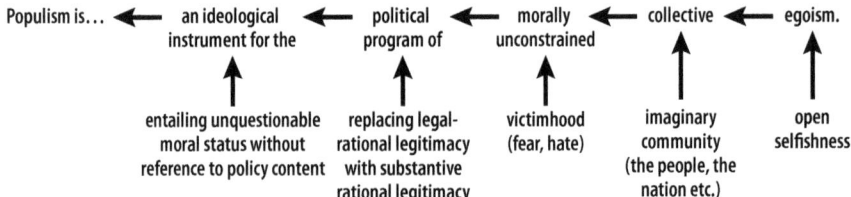

Figure 17: Populism summarized.

104. **POPULISTS OFFER problem-solving without moral constraints; dogmatic liberals offer moral constraints without problem-solving.** The weakness of rational criticism against populism stems from misunderstanding and also disregarding the position of the populist voters. It is a misunderstanding when the mushrooming of fake news and "the post-truth era" is described as

a supply-side phenomenon, with populists wanting to present their conspiracy narratives and fabricating news accordingly. Indeed, there is demand for fake news and conspiracy theories in the populist voters.

The audience that views the world through the eyeglasses of the populist narrative will structure, interpret, and even supplement reality accordingly, with the help of real as well as non-real "facts"—which, as they fit into their worldview, will be considered just as real as the "actual" facts. The narrative creates its own reality: the news and facts, real or otherwise, are not the backbone of the narrative but it is the other way around, they are optionally changeable illustrations to pre-ordered judgments.

The post-truth era means not simply the spreading of fake news by the populists: it means that whether a fact, news, or explanation is "false" or "delusional" is only determined by the person's beliefs, narratives, and preconditions which they believe to be true and want to see confirmed. This is why rational criticism, focusing on factuality of the populists' claims, is ineffective.

Beyond misunderstanding them, we need to speak about disregarding the position of the populist voters as well. We have seen that populists, be they Western ideology-driven or post-communist ideology-applying, reflect real social problems, or past and present phenomena that the voters recognize as endangering their material interests, as well as their feelings of safety and comfort. In this situation, populism offers problem solving without moral constraints—while dogmatic liberals offer moral constraints without problem solving.

Dogmatic liberalism tends to taboo and negate certain problems related to globalization and domestic social tensions, morally stigmatizing people affected by these problems that challenge their feelings of safety. In a way, what we can see is reciprocal stigmatization: populists call out "them" as the cause of all their problems, and dogmatic liberals call the voters resonating with populist messages "xenophobic," "homophobic," or worse. No wonder the people affected become receptive to the populists' more convenient solutions, which also offer them absolution from the moral stigmatization of dogmatic liberals.

This process undermines the possibility of rational discourse about the people's problems: people become stuck under the spell of populism as they perceive the other side, not simply not caring about their problems but even insulting them. The limits of this book do not allow us to delve into this issue any further, but the general point is that, when we analyze why populism is popular, the "pulling effect" of the populist narrative needs to be assessed in unison with the "pushing effect" of dogmatic liberalism.

Beyond Regime Specificities: Country-, Policy-, and Era-Specific Features

WHILE REGIME-SPECIFIC FEATURES DESCRIBE the workings of power and autonomy, country-specific features are cultural, historical, or natural features of the regime's environment. So far, we have discussed regime-specific features: we have provided analytical aspects for the regime, that is, the institutionalized set of fundamental rules structuring the interaction in the political power center and its relation to the broader society. Simply put, regime-specific features regard power and autonomy: they answer (1) which actor has and does not have power and/or autonomy in either sphere of social action; (2) what the character of the exercise of power and autonomy is; (3) in what arrangement holders of autonomy and power coexist; and (4) how the given arrangement is maintained, that is, how regime stability is achieved. Regime-specific features are the ones by which a regime is defined, and this is how we define the six ideal type regimes as well (Proposition 12).

On the other hand, each regime operates in a certain environment, related to a country's culture (national and ethnic cleavages), history (country size and the survival of nomenklatura), natural endowments (available resources), and geographical/geopolitical position. These are the country-specific features, which must be kept analytically distinct from regime-specific features. Naturally, there are connections between them, for certain country-specific features influence the sustainability of regimes and might create local peculiarities of certain regime-specific features (like the composition of the adopted political family; Proposition 36). But keeping the two sets of features analytically distinct is fundamental to realize similarities, as well as genuine differences, between certain regimes and countries.

Let us take the example of Russia and Hungary. On the one hand, they are vastly different: Russia is a multiethnic, multilingual nation more than 180 times bigger and 14 times more populous than

Hungary; it is rich in natural resources; and it is outside the EU, unlike Hungary. But there is no bigger difference between Putin's Russia and Orbán's Hungary in 2022 than the difference was between Brezhnev's Soviet Union and Kádár's Hungary before 1989. While two different countries, the regimes of the latter pair could be described by the framework of communist dictatorship, whereas the former pair, by the framework of patronal autocracy.

With simple metaphor, we can say that the regime-specific features define whether the subject is a cat or a dog, while country-specific features differentiate Chihuahuas and Great Danes. While "intra-species differences" may be significant, they do not make the respective "animals" members of different species.

106. Ethnic cleavages can be sources of pluralism or disorder as the organizational basis of informal patronal networks and social identity groups.

We can speak about ethnic cleavages when ethnic identity provides a cohesive force on the level of elites, and/or when it is a source of mass mobilization. In the post-communist world, ethnic cleavages often guarantee of pluralism, but sometimes they can lead to violent conflicts.

The first dimension of analysis is whether ethnically divided countries disintegrated into more homogeneous units after the regime change. Members of the Soviet Union seceded peacefully, forming new countries and along the pre-existing federal divisions; the dissolution of Yugoslavia also resulted in new countries along the lines of pre-existing territorial subdivisions, but it broke up violently.

Second, if the ethnically divided country did not disintegrate, the question is whether ethnicity based clans, i.e. informal patronal networks, have dominated the political landscape. The Hungarian minority in Romania (and its party, RMDSZ), for instance, is a minor player compared to the large patronal networks, but ethnicity-based clans have been the major players in the post-communist countries of Soviet Central Asia. Traditional clans mostly come together to form tribes, and at times the tribes will form tribal unions, which in Kazakhstan are called *zhuz*.

When ethnicity-based clans are the dominant political-economic actors, the third analytical dimension enters, concerning the presence of a clan pact: an informal agreement to stabilize relations between the clans. As Kathleen Collins writes in her book *Clan Politics* (2006), such pacts are likely to be made when "(1) a shared external threat induces cooperation among clans who otherwise would have insular interests; (2) a balance of power exists among the major clan factions, such that none can dominate; and (3) a legitimate broker, a leader trusted by all factions, assumes the role of maintaining the pact and the distribution of resources that it sets in place" (50). Collins persuasively shows that clan pacts were necessary to create a stable regime after the transition in Soviet Central Asia, and where it was not concluded—namely Tajikistan—its absence led to a civil war.

Fourth, if a clan pact is in place, the question is whether it stabilizes a single- or a multi-pyramid patronal network. The chief patron will sometimes be balancing between a few such large ethnicity-based clans, including them in the regime and thereby precluding serious clan opposition to the regime. Elsewhere the clans will form six or seven regional groups, and one or two stronger regional groupings will rise to more-or-less monopolizing the available positions (Tajikistan, Turkmenistan, Uzbekistan).

At other times, plenty of independent tribes competing in the political arena drive the political system towards a parliamentary bargain-mechanism (Kyrgyzstan). This latter example shows that ethnic cleavages may be the source of pluralism: the high number of competing ethnicity-based clans leads to a functioning patronal democracy, preventing the development of a single-pyramid, autocratic setting.

107.

THE SURVIVAL OF COMMUNIST SECRET SERVICES could result in a deep state, or a specific type of nomenklatura-based clan in patronal regimes. While every sovereign state maintains an intelligence agency, it is a country-specific phenomenon when agencies tasked with issues of national security start acting as a deep state. In other words, an intelligence agency can informally become an autonomous unit, a "state within the state"—or rather a "mafia within the mafia" in some post-communist countries. Historically, agencies like the KGB in the Soviet Union, the StB in Czechoslovakia, or the Securitate in Romania constituted large networks that suffused state and society. The knowledge and social capital represented by the members of these networks could be converted to political and economic capital after the regime change.

In some countries, domestic survival of the network did not produce a "deep" state but the state itself, that is, the new ruling elite. Examples include Azerbaijan with Heidar Aliyev, who became chief patron after pursuing a career in KGB, as well as Russia with Putin and his so-called *siloviki*. In countries where some sort of deep state did develop, the survival of secret service often happened through continuity of personnel in the freshly founded intelligence agencies of liberated countries. Ukraine is a good example of such continuity: although the Ukrainian Security Service (SBU) replaced the Ukrainian branch of the KGB, experts estimate that 35 percent of the SBU was composed of KGB professionals who had been trained by and retained contacts with Moscow.

Building on the accumulated knowledge and social capital, a deep state could be formed as an informal extension of the powers formally vested in the secret service. In some cases, the formal and informal powers of the deep state are used for blackmail, extorting monies out of people by coercion. In other cases, the deep state is entangled with politics, whereby it can either act as (a) a server of politics, meaning it informally offers its services to interested patronal networks (e.g., Hungary before 2010), or (b) a maker of politics, meaning it uses its means to influence policy-making and appointments, as well as enthroning and dethroning political actors in accordance with informal agendas (e.g., Romania).

As a special type of nomeklatura-based clan (Proposition 36), the situation of the deep state is analogous to that of autonomous oligarchs (Proposition 41). In a multi-pyramid setting, it can retain a relative autonomy, maintaining equal distance from the competing networks while avoiding subjugation to either of them; in a single-pyramid setting, it may be temporarily recalcitrant or have a positive (adopted), negative (rival), or neutral (fellow traveler) attitude toward the chief patron, but it will eventually lose its autonomy should the single-pyramid patronal network consolidate. It is patronal competition that allowed a deep state to function in patronal democracies like Ukraine and Romania, while the secret service has not been an autonomous server of politics but a client organization in Hungary since 2010.

108. **PATRONAL COUNTRIES WITH LARGE TERRITORY feature multi-tier single-pyramids, with local governments becoming sub-sovereign mafia states.** Single-pyramid systems must have control over the whole country, not only in terms of mere stateness but also in terms of monitoring the activity within the patronal network. The larger and more populous the country is, the higher the costs of monitoring are, and the more difficult it is for the chief patron to supervise the activity of clients directly.

In regimes with smaller territories and populations, one-tier single-pyramids are typical. This is not to say that there is no stratification of the patronal network: there are sub-patrons (as in every post-communist patronal network), and they also compete against each other. But they do not have a territory or region which they would rule with relative autonomy. Chief patrons of one-tier single-pyramids have strong direct control over their polity as they do not have to balance between relatively autonomous regional sub-patrons (local top patrons).

Balancing is typical in multi-tier single-pyramids, which develop in countries with territory so large that the costs of direct monitoring would be too high. The obvious example is Russia, where there are basically regional "sub-pyramids" within Putin's single-pyramid. The sub-patrons who lead these sub-pyramids are simultaneously clients of the chief patron and the top patrons in their own localities. The chief patron has kept certain competences, or taken them away from the hands of local governors; in particular, the control over natural resources was centralized when Putin seized the regional governors' tax revenues from the country's resource companies. But otherwise the sub-patrons are granted the right to rule their geographically limited region, in many ways with greater independence from Moscow than during the Brezhnev period.

Local rule is isomorphic to the central rule: the sub-patrons follow the same patterns of behavior with regard to their locality as the chief patron does with regard to the country. In other words, in a patronal autocracy, the central mafia state of the chief patron is accompanied by sub-sovereign mafia states of lower-tier patrons. The similarity of local and central mafia states in their regime-specific features was inadvertently revealed by the Russian Investigative Committee, which arrested, after several years of top-down authorized corrupt functioning, Vyacheslav Gazier, the governor of the Komi Republic in the Russian Federation. The official description of Gazier's "criminal organization," which involved the entire machinery of local state power, clearly outlines the contours of the mafia state: "the purpose of the criminal organization […] was to seize state property in a criminal way"; "distinguished by […] the hierarchical structure of the criminal organization"; "the cohesion and close relationship of the leaders and participants"; "the strict subordination of lower members to their superior"; "the well-developed conspiratory system of protection from law enforcement."

109. China and Russia have imperial ambitions stemming from a strong will to balance the size and civilizational core nature of the country and its role as a global superpower.

China and Russia are not simply large countries, but civilizational core states as well (Proposition 7). Their historical legacies of many centuries of imperial existence shape the perception and identity of current leaders and peoples. The resultant imperial ambitions aim at balancing the size and civilizational importance of the country and its role as a global superpower, manifesting in the expansion of global economic and/or political roles.

China represents a case of enormous country size, still with larger economic than political weight. The second largest economy in the world (in GDP), China's expansionist policies are also mainly driven by economic means, including the slow but steady state-supported investment and trade expansion in Africa and post-communist Europe. Potentially, economic expansion creates the necessary conditions for political expansion, but as of now, the signs of such ambitions are overshadowed by China being an economic superpower.

As opposed to China, Russia has larger political than economic weight, which economist László Csaba vividly captures by calling it "Kuwait with nuclear weapons" (*Válság-Gazdaság-Világ*

[Crisis-Economy-World], 2018). An economy relying mostly on the export of oil and gas instead of innovation and investment, the GDP of Russia with its 147 million people is smaller than that of South Korea with its 51 million people and only slightly surpasses that of the Benelux countries with 29 million people (in 2018). While Russia's nuclear arsenal and permanent membership on the UN Security Council guarantee its political weight on a global level, Putin has applied various kinds of strategies in an effort to restore the country's imperial influence.

First, Russia engages in autocracy promotion, supporting autocratic breakthroughs (Proposition 68), local chief patrons, and the longevity of established patronal autocracies in general. Unlike the democracy promotion of the West, Putin's commitment to autocracy is not value-coherent but functionality-coherent: he is not interested in spreading autocracy as the ideal model for the world but as an insurance policy for Russia, trying to prevent the negative externalities that would come with democratization in the region. Russian autocracy promotion might involve direct influence with military presence as well, as we could see in the cases of Belarus (which has been practically subordinated to Russia before and during the 2022 invasion of Ukraine) and Kazakhstan (where elite change within the single-pyramid patronal network was facilitated, in 2022, by Russian influence).

Second, Russia uses so-called "Gazprom diplomacy" which means that Putin uses the bargaining power stemming from the unilateral dependence of partner countries on Russia's natural gas and oil. Russia keeps former Soviet countries on a leash through the control of supply prices (e.g., Ukraine, Moldova, and Belarus), while outside the post-Soviet region Gazprom is used for direct bribery and money laundering with the help of cooperative populists (e.g., Orbán in Hungary and Matteo Salvini in Italy).

Trying to internally destabilize other, potentially threatening global players, Russia has supported populist parties and paramilitary groups and attempted to intervene in elections in several Western countries as well. Putin's political foothold is further strengthened by the co-optation of high-ranking Western politicians in the boards of Russian companies (including a former German chancellor, two ex-chancellors of Austria, and a former prime minister of France).

Autocracy promotion is for the benefit of local incumbents; Gazprom diplomacy and gaining influence in Western countries are against local incumbents who face Russia's soft power and covert destabilization attempts, respectively. The final strategy of Russia, which is military intervention, involves directly attacks on an incumbent government, either trying to replace it or ripping out a piece of its territory. The 2008 war with Georgia over South Ossetia and Abkhazia, the 2014 annexation of Crimea, and the 2022 invasion of Ukraine indicate Putin's ambition to restore the position of Russia both as an imperial power and the civilizational core state of the Orthodox civilization.

110. INTERNATIONAL POLITICAL INTEGRATIONS like the EU can remain stable if they have defensive mechanisms to maintain homogeneity in terms of the members' regime-specific features.

Geopolitical orientation is greatly influenced by civilizational gravitational fields, exerted by core states of civilization. International integrations around Russia, the core state of the Orthodox civilization (Proposition 7), include the Commonwealth of Independent States (CIS), the Eurasian Customs Union (EACU), and the Eurasian Economic Union (EAEU). These integrations are stable for two reasons. First, they are shallow: while CIS would theoreti- cally be a force to integrate post-Soviet countries, less than 10% of the thousands of documents and resolutions adopted by its bodies have been actually ratified by the member states. Second, CIS and the other integrations feature regime homogeneity.

For an integration to be stable, participating governments do not have to share policy preferences; they only have to be able to reconcile their interests, to be on the same page about the role of formal policy and informal norms and influences. Similarly, it is not required to have the same country-specific features, like—in case of liberal democracies—the same kind of welfare state or the same pattern of democratic institutions, but to respect the community's basic values—to be in essence a liberal democracy. The above-mentioned integrations tied to Russia are regime-homogeneous: they all have patronal leaders, who can conclude family businesses without broaching human rights or the infringement of democratic values.

In sharp contrast, the European Union (EU) is a deep but fractured integration, and it features regime heterogeneity. Among its members, a majority of Western liberal democracies is accompanied by a conservative autocratic attempt (Poland), patronal democracies (Bulgaria, Romania, Slovakia), and a patronal autocracy (Hungary). From these, patronal autocracy is the most subversive because it is incompatible with Western members, as well as with both the EU's political foundations (liberal democracy) and economic foundations (market economy).

A structural-design flaw of the EU is the lack of effective defensive mechanisms that would foster regime homogeneity. To underline this, let us compare the logic of EU and U.S. sanctions against patronal regimes (Table 37). The EU's existing sanctions related to the misuse of EU transfers punish the victim, not the perpetrator: they threaten taxpayers' money and public spending, rather than targeting the corrupt practices and personal wealth of the adopted political family. Like the military tactic of carpet-bombing, the victims are mostly civilians.

Table 37: The disparate logic of EU and U.S. sanctions.

	EU sanctions	U.S. sanctions
launch of sanction proceedings	bureaucratic, cumbersome, may be subject to political bargaining;	partly based on political considerations, but the reporting obligation of the companies approached entails the mandatory launch of proceedings;
suspension of sanction proceedings	may be subject to political bargaining;	the proceedings cannot be suspended; once they are launched, they are no longer within the reach of political bargaining;
targets of sanction proceedings	institutions committing the presumed infringements, making the link between the perpetrator and the crime more difficult to personify and communicate;	persons committing the presumed infringements, allowing the personification of narratives;
underlying message of the selection of targets	it does not address the matter of personal liability, enabling the mafia state's patronal servants to continue taking part in operating unlawful mechanisms; the chief patron still has the unscathed capacity to maintain krysha;	erosion of the integrity of the adopted political family and the protection provided by the chief patron, dissuading the mafia state's patronal servants from participating in infringing procedures;
criticism horizon of the sanctions	target the government	target the regime

In contrast, U.S. sanctions are more similar to guided missiles, attempting to penalize the breaches and the perpetrators of corruption with laser-like accuracy. Means like the Magnitsky Act or Presidential Proclamation 7750 make it possible to deny visas and freeze foreign bank accounts. A criminal organization, whether private or public, has three crucial needs: sources of money, the ability to launder it, and impunity for its members. U.S. sanctions overrule the last point, the chief patron's krysha (Proposition 38), striking the mafia state at its Achilles' heel.

111. INTERNATIONAL ECONOMIC EMBEDDEDNESS carries both regime-stabilizing and regime-disrupting potential, the realization of which depends on the policies the chief patron uses to exploit them.

After the collapse of the Soviet Union, post-communist countries which opted for Western integration soon became entangled in global trade, much more so than countries that remained in the gravitational field of Orthodox civilization. However, the patronal regimes in both groups have developed either or both types of economic dependences: FDI (foreign-direct investment) dependence or export dependence.

Export dependence refers to the fundamental role of export revenues to the stability of the domestic economy in general and to the balance of the budget in particular. While vulnerability to foreign markets has obvious regime-disrupting potential, export dependence can also be regime stabilizing if it creates asymmetric interdependence, as explained above with respect to Russia's Gazprom diplomacy (Proposition 109). On the other hand, FDI in Russia has been restricted to some technologically unavoidable areas, while foreign ownership has been undesirable in most other sectors, from financial intermediation to trade and education. Under such circumstances, Lennart Dahlgern, the former head of IKEA Russia—by his own admission—tried to convene a meeting with Putin, but a high-ranking official told him that such a meeting would cost $5-10 million (which Dahlgern reportedly did not accept).

The situation is different when export dependence is accompanied by FDI dependence. In countries with relatively higher levels of foreign investment and economic activity, lobbying efforts, targeted at not individual members of the parliament but the patron's court (Proposition 18), can be more welcome. What needs to be seen is that, when a chief patron tries to appease local transnational corporations with subsidies, tax cuts, or weakening the labor code, he does not do so out of (neoliberal) policy preferences. Rather, he attempts to neutralize a regime-disrupting element. In the eyes of the chief patron, strong transnational corporations are autonomous major entrepreneurs who cannot be patronalized, partly due to their mobility and partly because of their foreign political background outside the chief patron's reach. It is in the interest of the chief patron to make these companies reluctant to support a regime change with their autonomous resources.

True, foreign companies and investors are generally uninterested in any fundamental change that would put their profitability at risk. Some foreign companies can also be crowded out and their place, taken over, particularly if their activity is immobile (Proposition 84). But those who cannot be forced to leave are offered benefits or, in Hungary, even so-called strategic agreements: Audi, Coca-Cola, Daimler, GE, Microsoft, Richter, Samsung, Sanofi, Synergon, and so on. Co-optation of transnational corporations by Orbán has been a successful strategy of pacification. Foreign companies do not question the basic operation of the single-pyramid system: the members of the car industry, the IT industry, or the telecommunications industry constitute lobbying business groups in Hungary, not a separate informal patronal network (Table 38). Despite their autonomy, they even contribute to the stability of the regime, both economically at the domestic level and politically at European level.

Table 38: The main features of a business group and an informal patronal network.

Business group	Informal patronal network
composed of actors of **separated spheres** (**entrepreneurs** from the sphere of market action)	composed of actors of **colluding spheres** (**oligarchs and poligarchs**)
activity of participants is **homogeneous**	activity of participants is **heterogeneous**
sector specific	**sector neutral** ("all-eater")
uses **lobbyists** to carry out **interest representation**	uses **corruption brokers** to carry out **interest collusion**
cohesion of the group is provided by **sector specific activity and benefits**	cohesion of the group is provided by belonging to the **same chain of vassalage**
horizontal alliance of autonomous actors	**vertical patron-client relation** of **dependent** actors

112. **Ordinary criminality as unauthorized illegality** may not be tolerated by the adopted political family, which in turn is an integrated user of the global criminal ecosystem. The mafia state fights not corruption at large, but partisan acts of corruption that it is not carried out by its express permission. It acts in the way the classical mafia would within the scope of its interests, but on a national level: it eliminates private banditry. On the one hand, how the chief patron looks at such activities is regime-specific. In his eyes, cases from petty corruption to ordinary criminality represent unauthorized illegality, as opposed to the authorized illegality of the members of the adopted political family. On the other hand, the scope and forms of unauthorized illegality differ from country to country, just like the attitude of the chief patron toward it (Table 39).

In some cases, when the cost of repression or takeover would surpass the benefits, the chief patron will be tolerant, and leave the corrupt networks alone (the case is similar to the logic of "uncollectible surplus value"; Proposition 85). In other cases, the mafia state "settles over" an existing network and starts taxing it without breaking its autonomy. For example, the Uzbek criminal state settled over illegal currency exchange, using the police to collect "taxes" from those who pursue this activity, and delivering the monies through the police chief, a local sub-patron, to the chief patron. This is less typical in the post-communist regimes that are in the sphere of influence of the European Union, while in Russia the relationship of state and crime (from hackers to the organized underworld) is mutually beneficial, and leads to mutual reinforcement.

The mafia state, together with traditional criminals, forms a kind of criminal ecosystem. On the national level, the pattern of this ecosystem ranges from the coexistence of a strong criminal state and moderate unauthorized illegality (e.g., Hungary) to parasitic symbiosis, taxing the network but at the same time guaranteeing protection from law enforcement (e.g., Russia, Uzbekistan). But we can speak about a global criminal ecosystem as well, which involves illegal elements all over the world, interacting as a system. First, this means that poligarchs and oligarchs from different countries are connected to each other, either in voluntary connections for mutual benefit or as a result of coercive subordination to a larger chief patron. In the language of world-systems analysis, we can say that Putin's Russia is the core of a criminal ecosystem, while Orbán's Hungary, through deals like the Paks II nuclear power plant, is tied into it in a semi-peripheral vassal position.

The global criminal ecosystem involves international criminal organizations and networks as well, and oligarchs and poligarchs use them for laundering corrupt monies. Ironically, it seems that the proper functioning of criminal states requires non-criminal states: liberal democracies are limited in their access to private economic businesses, and private (patronal) buyers of luxury real estates and the owners of local shell companies are protected by all the institutions and laws that have been developed to separate the market and political spheres of social action. This situation has been exploited by adopted political families and private criminals alike, from Hungary through Russia to Central Asia. So far, Western countries have been able to implement countermeasures in an *ad hoc* way (such as the freezing of Russian assets during the 2022 invasion of Ukraine), but systemic solutions will require laws as international as the movements of illegal money are.

Table 39: Modes of control of unauthorized illegality and the result in a criminal state.

	Action of the criminal state toward unauthorized illegality	The form of coexistence (the result of state action)
Repression	attack/restraint	segregation (eliminated unauthorized illegality or "private banditry")
Toleration	leave alone	segregation (no more molestation of the illegal actors)
Facilitation	settling over it	negotiated connection (brokered autonomy of the illegal network / hiring criminal as violent entrepreneurs)
Takeover	breaking its autonomy	integration (illegal network managed by the adopted political family)

113. Natural resources serve as a source of rent in patronal countries when they are available; when they are not, their function is substituted by the state budget, booty companies and banks, and international transfers. While it is a regime-specific feature that informal patronal networks rely on top-down forms of corruption, they show country-specific differences in their sources of rent. The basic question with respect to rent collection is what is at the regime's disposal: what kind of resources are available that can be the subject of rent-seeking and later distributed within the adopted political family.

The lion's share of exports and budget revenues in countries like Azerbaijan, Kazakhstan, Russia, and Turkmenistan is produced by the selling of natural resources, particularly oil and natural gas. The lucrativeness of these resources is guaranteed both by their respective markets' demand side—there is a constant demand for these resources in every modern country—and supply side—natural resources are usually geographically concentrated, therefore a country can easily be a local monopolist in its neighborhood.

On the other hand, any network that controls the given territory may claim natural resources, as underlined by some exponents of the so-called "resource curse" literature. According to these authors, resource abundance has an effect on the given country's regime-specific features through contributing to either the consolidation of autocracies (when natural resources are utilized by a single-pyramid network), or the disintegration of the regime in civil wars (when the resources are utilized by a competing pyramid, conquering the geographical area the respective resource is concentrated in).

Not all countries with patronal regimes have rich natural endowments. In their case, international transfers may fill the role of oil and gas. One particular kind of transfer that has been instrumental to Central European adopted political families is EU funding. In Hungary, over 80 percent of the tenders won by Lőrinc Mészáros, Orbán's economic front man (Proposition 16), is financed from EU funds. The odds of winning, a metric proposed by István János Tóth and Miklós Hajdu ("Political favoritism in public tenders in Hungary," 2021), clearly indicate the presence of guided bids in public procurements: in the 2011-2020 period, Mészáros won 8 out of 9 EU-funded bids he applied for, while the industrial average was 1 out of 3.

While the previous sources of distributable rent exist by virtue of geographical and geopolitical position, there are also created sources of rent in a relational economy. First, institutions of rent-collection can be founded, particularly (a) booty companies, owned by oligarchs or economic front men and enjoying the benefits of discretional state intervention (Proposition 84), and (b) financial institutions like banks, conglomerates, and perhaps state loans to finance booty companies. Second, the state budget can be a source of rent as well.

In the traditional macroeconomic approach, cutting budget deficits or increasing tax revenues by curbing the black and grey economy all point to healthy economic functioning. However, if we give up the axiom of the state being an agent of the public good (Proposition 5), we will see that the "whitening" of the SME sector may feed the budget of a "darkened" mafia state. By dismantling budgetary controls and systematically influencing the public procurement system from the top down, the chief patron can exercise discretional control over the distribution of state revenues.

114. THE POLICIES OF PATRONAL AUTOCRACIES may differ in content, but their direction is always patronalization and patrimonialization. Beyond regime- and country-specific features, we can distinguish policy-specific features as well. In contrast to the regime specificities of power and autonomy and the country specificities of unchosen or culturally/historically rooted factors, policy-specific features are (1) the exact content of the programs chosen and formally enacted by governments and (2) the result of these programs, including both success and the public-policy consequences typically measured in statistical measures and socio-economic indices.

In Proposition 56, we have already explained that, in a patronal autocracy, policies like education, social policy, or cultural policy should be observed through "regime-specific glasses": they are not public policies, whose success is measured from the perspective of the public, but patronal policies, whose success is measured from the perspective of the adopted political family. This provides an alternative analytical paradigm for policy analysis, illustrated in Table 40. We chose Hungary for illustration because it has been the subject of our earlier research (see *Post-Communist Mafia State* [2016] and *Twenty-Five Sides of a Post-Communist Mafia State* [2017], published by CEU Press).

In the analytical framework, education, culture and research, and social policy are analyzed by how they integrate people and institutions into the single-pyramid patronal network through institutional, financial, and personal dependence. Institutional competences that have belonged to autonomous units like the schools and local governments was centralized in the hands of newly formed entities, filled up with patronal servants (Proposition 20). Financial dependence was created in unison, delegating financial resources and the distribution of tax monies to these institutions, which can redistribute it on a discretional basis. Finally, personal dependence was created by the centralization of appointments (education), by making alternative options outside the power network economically unviable (culture), and by forcing the poorest people *de facto* servitude, with no labor rights, to local adopted-family members in the framework of public work (social policy).

This analytical framework also draws a clear line between patronal and public policy consequences. In education, a patronal policy consequence is the control of channels of social mobility, whereas it also causes—on the public policy side—decreasing student performance, increasing segregation and a diminishing number of new university students every year. Culture becomes subordinated to symbolic politics and propaganda, while this also means a decline in the diversity of culture. And at social policy, the creation of clientage society (Propositions 94-97) brings about the weakening chances of social mobility and social security.

Public policy consequences may be important to the chief patron if they influence the regime's stability, as explained in the next proposition. At any rate, regimes with the same regime-specific features may excel at different rates in their policies. Just as a country can be a patronal autocracy with small territory just as with large one, a patronal democracy may be lagging or feature a stable, successful economy while still belonging, by the logic of its internal processes, to the group of patronal democracies.

Table 40: An analytical framework for patronal policies, with the case of Hungary as an illustration (2010-2021).

		Patronalization and patrimonialization			Patronal policy consequences (rationale)	Public policy consequences
		Institutional dependence	Financial dependence	Personal dependence		
Education	Public	Centralization and takeover of public schooling from local governments	Financial decisions delegated to a central body	Ministerial appointment of school principals, employment decisions transferred to district-level authorities	Control of channels of social mobility, restricting freedom of speech of teachers and professors; discretional control over the distribution of budgetary resources	Decreasing student performance (PISA), increasing segregation and dropout
	Higher	Appointing omnipotent chancellors over the institutions by the chief patron, then placing them under the control of patronal asset management foundations	Making normative financing a question of institutional bargain, relegating intra-institutional financial decisions to chancellors and the newly appointed board of trustees	Minister can overrule the Senate's proposals for Rectors		Decreasing number of university students in Hungary, increasing number of emigrating university students
Culture / research		Takeover of research institution network of Hungarian Academy of Sciences; establishment of a pro-government academy of arts	Making formerly normative and competitive resource distribution a discretional right of the government	Making artistic life without state funding or membership at the new Academy of Arts economically unviable	Subordinating culture and research to symbolic politics and propaganda (camouflage)	Decreasing diversity of culture and research
Social policy		Centralization and takeover of certain social public services from local governments	Resource withdrawal from local governments and NGOs, restricting social budget	Introducing public work in place of some social benefits as a de facto form of servitude	Maintaining patriarchal family order on social level	Decreasing chances of social upliftment, weakening social security, increasing social inequalities

115. THE SOCIAL LIMIT OF PATRONAL POLICY MAKING consists of the people's stimulation threshold, and their room for maneuver within the neutralized institutions of public deliberation.

Elections force some accountability upon leaders even in an autocracy with restricted political freedoms. As a bandit, the preference of the chief patron would be to wholly devote state functioning to power concentration and wealth accumulation; but as a stationary bandit, who wants to rob the same subject, his own country, repeatedly and also enjoy impunity, he needs to achieve sustainability of the regime. The chief patron must treat his people not only as sources of revenue but also as voters.

How much the preferences of the people can influence state functioning depends on two factors: the openness of the public deliberation process, and the people's stimulation threshold (Figure 18). In a liberal democracy, the public deliberation process is open: it allows the people to voice their concerns, and for the concerns to be turned into political capital by the opposition. Thus, even slightly stepping over the stimulation threshold makes democratic leaders lose power to the opposition, who have the incentive and the means to capitalize on the people's resentment. In contrast, the chief patron can step way over the stimulation threshold without starting to lose power, as a result of neutralized public deliberation.

Normally, the leading political elite in both regimes tries to act within the amplitude of zero level of irritation and the level where it starts losing power. But even if they rely to a great extent on opinion polls, the leaders are not perfectly informed: they can make mistakes in assessing policy effects, the stimulation thres-hold, as well as the point where they start losing power. The question that arises is what the leaders can do when they reach this point. In a liberal democracy, where the factors the people react to may be either intended or unintended consequences of public policies, the obvious thing political leaders can do is change policy. In a patronal autocracy, however, where the public-policy consequences to which the people react are the unintended side effects of patronal policies, the chief patron can either change policy or try to expand his room for maneuver by the means of public authority.

On the one hand, expanding the room for maneuver can be achieved by further neutralizing the process of public deliberation.

This may include further one-sided changes in the electoral system, harassing the opposition, or launching floor-monopolizing campaigns to reframe the public discourse (Propositions 52-53). On the other hand, the chief patron may use violence, meaning either insourced state coercion (e.g., the police) or outsourced state coercion (e.g., paramilitaries or the organized underworld) (Proposition 63). What the chief patron needs to consider is two: first, how important the given policy is; and second, how far he can go in neutralizing public deliberation or using violence.

The level of violence in countries like Hungary is lower, mainly because of EU membership, as well as the people's generally low stimulation threshold for violence. In countries like Russia or Turkmenistan, violence is more available as an effective tool for the leaders. And yet all of these countries can be regarded as patronal autocracies; while the permanent use of mass terror remains a regime-specific feature of dictatorships, the occasional and targeted use of violence becomes a country-specific feature of autocracies. What is regime-specific is the chief patron's aim to neutralize public deliberation; whether he can and needs to use violence to do so, although it greatly determines the livability of the system, is a question of technique rather than the internal logic of the regime from an analytical point of view.

Figure 18: Losses for the leader and policy-making in liberal democracy and patronal autocracy.

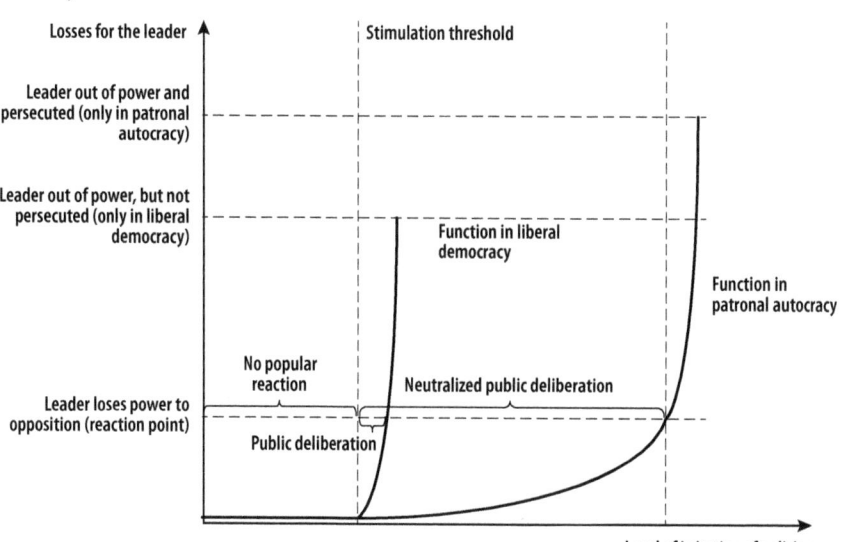

116.

THE CONCEPTUAL FRAMEWORK OF THIS BOOK can be expanded spatially—for other regions—and temporally—for future times. The conceptual framework provided in this book focuses on the post-communist region and its development since 1989-1991. If it was to be expanded to other regions, it should be started by the same way we departed from the mainstream Western approach: by dissolving some basic axioms. There were factors that we treated as constants because they are constants in the post-communist region, at least to the degree that they do not generate system-constituting differences. But this is not necessarily true in other regions.

There are at least five axioms of our framework that could be dissolved. First, the genesis axiom: that regime development starts from the collapse of the monopoly of public ownership. Post-communist countries all started from the same "Square One": communist dictatorship and the merger of the spheres of social action. But there are other parts of the world, like post-colonial countries, which start from a markedly different "Square One," and a different history of development of social spheres.

The second axiom is the stateness axiom: that the center of the regime is the state as a stable entity. With the exception of oligarchic anarchy, which was a temporary situation of transition in some countries (Proposition 30), we did not conceptualize civil wars or regimes where state failure becomes a permanent condition.

Third, the secularism axiom holds that the regime is dominated by secular power. Treating religion as the integrating force of society, on the one hand, and the primary principle of the state, on the other hand, would be needed to conceptualize theocracies and other kind of regimes dominated by religious power.

The fourth axiom to be dissolved is the party axiom: that the highest formal positions are occupied by *de jure* politicians of political parties. Military dictatorships, as well as kingdoms and hereditary monarchies require concepts beyond those of our framework, including the conceptualization of the military and the aristocracy as specific forms of ruling elite.

Finally, the tutelage axiom holds that the strongest *de facto* political actor in the regime is a *de jure* political actor. Particularly, the chief patron is typically the president or the prime minister, but even when he is not—like it was the case with Vladimir Plahotniuc in Moldova—he still is a *de jure* political actor. However, hybridology knows so-called "tutelary regimes," where *de jure* political actors become practically political front men to nonelected religious (e.g., Iran) or military (e.g., Pakistan) authorities without becoming explicit theocracies or juntas. We did not consider the regimes of militarily invaded or "puppet" states either, where the *de jure* sovereign government is subordinated, not to a domestic, but to a foreign power.

While the dissolution of these five axioms allows for the spatial expansion of our framework, it can also be temporally expanded by introducing the concept of era-specific features. Information technology and climate change are but two factors that anticipate both challenges and opportunities for the self-sustaining capacity of post-communist regimes, which may start new trajectories in hardly foreseeable directions.

Post-Communist Regime Trajectories: A Triangular Framework

COUNTRIES CAN BE PLACED IN THE TRIANGULAR FRAMEWORK OF REGIMES by dividing it up by different dimensions, and placing the country in each dimension coherently. Our regime typology consists of six ideal-type regimes: two democracies, two autocracies, and two dictatorships. These define a triangular framework, shown above in Figure 6 with a number of post-communist examples (Proposition 12).

In the triangle, the closer a country is to an ideal type regime, the more similar it is to it (and conversely, the farther it is from it, the less similar). This can be operationalized by dividing up the triangular framework by different analytical dimensions, and showing which section of the triangle represents which concrete feature. To illustrate this, let us choose one dimension—patronalism of rule. We know its value precisely in the case of the six ideal types: liberal democracy and conservative autocracy are non-patronal, patronal democracy and patronal autocracy are informal patronal, and the two dictatorships are bureaucratic patronal.

Next, what we have to put into the triangle are the so-called dominance boundaries. These boundaries delimit from each other dominance sections, i.e., parts of the triangle where a certain characteristic feature is dominant. This is shown in Figure 19 below.

A dominance section does not mean the level of patronalism is the same in the whole section: for instance, informal patronalism is much more dominant in patronal autocracy than in patronal democracy. But both of them are on the informal patronal side of the dominance boundary, whereas liberal democracy is on the non-patronal side. When a country is placed, based on its patronal character, in the triangle, it is not assigned to a *point* based on the exact *level* of dominance, but it is assigned to a *section* based on the *fact* of dominance.

In *The Anatomy of Post-Communist Regimes*, we divided up the triangle by eleven dimensions; below, we show only six of them for the sake of illustration. Besides the already mentioned patronalism of rule, Figures 19-24 also show the dimensions of formality of institutions, dominant economic mechanism, ruling party's function, corruption, and ideology.

As a country is assigned to a point in the triangular framework, it must be in the same point in every triangle. As if all the triangles, divided up by different dimensions, were stacked on each other, and one pinned down a needle at the point the country is assigned to: the points the needle goes through in each layer will belong to a certain dominance section (or sometimes a boundary). The features that these pinned dominance sections represent describe a regime at its current state coherently along the dimensions. Unlike historical analogies like (neo-) feudalism or fascism which try to capture the "essence" of a regime by focusing on a single dimension (patronalism of rule and ideology, respectively) but do not fit when it comes to other aspects, the triangular framework entails a strict criterion of coherence in terms of the definitive features of the regimes, while also concerning all spheres of social action and the level of separation thereof.

Figures 19-24: The triangular framework divided up by six dimensions (row by row, from the upper left): patronalism of rule, formality of institutions, ruling party's function, dominant economic mechanism, corruption, and ideology.

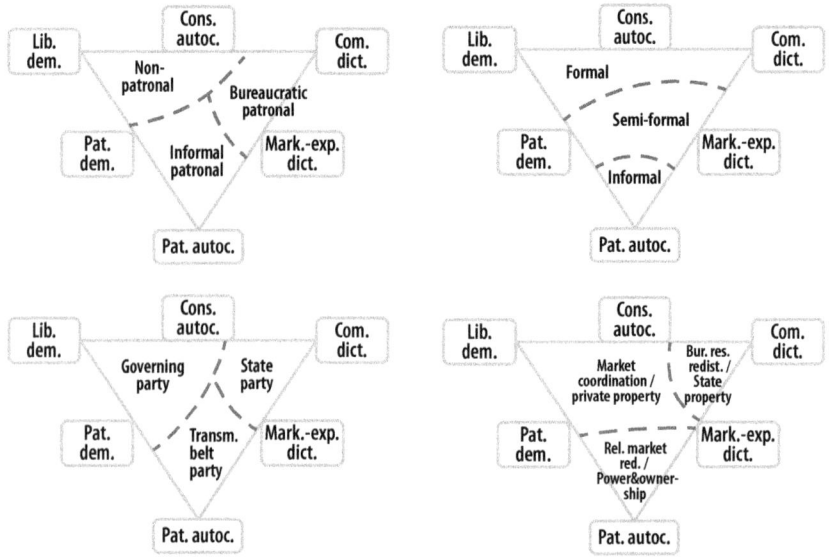

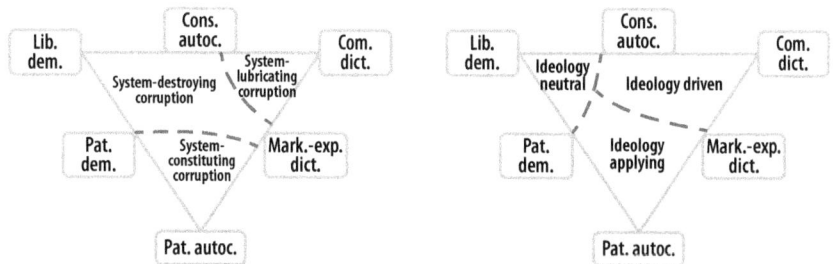

118. **THE PRIMARY TRAJECTORIES** of post-communist regimes constituted regime change to a democracy or autocracy, or model change to market-exploiting dictatorship. When a country is placed in the triangle, it is done by one set of features it shows at a given time. When these features change, the country can be assigned another point. Connecting consecutive points creates sequences, and the sequences create the development trajectory of the given country. In the second part of the book, after the 120 propositions, we will show the modelled trajectories of twelve post-communist countries, each representing a different type of trajectory; now, in the last three propositions, we provide the theoretical toolkit for their analysis.

First, one can make a distinction between regime change and model change. Regime change means the change of Kornai's general regime types, i.e., democracy, autocracy, or dictatorship; while model change is the change within a general regime type, i.e., from one type of democracy/autocracy/dictatorship to another. In all three historical regions of the former Soviet empire (Proposition 7), the primary trajectory of the regimes, meaning the path leading to the "first station" after communist dictatorship, brought regime change to either democracy or autocracy. In the case of China, its primary trajectory was a model change: without changing the framework of the one-party dictatorship, the country became a market-exploiting dictatorship (Proposition 88).

Second, regime changes can be analyzed by two dimensions of pluralism and patronalism. Thus, we can distinguish ideal typical primary trajectories (Table 41). The first one is changing the single-pyramid bureaucratic patronal regime (communist dictatorship) to a multi-pyramid non-patronal regime (liberal democracy). The trajectories of the Western-Christian historical region fit into this pattern. Eminent examples include the Baltic states (e.g., Estonia), but the primary trajectory of the Czech Republic, Hungary, and Poland pointed at this direction as well after the collapse of the communist system. The second ideal type trajectory leads from the single-pyramid bureaucratic patronal regime (communist dictatorship) to a multi-pyramid informal patronal regime (patronal democracy). Examples can be found in both the Orthodox and Islamic historical regions, such as Romania, Ukraine, and Kyrgyzstan. The final ideal typical regime changing trajectory leads from the single-pyramid bureaucratic patronal regime (communist dictatorship) to a single-pyramid informal patronal regime (patronal autocracy). The prime examples can be found in Soviet Central Asia, such as Kazakhstan.

Table 41: Ideal typical primary trajectories in the post-communist region.

	Primary trajectories	
	from	to
A Regime change (e.g., Estonia, Hungary)	Communist dictatorship	Liberal democracy
	Single-pyramid bureaucratic patronal	Multi-pyramid non-patronal
B Regime change (e.g., Romania, Ukraine)	Communist dictatorship	Patronal democracy
	Single-pyramid bureaucratic patronal	Multi-pyramid informal patronal
C Regime change (e.g., Kazakhstan)	Communist dictatorship	Patronal autocracy
	Single-pyramid bureaucratic patronal	Single-pyramid informal patronal
D Model change (e.g., China)	Communist dictatorship	Market-exploiting dictatorship
	Single-pyramid bureaucratic patronal	Single-pyramid bureaucratic patronal

119. THE SECONDARY TRAJECTORIES of post-communist regimes constituted democratic backsliding to more patronal and/or autocratic regime types. Moving on to typing secondary trajectories, or the movement after the country's primary trajectory,

the term we need to consider is democratic backsliding. In hybridology, democratic backsliding or decay is used for deterioration of a democratic polity in terms of freedom, civil rights and liberties, and the constitutional functioning of the institutions of public deliberation in general.

At first sight, the concept is a normative one, and it seems to carry implicitly the presumption of transitology as well: the country is sliding "back," as if there was a single street—the democracy-dictatorship axis—where movement from democracy was only possible toward the original starting point (dictatorship). However, in our understanding democratic backsliding is a descriptive concept, and it means movement from a democracy to (a) conservative autocracy, (b) patronal democracy, and (c) patronal autocracy. Changes to dictatorships are possible but highly unlikely, for democracies and even autocracies rely on electoral civil legitimacy, which cannot accommodate an outright one-party system (Propositions 42-46).

Table 42 sums up secondary trajectories, each showing one form of democratic backsliding. In Poland, Kaczyński's autocratic attempt has aimed at moving from a multi-pyramid to a single-pyramid non-patronal regime (i.e., from liberal democracy to conservative autocracy); in the Czech Republic, Andrej Babiš aimed at moving from a multi-pyramid non-patronal to multi-pyramid informal patronal regime (i.e., from liberal democracy to patronal democracy). In Russia, Putin achieved autocratic breakthrough in 2003, after which the multi-pyramid informal patronal regime (patronal democracy) was changed into a single-pyramid informal patronal regime (patronal autocracy). Finally, Hungary shows a two-part secondary trajectory. Under the first Orbán government in 1998-2002, the country moved from the multi-pyramid non-patronal to a multi-pyramid informal patronal regime (i.e., from liberal democracy to patronal democracy). Then, in 2010, the second Orbán government achieved autocratic breakthrough, and transformed the country from the multi-pyramid informal patronal regime (patronal democracy) to a single-pyramid informal patronal regime (patronal autocracy).

Table 42: Ideal typical secondary trajectories (of democratic backsliding) in the post-communist region.

	Secondary trajectories: democratic backsliding	
	from	to
A Regime change (e.g., Poland after 2015)	Liberal democracy	Conservative autocracy
	Multi-pyramid non-patronal	Single-pyramid non-patronal
B Model change (e.g., Czech Republic after 2013)	Liberal democracy	Patronal democracy
	Multi-pyramid non-patronal	Multi-pyramid informal patronal
C Regime change (e.g., Hungary after 2010)	Liberal democracy	Patronal autocracy
	Multi-pyramid non-patronal	Single-pyramid informal patronal
D Regime change (e.g., Russia after 2003)	Patronal democracy	Patronal autocracy
	Multi-pyramid informal patronal	Single-pyramid informal patronal

120. Regime cycles are a result of changes on the level of impersonal institutions without anti-patronal transformation.

When Western observers examine different regime trajectories, they tend to focus on the impersonal institutional framework. Of course, they are quite aware of the importance of individuals and personal connections, at least on the level of the elites. But usually the actors are identified by their formal titles and competencies: they see a president or prime minister rather than a chief patron, and a multi-party system, not a competition of patronal networks.

Dissolving the axiom of coincidence of *de jure* and *de facto* positions (Proposition 5), we can achieve a dual-level approach necessary for the examination of post-communist regimes. That is, we must consider both (1) the level of impersonal institutions, where we can talk about democratic or anti-democratic transformation in terms of *de jure* guarantees of rule of law and the separation of powers; and (2) the level of personal networks, where we can speak of a patronal or anti-patronal transformation in connection with the degree of *de facto* separation of spheres of social action and, accordingly, the emergence or liquidation of informal patronal networks.

When we spoke of stubborn structures above, we indeed meant this: some of the region's regime transitions succeeded only on the level of impersonal institutions, while on the other level no anti-patronal transformation accompanied the process of democratization (Proposition 10). This leads us to the concept of regime cycle, pioneered by Henry E. Hale. The term "regime cycle" was developed for the so-called color revolutions in the region, and intended to capture that they were mostly characterized by single-level transformations. In a patronal democracy, characterized by competing patron-client networks, the network in power tries to monopolize power, moving towards autocracy. But when the experiment is reversed, it is not the non-patronal world of Western-type liberal democracy that is coming, but the competitive order of patronal democracy. In short, the anti-democratic transformation is followed by a democratic transformation, which is not accompanied by an anti-patronal transformation (Proposition 70).

Table 43: Processes of regime dynamics and cycles.

From \ To	Liberal democracy	Patronal democracy	Patronal autocracy
Liberal democracy		patronal transformation (without anti-democratic transformation)	anti-democratic + patronal transformation
Patronal democracy	anti-patronal transformation		anti-democratic transformation
Patronal autocracy	democratic + anti-patronal transformation	democratic transformation (without anti-patronal transformation)	

We have seen this, for example, in Ukraine, when Leonid Kuchma's single-pyramid patronal network was overthrown in the Orange Revolution in 2004, and when Viktor Yanukovych's autocratic attempt was stopped at the Euromaidan Revolution in 2014. Among the few exceptions to this rule was Georgia, where the government of Mikheil Saakashvili, elected after the 2003 Rose Revolution, attempted an anti-patronal transformation. But it was not accompanied by democratic transformation: while curbing state control—on an ideology-driven, libertarian basis—was anti-patronal, eliminating the power component of power&ownership (Proposition 86), Saakashvili took Georgia in the direction of not liberal democracy but conservative autocracy. Table 43 sums up regime cycles, the processes of regime dynamics, and shows the type of transformation required to change from liberal to patronal regime types, and vice versa.

II. Trajectories of Twelve Post-Communist Regimes

Estonia: Regime Change to Liberal Democracy

The primary trajectories listed in Table 41 can be depicted in the triangular framework as four ideal typical routes, leading from communist dictatorship to liberal or patronal democracy, patronal autocracy, or market-exploiting dictatorship (Figure 25). While every post-communist country had a primary trajectory, we may **illustrate the four ideal type trajectories by four countries that had no secondary trajectories**. That is, the following countries changed from communist dictatorship to another regime type and have stayed there ever since (as of 2022), either in a stable or a dynamic equilibrium.

Figure 25: Ideal typical primary regime trajectories. A, B, C, and D on the arrows correspond to the trajectories in Table 41.

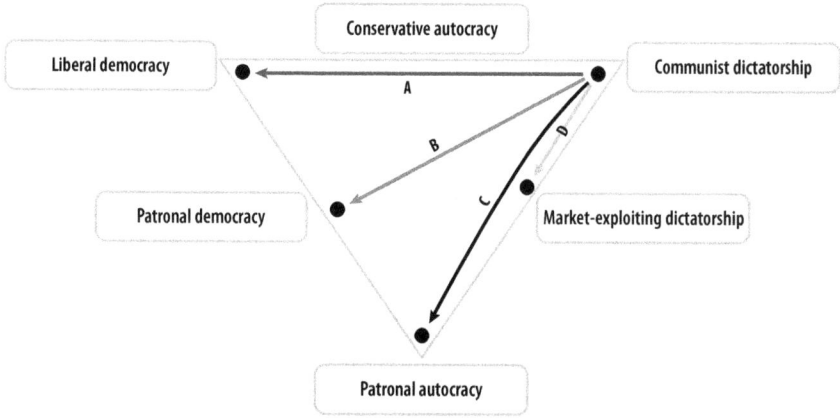

Estonia is an example for changing to a stable equilibrium, namely liberal democracy. A former member of the Soviet Union, Estonia regained independence in 1991.[1] Figure 26 shows this, with a new point starting in 1992 and lasting since. Indeed, the country has shown remarkable **stability in terms of normative and free-market oriented economic policy**, on the one hand,[2] and **non-patronal, multi-pyramid ruling elite** with numerous politicians' parties and limited power, on the other hand. In 1992, a new constitution was approved and suffrage was extended to people registered as citizens in a referendum.[3] In early years, this also meant the exclusion of a major segment of the Russian minority from suffrage.[4] However, since 1996 the country has gained the highest country rating for political freedom in Freedom House reports,[5] and it has done similarly well by the Liberal Democracy Index of the V-Dem project.[6] According to Hale, Estonia is among the less patronalistic countries of the post-communist region, and even existing patronal tendencies have been limited by a parliamentarist constitution.[7]

Nevertheless, the Estonian transition has been described as elitist and even "tutelary," "characterised by the dominance of political elites in making decisions and steering society in a direction that the elites see as necessary for the development of society and the good of the people."[8] Yet this has resulted neither in a dominant-party system[9] nor in systemic corruption and the prevalence of oligarchs and poligarchs devoted to power monopolization and personal-wealth accumulation.[10] According to a Freedom House report, Estonian media are legally protected and largely free of overt political influence, whereas media ownership is also dominantly private and subordinated to business interests rather than political interests (FH notes "increased commercialization and undeclared advertising" as problems).[11] The economy has been dominated by entrepreneurs, and not oligarchs, in competitive markets. Naturally, these entrepreneurs engage in lobbying, the reform of which has long been a topic in Estonian politics. There have also been corruption scandals—the most serious ones being those of former Minister of the Environment Villu Reiljan who was convicted by Estonian courts for seeking a bribe of ca. €100.000 and favored a long-time supporter of his party in a land swap case, too.[12] The magnitude of such cases, of course, pales in comparison to the stream of corrupt monies and assets in a relational economy. In contrast to the practice of informal patronal networks, the Estonian political elite has not annexed the economy, and it did not use the state to create or feed oligarchs either. Opposition parties have been strong, law enforcement is normative, and due to the proportionate electoral system, Estonian governments have usually been coalitional, with numerous changes of government.[13]

Figure 26: Modelled trajectory of Estonia (1964-2022).

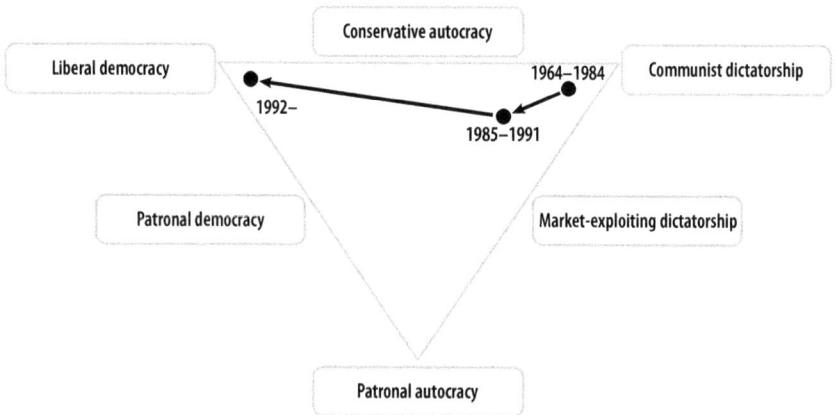

Adding to these features the internal dynamics stemming mainly from ethnic conflicts,[14] as well as the emergence of identity politics and right-wing populism,[15] we can say that **Estonia is generally not unlike Western liberal democracies**. The major difference, of course, that also causes its modelled trajectory's deviance from the ideal type, is that it is a post-Soviet country, meaning its development was closely tied to that of the Soviet Union before 1991. Indeed, in Figure 26, the first two points belong to the Soviet Union. In the following, every post-Soviet country we use as an illustration involves the same two points, referring to the Brezhnev era of hard dictatorship (1964-1984) and to the Gorbachev era leading to the Soviet Union's dissolution (1985-1991). The primary trajectory of post-Soviet countries starts from this latter point—in the case of Estonia, a regime change to liberal democracy and **consolidation in a stable equilibrium situation**.

Romania: Regime Change to Patronal Democracy

While Estonia represents a case of stable equilibrium and change to liberal democracy, **Romania is a country with a primary trajectory to the dynamic equilibrium of patronal democracy.** After a violent dictatorship collapse, involving the execution of general party secretary Nicolae Ceaușescu in 1989, Romania approach patronal democracy, and it has oscillated around this ideal type since.[16] This is depicted in Figure 27, showing Romania's regime trajectory.

Figure 27: Modelled trajectory of Romania (1964-2022).

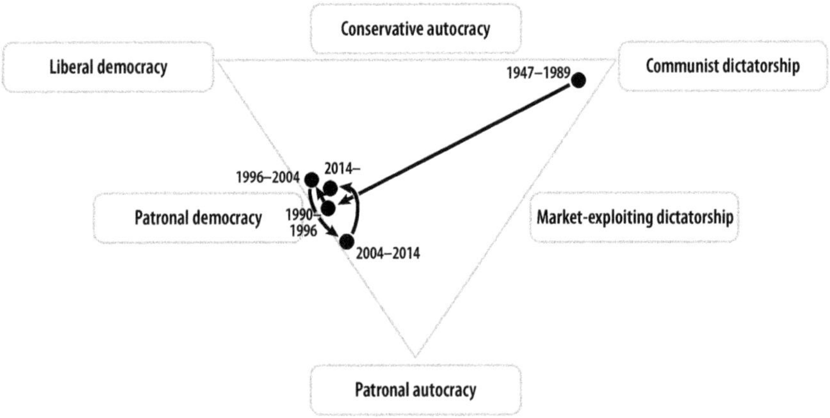

```
                    Conservative autocracy
   Liberal democracy                         1947–1989      Communist dictatorship

                    1996–2004   2014–
   Patronal democracy  1990–                 Market-exploiting dictatorship
                       1996
                            2004–2014

                    Patronal autocracy
```

The first point in the trajectory depicts the period from World War II to the collapse of the regime (1947-1989). This period started with rapid communist nationalization, after which the dominance of state ownership, bureaucratic resource-redistribution, and bureaucratic patronalism of the state party were maintained.[17] From 1990 to 1996, there was a transitional period under President Ion Iliescu. This period was characterized by institution building, as well as the creation of a divided-executive system, with the president and the prime minister both having important powers. This led to clashes between them in the 1990s: as Magyari notes, "[the] period of the Iliescu presidency was marked by antagonism between the President and the government, the most extreme case being the conflict with Prime Minister Petre Roman. In its aftermath, President Iliescu was a participant in, and initiator of, the forceful toppling of the government and the firing of the Prime Minister."[18] Indeed, this period already saw the development of multi-pyramid system of competing patronal networks. Hale goes as far as to describe Iliescu as Romania's "first patronal president" who however "did not significantly tamper with the 1996 parliamentary or presidential elections' despite having 'months of warning' that he was likely to lose."[19] This indicates electoral democracy with only unfair but not manipulated elections, and this setting has provided the framework for the competition of informal patronal networks since. "The two key parties, which tend to exchange one another in government, are not what they claim to be. The PSD is deeply integrated (Iliescu remains the party's honorary president) and built on the power of local power brokers. It is everything but not a social democratic party, as its policies are neoliberal and pro-nouveau riche, inconsistent, and serve the interests of small groups. [...] The 'New PNL' ('New' National Liberal Party) is controversial and not at all liberal, but is a populist/popular partly confused over its political philosophy. The third force is the ethnically organized Democratic Alliance of Hungarians in Romania (RMDSZ in Hungarian, DAHR in English), which does not accept any ideology but which ethnicizes politics. Ideology-free parties are marked by, on one hand, a move toward people's party features, attempting to address all, while on the other hand they are typically loot-acquiring parties, wholly characterized by 'party patronage' based on distributing available public life functions and taking advantage of such."[20]

The period from 1996-2004 was the most liberal period of Romania to date, under Prime Ministers Victor Ciorbea (1996-1998), Mugur Isărescu (1999–2000) and Adrian Năstase (2000–2004). However, that Năstase was later found guilty in two corruption cases[21] indicates that this period was not devoid of actors engaging in informal practices, while formal institutional constraints remained strong and actors were not able to simply step over them. This point is also illustrated by the presidency of Traian Băsescu from 2004-2014. He has clearly shown the intention of building a single-pyramid patronal network and transforming the country into a patronal autocracy.[22] Yet lacking an effective monopoly of political power, he faced strong balances from the formal institutional setting, particularly the National Anticorruption Directorate (DNA), the National Agency for Fiscal Administration (ANAF), and the Attorney General. By the end of his term, there were nearly eighty investigations of him, and for a few of these, the DNA and the Attorney General have even submitted official indictments.[23] Since 2014, the country has moved back to the more competitive landscape of patronal democracy under President Klaus Iohannis.[24]

All these changes illustrate the dynamic equilibrium of patronal democracy. **Unlike a stable equilibrium where dynamics remains internal and the country remains at one point, a dynamic equilibrium involves constant oscillation and attempts to alter regime-specific features.** These movements can be contained then by the social and institutional boundaries explained in Propositions 69-70, particularly divided executive power and the proportionate electoral system, which allows for the alteration of political forces in formal offices. Hence, in countries like Romania no regime change has happened in spite of the numerous sequences that are involved in dynamic equilibrium.

Kazakhstan: Regime Change to Patronal Autocracy

Kazakhstan represents the primary trajectory **from communist dictatorship to patronal autocracy** (Figure 28). The country's post-communist history started, not with a retreat or collapse of the dictatorship, but with a dictatorship transformation. Months before the country declared independence in 1991, general party secretary Nursultan Nazarbayev was named president by the dictatorship's legislature. Later, he ran alone in the country's first presidential election, winning 95% of the votes.[25] Formally, the communist party dissolved into two successor parties, the Socialist Party and the Congress Party, both led by Nazarbayev's clients while he remained formally independent. However, Nazarbayev could not consolidate his rule until 1994, meaning he could fully control neither the parliament nor some members of the ruling elite with considerable political and economic resources. Hale describes how members of parliament blocked some of Nazarbayev's bills and started collecting kompromat against him, while seemingly potent opponents (including the leader of the Congress Party) signaled presidential ambitions.[26]

Figure 28: Modelled trajectory of Kazakhstan (1964-2022).

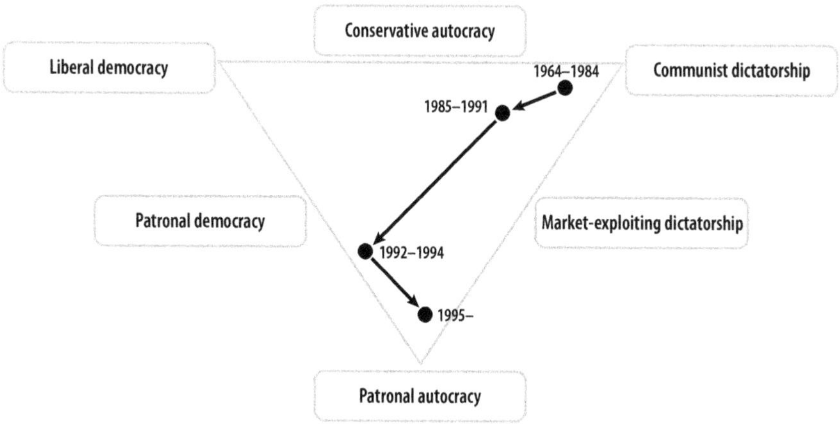

In 1994, Nazarbayev used the privatization process as well as his own state and presidential powers to promote oligarchs and build an informal patronal network,[27] and in 1995 he changed the constitution one-sidedly, expanding his competences, after the Constitutional Court suddenly declared that the parliament had been elected illegally and its powers were null and void.[28] From that year on, Nazarbayev instituted a stable equilibrium patronal autocracy. He remained "above party president" until 1999, when he became leader of his newly formed vassals' party, Nur Otan, which has won every seat in legislative elections since. Opposition parties do exist, however, operating in a typical landscape of domesticated parties (like Ak Zhol and Communist People's Party of Kazakhstan) as well as marginalized parties (like the Nationwide Social Democratic Party).[29] Kazakhstan's economy has also been under the control of Nazarbayev's adopted political family. As Hale reports, Nazarbayev has "presided over a massive consolidation of the country's assets under the control of his closest associates, including relatives. One noteworthy development was the emergence of the massive holding company Foundation for National Well-Being Samruk-Kazyna, which […] counted Nazarbaev son-in-law Timur Kulibaev among its top formal leadership. By some calculations, this entity controlled as much as 45 percent of the country's GDP."[30]

An opposition website visualized Nazarbayev's adopted political family as a Christmas tree, reflecting on the shape of the patronal pyramid he is leading.[31] Based on publications in the press, the website guides the reader through the patronal network, and one may note the variety of positions that are mingled: people with kinship ties (like his daughters) are present alongside people with quasi-kinship ties (like the head of state-owned oil and gas company KazTransGas), just as people with formal positions (like the Minister of Justice) are there with people with informal positions (like Nazarbayev's confidante). The website puts on the top of the Christmas tree Nazarbayev's brother and first and second wives as well as his (formal) trustee, assistant, middle daughter (the richest woman in Kazakhstan) and third daughter (Kazakhstan's largest developer). The extensive business interests of these actors shows how a lack of separation of the spheres of social action is present, with people holding a variety of formal and informal positions at the same time.[32]

On the one hand, it seemed that Nazarbayev achieved autocratic consolidation, creating informal patronalism out of bureaucratic patronalism. During his rule, he kept a tight grip on the most important political and economic resources, eliminating every threat and the autonomy of potentially dangerous resource owners.[33] On the other hand, **the problem of succession** reached the elderly chief patron who resigned, after three decades, in 2019. In the years before his resignation, the position "Leader of the Nation" was created for Nazarbayev, and the competences of one of his other titles, the Chairman of Security Council of Kazakhstan, were changed. He legally held both of these positions for life, which grant him (1) legal immunity and (2) veto rights and *de facto* executive powers over policy decisions. But giving up the formal position of the president led to the division of executive power, which allowed for divisions to emerge within the single-pyramid patronal network as well. **The new president, Kassym-Jomart Tokayev became a second center of power**, and he challenged the existing single-pyramid network by organizing a network of clients around himself. **The Kazakhstani revolt in early 2022** differs from earlier color revolutions: popular unrest, sparked by a sudden sharp increase in liquefied gas prices, is not backed by other competing pyramids who try to avoid domination of the ruling one but a new network which seceded from the single-pyramid through multiple defections. **Instead of the revolts leading to a regime change from a single-pyramid to a multi-pyramid setting, this revolt represents elite change within a patronal autocracy**, where one chief patron's single-pyramid system is to be replaced by that of another one, with the intervention and most probably increasing influence of Russia.[34]

We chose Kazakhstan as an illustration for this primary trajectory because it has been the closest to ideal typical patronal autocracy since the end of its primary trajectory in 1995. Yet **there were other dictatorship transformations in Soviet-Central Asia, too, which concluded somewhere between patronal autocracy and market-exploiting dictatorship.** As Hale reminds, "in Turkmenistan and Uzbekistan […] the Soviet Union's Communist Party structure remained intact during the last stages of perestroika and the local party bosses ruled through it during the transition to independence, effectively just renaming the party."[35]

Hale goes on to call these regimes "full-on dictatorships" with no genuine opposition party allowed. Moreover, Turkmenistan maintained its one-party system until 2008, after which a dominant-party system with fake opposition was created. As for real opposition, they are "not only prevented from getting on the ballot. In these countries, they are systematically jailed, tortured, or exiled and, more generally, effectively denied any outlet whatsoever to publicize their views in openly circulated print or electronic media. […] While some other patronal presidential systems […] features closed polities and harass and occasionally either jail or (informally) exile their critics, even the most closed of them (such as Belarus) feature nothing approaching this level of systematic repression, which strongly resembles what existed in the USSR but without the communist ideology."[36]

China: Model Change to Market-Exploiting Dictatorship

China is the paradigmatic case of the model change **from communist to market-exploiting dictatorship** (Figure 29). This was partially made possible by the fact that China's primary trajectory ran outside the Soviet Union, and avoided the third wave of democratization.[37] If we are to sequence Chinese developments, the country was near the ideal typical (heavy) **communist dictatorship under the leadership of Mao Zedong from 1949**. After his death, the next so-called "paramount leader" of China became Deng Xiaoping in 1978, the same year the Chinese Communist Party held its historic Third Plenum of the Eleventh Party Congress that put China on the course of market liberalization.[38] In the triangle, the point **from 1979-1991** represents **the period of power decentralization and production-structure opening**, as described in Proposition 88.

Figure 29: Modelled trajectory of China (1949-2022).

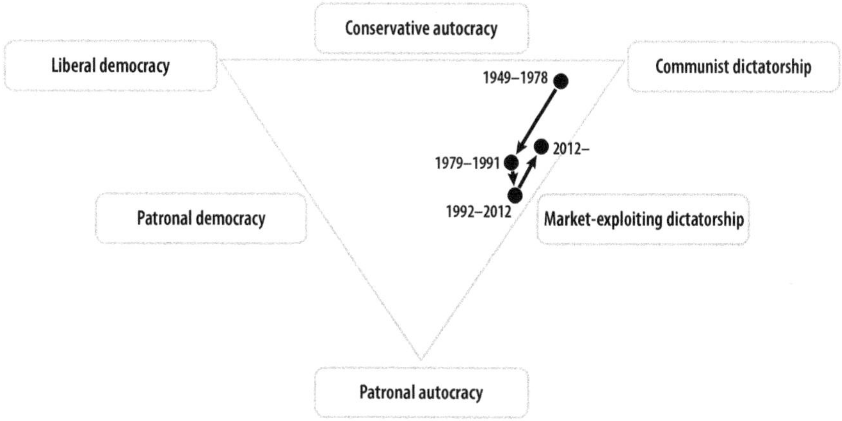

Stronger liberalization and decentralization followed after **Deng's Southern Tour of 1992**, consolidating the country at an equilibrium of market-exploiting dictatorship.[39] According to Szelényi and Mihályi, "during the 1980s China was building 'capitalism from below' and [...] many of the wealthiest people in China even during the early 2000 lists of rich Chinese came from humble background (like the Liu brothers or the Yang dynasty). Even those who seem to have fit the image of political capitalists (like Rong) were not political capitalists in the sense we know from post-communist Russia."[40] The economic elite's embeddedness is shown by the major entrepreneurs who either became rich due to party connections or needed party protection, but some of the wealthiest Chinese, like Jack Ma, made their wealth from innovative IT or other high tech industries. Recently, party organizations have been implanted at 60-70% of private companies of foreign as well as domestic owners, and there have been instances of coopting heads of large private companies into the state party.[41] Yet these are to be seen as guarantees, or opportunities for the party to intervene, augmenting legal accountability with an accountability regarding the party state's substantive-rational goals (referring to the so-called "party ethics"). Even if some of them are required to enroll in the state party, Chinese entrepreneurs still enjoy considerable autonomy in making executive decisions in their own companies, unlike state enterprise leaders in pre-regime change communist dictatorships.[42]

On the other hand, media and culture are heavily restricted in China, and the Communist Party of China (CPC) acts as a state party that dominates the political landscape.[43] While the people nominally have access to the internet, the so-called "Great Firewall of China" implements many different types of censorship and content filtering to control the country's internet traffic.[44] The Chinese party state does not allow free access to websites such as Google and Facebook, only to their Chinese variants. Also, beside the fact that it can ban local websites, the party has introduced a social-credit system to sanction behavior it finds improper, including the expression of non-accepted views.[45] This way, the formally less repressive Chinese state practically resurrects the situation of communist dictatorships, incentivizing self-censorship for the subjects whose existential positions are directly affected by the approval or disapproval of their opinions by the state. Experts have already described China as a "surveillance state" and a **"digital totalitarian state"**[46] because of its newly developed, big data-based systems of internet control. In a special issue of the *Journal of Democracy* entitled "The Road to Digital Unfreedom," Xiao Qiang explains that the Chinese state "has set up a series of mechanisms aimed at asserting its dominance in cyberspace. It has also increasingly combined an extensive physical infrastructure of surveillance and coercion with cutting-edge digital technologies. [...] By leveraging information and resource asymmetries, state agencies and the companies that cooperate with them can turn these innovative technologies into tools for manipulating ordinary citizens. Big data, for instance, is an invaluable resource for making predictions. Officials can draw on this capacity to anticipate protests and even major surges in online public opinion, enabling them to act preemptively to quash opposition. In another authoritarian application of big data, [Chinese] authorities are working to integrate information from a wide array of sources into a nationwide Social Credit System (SCS) that would assess the conduct of every person in the country, an innovation worthy of George Orwell's *Nineteen Eighty-Four*. As Wired magazine has put it, China's new generation of surveillance operations is indeed where 'big data meets Big Brother.'"[47] While modern autocracies and dictatorships have already done away with the bloody methods of oppression, such efficiency of big data and IT offers completely new levels of discretional punishment on the road from direct violence to existential vulnerability.

The development of SCS already belongs to the last point in the triangle, which shows backlash toward dictatorship: **strong centralization started under General Secretary Xi Jinping since 2012.**[48] Heilmann interprets Xi's reforms as a return to "crisis mode," which is a temporary reintroduction of stronger dictatorial functioning to counter an extraordinary situation. As he writes, Xi "obviously sensed that the decision-making and loyalty crises in the Politburo under General Secretary Hu Jianto (2002-12) and the corruption and organization crises in the Communist Party had collectively reached a dangerous level [...]. Therefore, the best way to achieve [...] organizational stability [...] was through a concentration of political power and centralized decision-making, organizational and ideological discipline, extensive anti-corruption measures, and the prevention of any attempts to form factions or cliques within the party, coupled with a campaign against Western values and concepts."[49] In the triangle, this means a movement to the dominance section of ideology-drivenness, as well as closer to bureaucratic-resource distribution and totalitarian rule. Yet this is still not a secondary trajectory, that is, not a (emerging) change toward communist dictatorship.

Xi's reforms remain within the logic of market-exploiting dictatorship, and mainly decrease the share of relational market-redistribution, not market coordination, in the country's markets. China has exploited markets for decades, and understood its benefits: the reformed nomenklatura will not break down the reforms and return to a setting that only had a stronger grip but not a stronger economy or legitimation. **The essence of Xi's reforms is strengthening bureaucratic patronalism to avoid informal patronalism, not to return to communist dictatorship.** Hence, China remains an example of market-exploiting dictatorship and its modelled trajectory, an example of dictatorship reform.

Czech Republic: Backsliding Toward Patronal Democracy

The Czech Republic is a country that saw a relatively long period of liberal democracy without an attempt at model or regime change (Figure 30). After the so-called Velvet Revolution in **1989**, the Czech Republic (then Czechoslovakia) was among the countries with least patronal legacy in the region,[50] which combined with a parliamentary constitution[51] **produced a vivid but stable democratic regime**. This has been evident from Freedom House ratings[52] and V-Dem indices,[53] while vividness also manifested in frequent changes in government, including an almost complete renewal of the party system in 2010.[54] True, parties have been accused of having weak linkage to the masses[55] and strong ties to the economic elite,[56] whereas Hanley and Vachudova describe so-called "regional godfathers," oligarchs and "smaller corrupt business groups whose more publicized capture of the regional organizations of key Czech parties gave them growing political influence in mid-2000s. [They] are expected to assert [their] interests […] using the services of lobbyists and lawyers in the wealth defence industry or by bankrolling non-governmental organizations (NGOs), politicians, or parties."[57] In several cases, Czech parties and their local organizations were packed with so-called "dead souls": political front men of private economic actors who were sent in to tilt intra-party votings and decision-making according to the oligarchs' wishes.[58]

While economic actors targeted parties with considerable state power, and practically privatized them in a bottom-up fashion, such activity mainly falls, in our terms, under the cases of lobbying and cronyism, without top-down patterns of corruption appearing. The non-patronal, bottom-up, and multi-pyramid nature of Czech informal networks is also obvious from the detailed analysis of Michal Klíma in his book *Informal Politics in Post-Communist Europe*. According to him, Czech political life is characterized by "client-client relations," or mutually beneficial alliances between major entrepreneurs and party members. These relations constitute nationwide networks of cronyism, realizing a collusion of spheres as political actors become definitive in market action and economic actors become definitive in political action. As Klíma writes, "decisions are made behind closed doors on a wide range of informal exchanges of favours. In addition to the classic allocation of the largest domestic tenders and projects from European funds, these networks also decide upon the post-election composition of the cabinet or alternatively the fall of the government."[59] However, the lack of complete state capture and top-down forms of corruption (as explained in Proposition 78) indicate that **the ruling elite *per se* was not dominantly subordinated to the principle of elite interest**, power monopolization and wealth-accumulation. At the same time, both civil society and formal institutions remained strong in this period. Hence, the point in the triangle from 1990-2013 is nearer to liberal than patronal democracy.

Figure 30: Modelled trajectory of the Czech Republic (1964-2022).

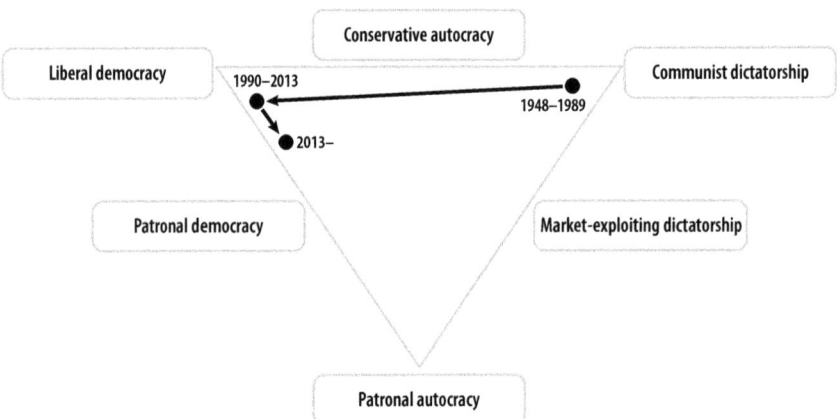

In 2013, however, **Andrej Babiš**, a member of the Czech Republic's "half a dozen billionaire oligarch 'families,'"[60] decided to enter politics. ANO (YES), a vassal's party founded only two years earlier and backed by Babiš' vast business and media empire,[61] won seats in the Czech parliament and became the coalition partner of the Social Democrats. In this government, Babiš held the post of finance minister until 2017, when he managed to form a minority government with himself as prime minister.[62] **In spite of the lack of monopoly of power, ANO,** according to Hanley and Vachudova, **managed to accumulate power in the state administration, as well as in state-owned enterprises, in the police**

and secret services, in the economy, and in the media. "The positions that Babiš and his ANO associates held in government gave them the power to shape institutions and policies that regulate economic actors. By controlling the Ministry of Finance 2014–17, for example, Babiš controlled the state bodies tasked with inspecting the financial activities of Czech businesses and their compliance with tax laws. This gave Babiš access to information about his political and business competitors and thus potential leverage over them. […] Concerns about Babiš misusing state power have also centred on his close relationships with police officers, prosecutors and the secret services, and the implications of these relationships for safeguarding the rule of law. [Moreover,] it has long been striking how many former high-level police and secret service officers have moved to the security division of Agrofert [Babiš' main company] or to the helm of one of its companies over the past two decades […]. Babiš used Agrofert to gather a critical mass of individuals with the power to misuse state information and blackmail state officials. These individuals have, with the rise of ANO, made a smooth transition to party politics and to government."[63] The authors report that Babiš appears to have used his power to make a threat to the outlet Echo24 (which he considered a hostile publication) that its main investor, Jan Klenor, could soon become the target of a financial investigation by the state.[64] He was also accused of channeling public funds from the EU to his business, which in 2019 spurred the largest demonstrations in the country since the regime change.[65]

On the one hand, **the fact that an oligarch becomes a poligarch, turning an economic venture into a political venture is a clear step toward informal patronalism**, with a head of executive running on the principle of elite interest. On the other hand, backsliding in the Czech Republic has only led toward patronal democracy. Aside from patronalization attempts in public administration, Babiš has not attacked formal checks and balances, in spite of formal control mechanisms being rather active (Czech law enforcement investigated against Babiš and he was also stripped of his parliamentary immunity in 2017).[66] Indeed, he has tried to use the state to promote his own network while suppressing opponents, just as a competing patronal network of patronal democracy. This may lead to rival oligarch's networks entering into the party competition, too, increasing the number of patron's parties and pushing the country closer to patronal democracy. But politicians' parties capitalizing on popular resistance can hinder such developments in the long run, whereas backsliding to autocracy seems unimaginable without monopoly of political power and with strong autonomous oligarchs, as well as formal institutions and civil society. This theoretical conjecture is underpinned by the fact that, **in 2021, Babiš was defeated in elections,** with his patronal network being forced in opposition.

Poland: Backsliding Toward Conservative Autocracy

While **Poland** represents the only case for a **conservative autocratic attempt** in the post-communist region, it was a consolidated liberal democracy until 2015 (Figure 31). Previously, it was a communist dictatorship from 1949-1989, with a period of softening from 1980.[67] Besides the stronger presence of the so-called second economy of moderately tolerated private enterprise, Solidarity Movement, growing out of the Shipyard of Gdańsk under the leadership of Lech Wałęsa was no longer just a parallel society, but also an embodiment of a parallel political power. Even a few years after the introduction of martial law, it started to play a definitive role in the revitalization of civil society. The Solidarity Movement was unique in the region not only for its size (10 million members), but also its heterogeneity: it joined individuals and groups of various worldviews, of different social positions, and was strongly supported by the Catholic Church as well as Pope John Paul II, former archbishop of Cracow.[68] A constellation of this sort was unimaginable in any other socialist country, although other reform-communist dictatorships did exist in the Western-Christian historical region.

In 1989, Poland experienced a "lawful revolution," involving negotiations between the ruling communist parties and the actors of the political opposition. In this country, just like in Hungary, the part of the communist party ready to be compromised by the talks was the one ready to face realities. In neither country was transition or a regime change the aim of these members of the communist party, but rather the legitimization of measures required to deal with the economic crisis made it seem worthwhile to involve an opposition they believed was weak. Yet it was the broadly supported Solidarity, as trailblazer of the process and a movement gathering the actors critical of the system, who negotiated with the regime—with the mediation of the Catholic Church.[69] After the first democratic elections of the eastern bloc took place in 1989, a number of parties formed out of the Solidarity Movement, while Solidarity began to function as a real labor union.[70]

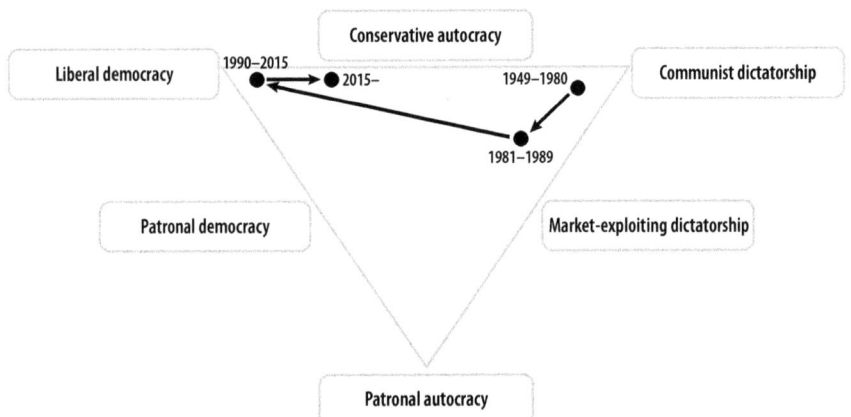

Figure 31: Modelled trajectory of Poland (1949-2022).

From 1990-2015, three right-wing or center-right governments carried out shock therapy reforms, trying to institute market coordination as the dominant mechanism of the economy.[71] The first one was conducted by the finance minister of the Mazowiecki government, Leszek Balcerowicz in 1990, which helped complete a relatively quick switch from a state socialist shortage economy to market competition based on private ownership. The second shock therapy is attributed to the Buzek government (1997-2001), in which Balcerowicz was deputy prime minister and finance minister. Significant reforms were introduced in four major fields: education, pensions, public administration, and healthcare. Finally, under the first government formed by the PiS (Law and Justice, the party of Jarosław Kaczyński; 2005-2007), new radical changes were introduced in the battle against corruption, for lustration, and to "clean up" the secret services. The leading politicians, and intellectuals/experts of PiS, in government between 2005 and 2007, and the Civil Platform, in government from 2007-2015, were all the legacy of the Mazowiecki and Buzek government. The Polish right wing has represented free market and capitalism right from the start, and they have not changed these fundamental principles even after both the Mazowiecki and the Buzek governments essentially suffered huge defeats.

Although Kaczyński started an autocratic attempt with PiS in 2015,[72] the lack of legitimacy of statist interventionism in the economy, as well as the lack of substantial oligarchs and poligarchs explains why **Poland's democratic backsliding did not lead to patronal regimes but toward conservative autocracy**. With a 51% majority in the parliament (i.e., without an effective monopoly of power), Kaczyński introduced politics that were subordinated to the principle of ideology implementation. For him, the concentration of power goes hand in hand with the goal of achieving a hegemony of a "Christian-nationalist" value system. It follows from this that the liberal value system built on the autonomy of the individual is viewed as an enemy, since the nation considers the interests of the Polish collective as higher than the interests of the individual. In the economy, this has manifested in preferring centralized regulation and state investment as the main vehicles of development instead of FDI, accompanied by economic xenophobia and "crawling renationalization."[73] Yet this has not included post-communist ownership redistribution, and no new layer of owners has been brought up. There are no inner-circle "Kaczyński oligarchs," nor ones that are systematically built through shelter provision. Actual decision-making also remains centered within the framework of formal institutions, with Kaczyński occupying the peak of the power pyramid as the president of PiS. An oddity of Kaczyński's rule is that he chose to be a simple MP, not a prime minister,[74] but he still acts within the formal institutional setting of the party and does not decide on matters like personal-wealth accumulation that would reach beyond formal competences. Loyal members of the power pyramid are rewarded with office and not wealth, and the economy is—in line with Kaczyński's ideology—not informally patronalized and only in some parts did the state expand its ownership.

Chances of the Polish conservative attempt at building an autocracy being defeated are strong even under the current democratic institutional framework. This is ensured by strong defensive mechanisms, like the proportional electoral system, constitutionally preventing excessive power concentration,[75] and strong civil society. The latter involves the social traditions of resistance to authority, the civil movement building on these traditions, the existence of moderate right and liberal parties constituting the main body of opposition forces, PiS being forced onto the extreme right of the political spectrum, the political diversity offered by the municipal governments, and the firm media-platforms for the freedom of expression. At the same time, the possibility of turning toward patronal autocracy is also prevented by the very character of PiS, its personal composition, principles, and program, as well as the tradition and present of the Polish right. In its current form PiS is not capable of following a downward tertiary trajectory in the triangle, for many circumstances and components are missing for it to do so.[76]

Despite constant critique and the launching of an infringement procedure by the EU for the violation of the rule of law, Poland has gained political weight in Europe and the NATO thanks to its response to **the 2022 Russian invasion of Ukraine**. The Three Seas Initiative (with the dominance of Poland, Romania, and, as a partner-participant, Ukraine) emerges as a real regional force, replacing the Visegrád Four alliance which practically collapsed after Orbán's pro-Putin response to the invasion and denial of solidarity to Ukraine. Moreover, Orbán viewed the Visegrád Four as a blackmailing alliance within the EU, and wanted to use it to position himself in the political scene; in contrast, the Three Seas is not a blackmailing alliance but the platform of actual political, economic and military cooperation, and Kaczyński does not position himself but he positions Poland. The lack of personalism is characteristic of his conservative regime as well, which also makes it easier to imagine that Poland will eventually meet some of the EU's democracy criteria. For unlike Orbán and his adopted political family, Kaczyński and his fellow party members are not corrupt criminals who would cling to their system as a means to avoid the risk of criminal prosecution.

Hungary: Backsliding to Patronal Autocracy from Liberal Democracy

Hungary has probably the "longest" trajectory of the post-communist countries, in the sense that is has seen model and regime changes **from communist dictatorship to liberal democracy (primary trajectory) and from liberal democracy to patronal autocracy (secondary trajectory)**. This is depicted on Figure 32, starting from 1949-1968, the years of hard, communist dictatorship with forced collectivization and industrialization.[77] **In 1968, the New Economic Mechanism (NEM) was introduced**, involving reforms toward decentralization, price liberalization, wage liberalization, and the development of an extended system of secondary manufacturing branches and small farms attached to state cooperatives. NEM resulted in the softer, reform socialist model known as "Goulash communism,"[78] which increased the income of the workers and eased the inflexibility of the rigid planned economy. Indeed, the controlled coexistence of the first and second economies meant a step toward market-exploiting dictatorship, and China can be seen as a mature follower of these early socialist reforms.[79]

Hungary was the other country (beside Poland) that **experienced a dictatorship retreat. The establishment of the Opposition Roundtable in 1989** unified the opposition for talks with the communist party to ensure a peaceful transition.[80] In the course of the negotiations the reform-communists no longer had the chance to ensure themselves a guaranteed powerbase unaffected by political competition, as the Polish Sejm did, but aimed instead to have a semi-strong presidential position installed with similar authorities vested in it. A separate deal between the MDF (Hungarian Democratic Forum) and the reform communists was forestalled by a referendum at the end of 1989 initiated by the SZDSZ (Alliance of Free Democrats) that preceded the first free elections in 1990. In the 1990s, Hungary was treated as a forerunner of democratization, involving both economic liberalization and a strong formal institutional framework: the Constitutional Court, a competitive party system and continuous changes of government in elections.

Figure 32: Modelled trajectory of Hungary (1949-2022).

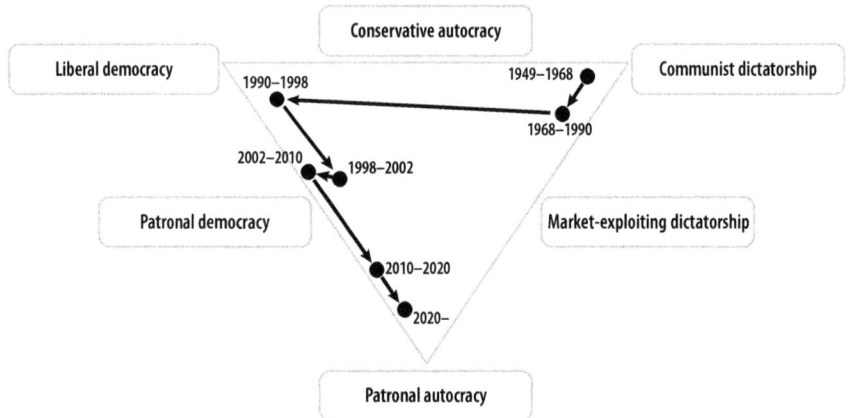

The first time Viktor Orbán and his party Fidesz came to power was in 1998. His program was summed up in the campaign slogan "more than change of government, less than change of regimes," and in the expression "all-out attack."[81] The slogan fairly describes what actually happened: a model change from liberal democracy to patronal democracy. Yet this was not simple backsliding but part of a strong autocratic attempt, breaking the autonomy of formal institutions and building an informal patronal network in the economy with inner-circle oligarch Lajos Simicska (who was also made head of the tax office in 1998-1999). Indeed, Orbán would have succeeded had he had a two-thirds majority, that is, an effective monopoly of political power.[82] Thus, the democratic institutional system was eroded, but it was nevertheless upheld—more or less—by the country's constitution and so-called "basic laws" that require supermajority.

Orbán was defeated in 2002 by the socialist-liberal coalition, which however did not lead back to liberal democracy. Let us go into some details here, because the functioning of Hungarian democracy in 2002-2010 illustrates an **unequal patronal competition** that lacked the dynamic equilibrium and broke down, degenerating into patronal autocracy. First of all, Fidesz retained informal dominance in the Prosecutor's Office, State Audit Office and the Constitutional Court, whereas President László Sólyom—who had weak formal powers—was also closer to the Fidesz on an ideological basis than to the governing coalition.

Populism became widespread in this period, too, resulting in a so-called "cold civil war:" both sides declared the other illegitimate (especially Fidesz did the governing MSZP, Hungarian Socialist Party), while any misstep of "one of us" was indulged in view of the threat of "one of them" coming to power (especially the MSZP feared Orbán).[83] On the other hand, Orbán's adopted political family collaborated with the rival government forces, evoking a friendly sense of "trench-truce." This has been widely recognized in the public by the term **"70/30," which meant that the illegitimate resources acquired (or simply acknowledged) in common would be divided with 70% going to the governing party and 30, to the opposition.**[84] The actors on the government side, however, were less disciplined and driven by uniform motives. Firstly, fields that promised revenues from corruption were assailed by "treasurers" of the party out on their own initiatives and local oligarchs (minigarchs), and secondly, others made repeated efforts to break the established ties of corruption collaboration of the two rival parties. In contrast, Orbán's political family relied on a single-channel order of accountability in the economy, penalizing private foragers cashing in under the Fidesz banner to ensure the unity of "taxation" on centrally sanctioned corruption income across all levels of the established order of patron-client relations. This manner of illegitimate taxation established expensive, but reliable conditions in corruption transactions: if someone paid the price, the service was delivered (unlike in the case of the MSZP government).

Until 2010 neither access to sources, nor means of sanctioning could be wholly monopolized by either political side. The parliamentary majority was normally surrounded by a colorful composition of parties in local government, and within the system, a number of joint, or at least multi-party committees had a say in the distribution of resources under state control. However, the second socialist-liberal government suffered decisive blows after 2006, the year of prime minister Ferenc Gyurcsány's tape scandal, and 2008,the year of losing a referendum and of the global financial crisis. Under such circumstances, Fidesz set out to secure a two-thirds supermajority in parliament already in campaign gear. With the help of the Prosecutor's Office, they succeeded in depositing the full weight of corruption cases at the doorstep of the government forces so far as public opinion was concerned.

In 2010, Orbán and Fidesz won a parliamentary supermajority, breaking the—already vulnerable—equilibrium of patronal democracy. Gaining enough power to change the constitution one-sidedly, Orbán **achieved an autocratic breakthrough** and approached patronal autocracy. Hungary has become **a paradigmatic case of the mafia state**, with an adopted political family (clan state), political, economic, and societal patronalization (neopatrimonial state), post-communist ownership-redistribution (predatory state), and politically selective law enforcement to make systemic corruption a constitutive element of the regime (criminal state).[85] While Hungary is often discussed together with Poland as the two "right-wing populist" authoritarian regimes of the EU, this is just an illusion created by the democracy-dictatorship axis. Focusing only on formal political institutions, the difference is that of an autocratic attempt and an autocratic breakthrough; seeing the informal, sociological background as well, we can observe the enormous qualitative distance between a conservative and a patronal autocracy (Table 44).

Since 2010, Orbán has managed to maintain supermajority in the subsequent manipulated elections. In 2020, **the coronavirus pandemic amplified the most essential features of the Hungarian mafia state.** Power concentration manifested as Orbán invoked a state of emergency and an enabling act allowed him to rule by decree.[86] At the same time, wealth accumulation has also been accelerated during the pandemic, with the adopted political family strenghtening its position in key industries from natural gas to banking and railways.[87]

The 2022 elections coincided with the Russian invasion of Ukraine and saw a campaign of denying solidarity in the name of collective egoism (Proposition 103), balancing between formal obligations to the EU and corrupt, informal ones to Putin, and helicoptering of ca. 3-4% of the GDP on the voters in the months before the election. The following economic crisis and international isolation were not a result of "bad" policy decisions but that the adopted political family had to ensure victory at all costs to avoid the risk of criminal prosecution (Proposition 54). A change of direction is possible on an ideology-applying basis, although this is yet to be seen at the moment of submitting the manuscript.

Table 44: Comparative summary of Poland and Hungary (in 2022).

	Conservative autocratic attempt: Poland	**Established patronal autocracy: Hungary**
The state	**A bureaucratic authoritarian state:** an incomplete attempt to establish conservative authoritarian rule through the capture of political institutions	**A mafia state:** a business venture managed through the monopoly of instruments of public authority
Actual decision-makers	**The head of executive and the governing party:** a formal body of leadership	**The chief patron and his court:** an informal body of leadership
The ruling party	**Centralized party:** decision-making centered in the leading bodies of the party, led by its president (a politician)	**Transmission belt party:** no decision-making in the party, just mediating and formalizing the wishes of the chief patron and his network
Ruling elite	**Party elite:** a political party determined by formal structure and legitimacy	**Adopted political family:** a patronal network (extended patriarchal family, clan) lacking formal structure and legitimacy
Dominance structure	**Non-patronal network:** a chain of command in the political sphere built around the formal structure of party loyalty	**Single-pyramid patronal network:** a centralized chain of command extending from the political sphere to every other sphere of social action, built on an informal patron-client network of vassalage and personal loyalty
Economic activity of the state	**Expanding state economy** but still respecting free market competition and freedom of enterprise (the loyal elite is mainly rewarded with offices and not wealth)	**Rent-seeking and centrally led corporate raiding:** wealth accumulation and patronalization of private property through the bloodless instruments of state coercion
Corruption	**State combating corruption:** sporadic cases of private actors corrupting public administration, against the will of the state authorities	**Criminal state:** top-down system constituting centralized and monopolized corruption, committing criminal acts according to current criminal code
Motives of the rulers	**Power and ideology:** accumulation of power and implementing ideology	**Power and personal wealth:** accumulation of power for wealth and vice versa
The role of ideology	**Ideology-driven regime:** "fanatic," willing to represent ideological issues against political rationality (acts follow the ideology, value-coherence)	**Ideology-applying regime:** "cynic," acting by political and economic rationality in the principle of elite interest (ideology follows the acts, functionality-coherence)

Russia: Backsliding to Patronal Autocracy from Oligarchic Anarchy

Russia represents the case of **democratic backsliding to patronal autocracy from oligarchic anarchy** (Figure 33). It may be objected that oligarchic anarchy does not appear in our triangle, which indeed does not account for the feature of state strength or failure (as pointed out in Proposition 116). However, in terms of regime-specific features, oligarchic anarchy is fairly similar to patronal democracy because of its multi-pyramid system of competing patronal networks, as well as a limited ruling elite holding unfair elections on the verge of electoral democracy and competitive authoritarianism.

Pomerantsev sums up Russia's regime trajectory quite neatly, writing that the country "experimented with different models at a dizzying rate: Soviet stagnation led to perestroika, which led to the collapse of the Soviet Union, liberal euphoria, economic disaster, oligarchy, and the mafia state."[88] From these, the period of economic disaster and "oligarchy" marks what we call oligarchic anarchy, which Russia became in the 1990s.

Figure 33: Modelled trajectory of Russia (1964-2022).

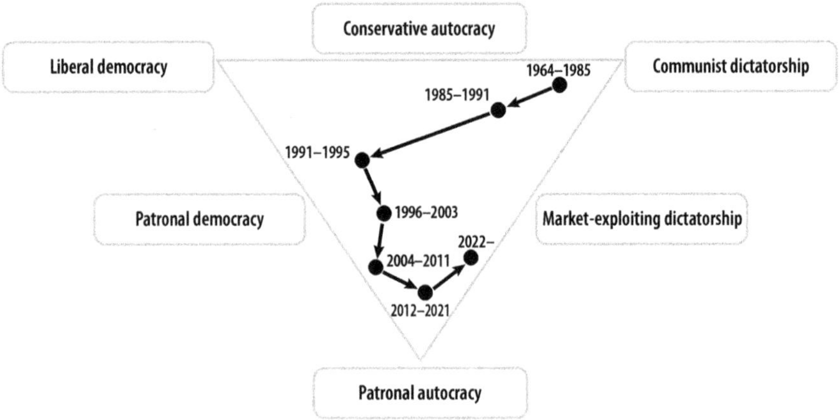

The regime change in Russia involved, on the one hand, system change: the change from socialism to capitalism.[89] As László Csaba writes, "Russia skipped the detour of real, comprehensive attempts at reform socialism, and made an attempt from 1992 at creating a real market economy." He goes on to explain that, while under the leadership of Gorbachev "substantial decentralization, liberalization, and the liberation of the market economy [...] did not happen," under the premiership of Boris Yeltsin the collapsing empire "had to reorganize public administration, and start [the market reforms] that they could."[90] In the two years between 1992 and 1994, Russia achieved almost complete liberalization of domestic prices and international trade, whereas half of domestic production was removed from the public sector through privatization, leading to the appearance of tens of millions of new owners. From a Western perspective, such achievements imply the emergence of a real market economy on the ruins on communist dictatorship.[91] However, oligarchic anarchy also featured a practically failed state, which, together with the newly formed private economy, was surrounded and partially appropriated by a disorganized, multi-pyramid setting of regional and nationwide-oligarchic networks.[92] But "[while] the moving parts of Russian politics [...] initially gyrated rather widely," Hale writes, "**the key moment in Russian post-Soviet political history occurred in 1996.** It was then when [president Boris] Yeltsin [...] deployed his arsenal of sticks and opened his cornucopia of carrots to mobilize regional political machines and major financial-industrial groups into a nationwide pyramid of patronal networks capable of defeating a major political opponent in the presidential race of that year. [...] The 1996 contest **proved to all that Yeltsin's presidential pyramid was superior**" (emphasis added).[93]

In the triangle, Yeltsin becoming a chief patron is represented by a clear step toward patronal autocracy and the dominance section of competitive authoritarianism, but not enough to cross the dominance boundaries of semi-formal institutions and relational-market redistribution. Yeltsin lacked the monopoly of political power as well as a strong state, which is a prerequisite for a successful mafia state to function. Moreover, he still ruled in the shadow of oligarchs, particularly Vladimir Gusinsky and Boris Berezovsky who owned substantial media empires, and Mikhail Khodorkovsky, who was the country's richest man and controlled much of Russia's natural resources as CEO of oil company Yukos. Vladimir Putin, who was named by Yeltsin as his successor in 1999, reformed the state so it regained strength, and also consolidated his power in the sphere of political action with a landslide victory of his United Russia party.[94] This 2003 victory enabled him to perform what Ben Judah describes as "the great turn." As he writes, it "closed the era where he ruled like Yeltsin's heir. It was the moment when Russia lurched decisively into an authoritarian regime."[95] Reportedly, Putin gathered a meeting with 21 oligarchs, informing them that they would be loyal to him and not interfere in politics on their own.[96] He also demonstrated what disobedience would mean: Gusinsky and Berezovksy were forced into exile, giving up their media empires to Putin's patronal network, whereas Khodorkovsky was jailed and his companies were taken over.[97] The 2003 meeting with the oligarchs brought a reversal of patron-client roles: while earlier the patrons had been the oligarchs, and political actors, their clients, Putin turned that upside down. State capture was replaced by oligarch capture, and Putin became the chief patron of Russia. Since that point, Russia has been a paradigmatic case of patronal autocracy. The strengh of Putin's grip over the regime notably manifested in 2008, when he faced a two-term limit but managed to avoid lame-duck syndrome, making his political front man Dmitriy Medvedev president and returning to power in 2012.[98]

In 2012, large protests were gathered in Moscow after 2011's fraudulent elections, with the possibility (as Putin most certainly saw it) of the outbreak of a color revolution.[99] The masses were not mobilized by an opposition party but by certain individuals like Alexei Navalny and Boris Nemtsov (who was assassinated four years later). The regime's GONGO, Nashi organized pro-government rallies in response, and the opposition protesters were criminalized in the patronal media that dominated the Russian sphere of communication. Eventually, large-scale protests ceased, the regime tightened non-balancing of rights against unauthorized demonstrations, and the adopted political family used kompromat to prosecute Navalny, who was sentenced to prison for embezzlement and fraud in 2013. **From this point on, the regime became more oppressive** in its state of autocratic consolidation, breaking civil society and neutralizing the autonomy of media, of entrepreneurs, of NGOs, and of the citizens.[100]

Normally, the more a regime has achieved autocratic consolidation, the more the chances of electoral victory as well as formal-procedural restitution wither away. However, **the regime may develop a state of "weariness," or it may otherwise become unable to maintain consolidation.** The consolidatedness of the regime means, ultimately, acceptance and resignation from the masses: elimination of the autonomies of civil society deprives the people of the means for effective organization and coordination, but a regime, no matter how oppressive it is, cannot rule over an actively hostile majority for a long time. During color revolutions, there are three factors that have provided the necessary spark for the people to start an uprising: (1) electoral fraud; (2) severe economic recession or stagnation; and (3) systemic corruption. The Russian regime has been on the verge of deconsolidation several times due to such factors. **In 2021, Alexei Navalny** released a documentary about "Putin's Palace," which provided not only the luxury castle with an estate as big as a smaller nation but also a description of the corrupt regime as a whole.[101] Formerly poisoned by the Russian secret service and spending his convalescence in Germany, Navalny was detained upon returning to Russia, at the same time when his documentary aired on YouTube. The video was seen by 20 million people in one, 60 million in three, and over 100 million people in a week. The Russian-language, English-subbed video combined with Navalny's detention created a wave of protests. Indeed, the video made (3), systemic corruption spectacular, which adds to (2)—that the Russian economy has been stagnating for almost a decade—and also (1)—that Putin had to staggering fraud to secure his victory at the constitutional referendum which guaranteed he would remain in power after the end of the two-term limit.[102] The coexistence of the three factors can be a breaking point in the regime's stability: electoral fraud erodes its legitimacy basis, corruption, its moral basis, and economic stagnation or decay, its material basis.

At the moment of submitting the manuscript, it is unclear whether **the 2022 invasion of Ukraine** will create another breaking point. As Russia's imperial expansionist instinct awakened with a perceived weakening of the West,[103] the invasion of Ukraine has created domestic crises in terms of legitimacy, economy, and the informal patronal network. First, legitimacy crisis manifests as **Russia becomes, from a criminal state with a core project of centrally organized and monopolized corruption, a criminal state with a central project of a crime against humanity**. The opposition of the Russian people to the war led Putin to initiate a series of repressive measures, including the blocking of social media, a censorship law against the use of the terms like "war" and "invasion" in the Russia-Ukraine context, and the detainment of thousands who have participated in anti-war protests. Second, international economic sanctions such as the exclusion of Russia from the SWIFT system, as well as the exodus of Western companies from Russia have devastating effect on the Russian economy and the life of ordinary Russian people. Third, the war brought an end to the "golden age" of oligarchs who could keep their assets abroad safely, under the protection of the rule of law and the respect of private property of liberal democracies. Western economic sanctions freezing the assets of the Russian elite and their family members show an X-ray image of Putin's adopted political family. Unlike a conservative autocracy, which creates state positions for party-based favoritism, top positions in the Russian state institutions are filled in by family lines, with sons and cousins receiving incomes way higher than those in similar positions in the West.[104]

In the triangle, Russia moves upwards from the informal to the semi-formal dominance section as the war brings formal organizations and chains of command (e.g. military, secret services, and state bureaucracy) to the fore, parallel to the devaluation and increasing vulnerability of oligarchic elements. **Putin repeated his 2003 meeting with the oligarchs** when he summoned 37 of them to the Kremlin a few hours after the invasion started. Only this time the meeting was not about the reversal of patron-client roles but delivering a threat in a war situation to curb possible critical instincts. And just as in 2003, Putin's words were accompanied by deeds: retribution against critical oligarchs like Oleg Tinkov (forced to sell his bank at 3 percent of its value) and disciplinary measures within the patronal network (e.g., a new decree allowing the confiscation of the savings of officials exceeding their income for three years) indicate the elimination of even limited bargaining capacity of informal power-holders.

Putin is taking a huge risk by the invasion. Rather than expanding his country's imperial role, the aggression can even shake its former indirect imperial influence. Moreover, as a civilizational core state, its role vis-à-vis other civilizations can be devalued: the unipolar world order is becoming not a tripolar but a bipolar one, with the US and China and without Russia. In terms of domestic regime stability, the accumulation and eruption of civil discontent is, at the moment, blocked by the lack of the autonomies of civil society. But as mass legitimacy-questioning and internal frustration of clients toward the chief patron appear, they may turn Putin into a "lame duck" and undermine even an otherwise consolidated patronal autocracy.

Ukraine: Regime Cycles with Color Revolutions

Throughout the 120 propositions, **Ukraine** was cited as a prime example of competing post-communist clans, and we also mentioned its color revolutions. Now we may take a look at Ukraine's complete regime trajectory, starting from its period under Soviet rule (Figure 34). **Already before the regime change,** Ukraine showed elements of clan politics within the state party. According to Minakov, **three regional groups from Kharkov, Stalino/Donetsk and Dnepropetrovsk represented the three largest party units and industrial clusters**, providing factional competition and alternately occupying the position of First Secretary of Central Committee of Ukrainian Communist Party and Chairperson of the Council of Ministers.[105] **A multi-pyramid system of competing patronal networks grew out of these roots after 1991,** with post-communist clans like the Kuchma-Pinchuk clan, the Lazarenko clan, and the Privat Group.[106]

The first attempt at building a single-pyramid power network happened in the first presidential term of Leonid Kuchma, who "consolidated his power by making the political system into a fully presidential one, by essentially coercing the parliament into agreeing to his constitutional 'reform' in 1996 [...]. At the same time, in the second half of the 1990s he formed a pact with emerging oligarchs that allowed him to concentrate economic power as well as media control [...]. He essentially established an alliance in which the oligarchs supported his political ambitions to continue to dominate Ukrainian politics, while he provided a 'krisha' [...] for them to illegally profit from the country."[107] The single-pyramid network he built proved successful in ensuring his re-election in 1999, despite the continually weak economic situation.[108]

Kuchma's model change to patronal autocracy was reversed by the Orange Revolution in 2004, leading the country back to patronal democracy via democratic but no anti-patronal transformation.[109] However, this was not the only regime cycle Ukraine saw. The period of **2005-2009** under president Viktor Yushchenko[110] was characterized by the **dynamic equilibrium of patronal**

competition, ensured by the new divided-executive constitution approved after the revolution.[111] It is worth noting that the president in the new system was not completely depowered: as Dubrovskiy and his colleagues write, "kept control over the secret service (endowed with the authority of investigating economic crimes and corruption) and law enforcement represented by the Prosecutor General's Office (PGO), which was empowered to perform all investigations of officials [...]. On top of this, a President had enormous control over judges. With these tools in his hands, he or she could potentially blackmail any elite member, so full (informal) control was only a matter of his/her willingness, skills, and impunity."[112] However, after Yushchenko was replaced, Viktor Yanukovych one-sidedly changed back the constitution to the initial, even stronger presidential arrangement, and made a strong attempt at creating a single-pyramid patronal network. As part of an anti-democratic transformation, **Yanukovych carried out autocratic breakthrough**, successfully neutralizing some of his opponents.

Figure 34: Modelled trajectory of Ukraine (1964-2022).

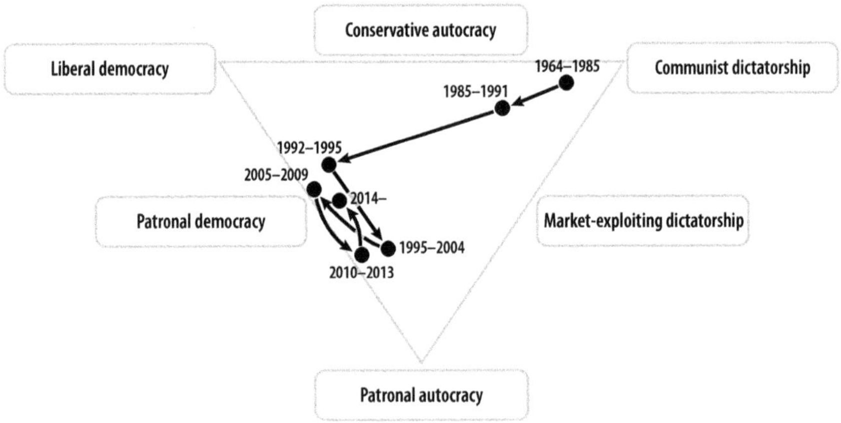

Yet **civil society in Ukraine was remarkably strong, making an autocratic consolidation impossible**. The presence of deeply embedded patronal networks on the one hand, and important socioeconomic changes that had given rise to a more open-access order oriented, so-called "creative" middle class on the other hand,[113] resulted in a resistance that culminated in the **Euromaidan Revolution in 2014**. The so-called "revolution of dignity" brought about not only the removal of Yanukovych but later also an election that was probably the fairest one in the country's history.[114] Yet, unsurprisingly, **the presidency of Petro Poroshenko brought only a single-level transformation**, as democratic transformation was not accompanied by anti-patronal transformation. Indeed, as we discussed in Proposition 70, it was the aforementioned clans that resisted the subjugation attempt and supported the revolution, only to return to the intense patronal competition that has characterized post-communist Ukraine since independence.[115] As Mizsei writes, "the Poroshenko presidency, without the ugly excesses of the Yanukovych regime, has returned to its default position: it works to advance the business interests and power of the President and his team, and it has strived to nominate people to positions in state enterprises according to the financial interests of the President and his entourage. Poroshenko delayed legislation and constitutional changes establishing the rule-of-law, and fought strongly against the independence of the prosecution service and for […] prosecutor generals […] who were not by any standards reformist, and refused to fight crime in an uninhibited manner."[116]

In April 2019, **Poroshenko lost the presidency to Volodymyr Zelensky**, who secured landslide victory in the parliamentary as well as the presidential elections. While this suggests a threat to the system of checks and balances,[117] Zelensky **is no chief patron and has no patronal pyramid** but only oligarchic backing from Ihor Kolomoyskyi, the leading partner of the Privat Group.[118] Apparently, Zelensky has an interest in anti-patronal transformation and breaking the power of oligarchs in the country, similarly to Mikheil Saakashvili in Georgia whose landslide victory after the Rose Revolution was followed by an anti-patronal attempt (see below). Initially, it seemed that Zelensky risked a conflict with Kolomoyskyi, while his attempts were obviously supported by the above-mentioned creative class, the emergence of which marked the increasing possibility (and, in part, reality) of a gradual but genuine change in the level of patronalism in Ukraine.[119]

At the moment of submitting the manuscript, the **2022 invasion of Ukraine by Russia** is an ongoing conflict, putting the country's independence at risk. On the other hand, the war seems to solidify the country's national identity. The traditional formula of nationalism, which equated nationality with ethnicity and language, dissipates as Russian-speaking areas like Kharkiv, Kherson, and Mariupol become sites of Russian bloodshed. Similarly to the Russian minority in the Baltic countries, the imperial Russian identity is replaced by a local—in this case, Ukrainian—Russian identity. While nation-building has been ongoing in the decades since Ukraine regained independence,[120] the "Ukrainian Patriotic War" accelerates this process on the basis of a stronger Ukrainian identity conceived in the heroic stance of the Ukrainian people against Russian aggression. This might also create the moral fundaments of a potential anti-patronal transformation in the future, which can be facilitated, from a sociological point of view, by the removal of the Russia-linked clans from the regime as well. It remains to be seen whether the power vacuum they leave will be filled by Ukrainian clans, or Western support, the prospect of EU membership, and Zelensky's robust charisma will be strong enough to prevent the clans from returning to their pre-war position.

North Macedonia: Regime Cycle with Intra-Elite Conflict

North Macedonia[121] is a highly patronalistic country where regime-specific features (divided executive power) and country-specific features (ethnic cleavages) together ensured **competition of patronal networks for more than a decade after the regime change**.[122] As William Crowther notes, North Macedonia declared independence in 1991 and was "confronted with serious economic development issues and ethnic divisions, [yet] democratic politics functioned moderately well. Structured completion and alteration in power occurred. Progress was visible in the development of civil society organizations, freedom of expression, and an independent media. [However,] reform lagged [in the economy], separation between the public and private economic activities was weak, and by all accounts clientelism and inappropriate privatization of state property were widespread. Complaints regarding voting irregularities arose recurrently. Despite these flaws, regular competition between rival elites occurred within the context of informally accepted parameters of behavior."[123] These features put Macedonia in the competitive authoritarian dominance section,[124] yet relatively close to patronal democracy because of prevailing informal patronalism among semi-formal institutions (Figure 35).

Figure 35: Modelled trajectory of North Macedonia (1964-2022).

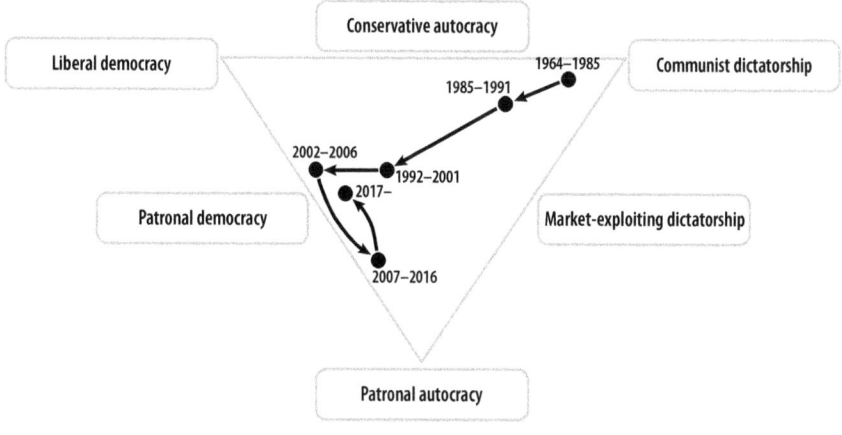

Besides **the former communists**, who appeared in the new multi-party system as the Social Democratic Party of Macedonia (SDSM), the two most important patronal networks were linked to **ethnic Macedonians** and **ethnic Albanians**. Both ethnic groups have tended to support separate ethnic parties, eventually 1-1 party achieving hegemonic position in their respective groups: Internal Macedonian Revolutionary Organization – Democratic Party for Macedonian National Unity (VMRO-DPME) and Democratic Union for Integration (DUI) for the Albanian population.[125] These parties and their nomenklatura- and ethnicity-based clans rotated in government; and until no group was strong enough to assume a dominant position, democratic pluralism in the polity prevailed. Moreover, **a period of stronger power-sharing and electoral democracy followed a brief period of civil war in 2001**. The ethnic conflict was concluded by the Ohrid Framework Agreement (OFA), which ensured more power to the Albanian minority, devolution of decision-making authority to local governments, and a proportionate electoral system, among other things.[126] Hale also notes the importance of Western leverage in diminishing the intensity of fighting between patronal networks in North Macedonia.[127]

Patronal competition was broken by a clan pact (Proposition 106): **a ruling coalition between the Macedonian and Albanian patronal networks was formed after the 2006 elections**. According to Crowther, this transformed the party system "from a situation of real, if limited, competition to one of hegemonic party rule,"[128] which critics described as "authoritarian consociationalism" and a "partocracy."[129] Indeed, this clan pact allowed the creation of a single-pyramid patronal network under head of executive **Nikola Gruevski**, whereby the two patronal networks could together carry out an **anti-democratic transformation**. In Crowther's study, we can discover signs of:[130]

- **turning both parties into transmission-belts** ("central party leaders monopolize policy making and decisions regarding advancement") and the legislature as well ("a compliant observer that mechanically translates decisions by Gruevski's inner circle into law");
- **system-constituting corruption** ("systemic corruption" and "a network of personal relationships around Prime

Minister Gruevski that are conducive to abuse of power for individual gain");[131]

- **ideology-applying populism** (characterizing "those Macedonians who reject Gruevski's program and adhere to the SDSM as traitors to the nation" and "NGOs critical of the government [...] as the pawns of foreign powers");
- **informal control of state institutions** ("Politically motivated prosecutions [...] directed against both opposition politicians and critical media," "NGOs engaged in democracy promotion and human rights advocacy were targeted for official and unofficial harassment," "the use of state resources for partisan advantage, and the sort of strategic manipulation of elections");
- **unconstrained power** (the networks' "ability to mobilize state resources and the national media made each nearly unassailable within their respective communities," "party leaders concentrated power in the executive, eroding checks and balances and reducing the ability of other branches of government or civil society to hold the ruling parties' leaders accountable").

The unusual formation of the Macedonian single-pyramid patronal network also engendered its vulnerability. Gruevski did not have singular control over the single-pyramid network, which remained internally fragmented between the two ethnic clans. Unable to overcome this cleavage, which had also been nourished by the two clans' divided voting bases, Gruevski had to face the **DUI leaving the coalition in 2016**, after the so-called wiretapping scandal made him unacceptable.[132] Eventually, **the country returned to patronal democracy** and Gruevski was forced to resign. And he was later sentenced to two years in prison for corruption—yet he avoided punishment by fleeing the country with the help of Hungarian authorities, which granted him political asylum in 2018.[133]

Moldova: Regime Cycles with Foreign Interference

While the regime trajectory of **Moldova** shares similarities with other countries with regime cycles, its concrete story is filled with country-specific idiosyncrasies, pointing out how much variation certain regime types can produce on the level of personal networks. A post-Soviet country landlocked between Romania and Ukraine, Moldova **declared independence in 1991, and it was not until 2001 that it faced a somewhat successful attempt at building a single-pyramid network.** Hale points out that, while the country had a strong patronal legacy and even a seemingly dominant agrarian/former-communist network, no single-pyramid was built in the first decade after transition. The first Moldovan president, Mircea Snegur (1990-1997) apparently lacked the ambition to create a dominant, subordinative patron-client network,[134] whereas the second president, Petru Lucinschi (1997-2001) "appears to have had much greater will and skill when it came to patronal politics [...] but the formal institutional changes [particularly the 1994, weak-presidential constitution] enabled parliament ultimately to undermine his attempts to create either a single-pyramid system or a more strongly presidentialist constitution."[135] Thus, the country remained a patronal democracy, with even the more-or-less dominant network facing internal fragmentation and the lack of a clearly dominant top patron (Figure 36).

In 2001, Vladimir Voronin became president and his vassals' party, the Party of Communists of the Republic of Moldova (PCRM) **gained a constitutional majority in parliamentary elections.** As Mizsei reports, "Voronin's strong mandate meant **he could easily begin to build a single-pyramid system**, in spite of the constitutional obstacles to a strong presidency [...]. First and foremost—somewhat like Putin in Russia—he **clipped the wings of the early oligarchs** in order to prevent them from limiting his power. [...] Voronin **developed his own oligarchic clans**. From today's perspective, the most skillful of them was Vlad Plahotniuc. However, in the early 2000s, he was not nearly the strongest player around Voronin; in fact, he only worked his way into the president's entourage around 2003. He gained his influence due to a business relationship with Voronin's son that over time proved the strongest mechanism to secure monopolistic access to business assets" (emphasis added).[136] While Plahotniuc would later become an important figure as chief patron, **Voronin's autocratic breakthrough was reversed by electoral means** in 2009. **This was possible mainly because of strong Western linkage and leverage**, with the EU representing the opposition and preventing—to mention only one example—the shutdown of the main television channel sympathetic to the opposition immediately before the elections.[137] As a result of foreign interference, the country could conclude its first regime cycle and return to the competitive regime of patronal democracy.

Figure 36: Modelled trajectory of Moldova (1964-2022).

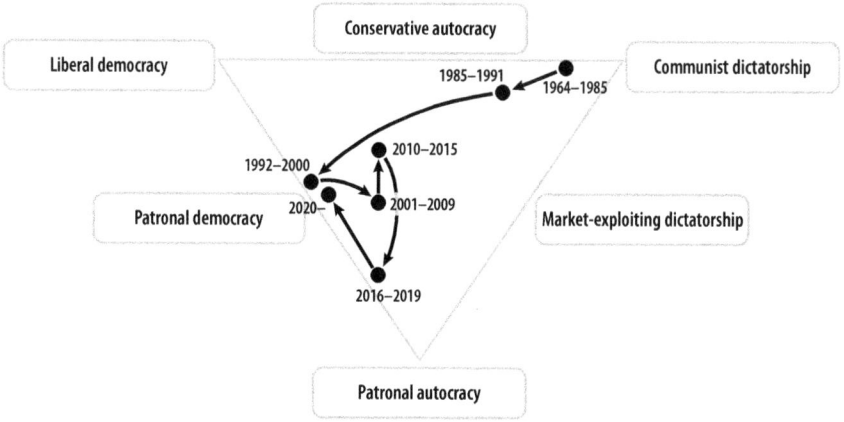

Already in this period, **Plahotniuc** initiated his plan that eventually led him to the position of chief patron. However, his origin and method of achieving the role of chief patron are unique in the post-communist region. First, Plahotniuc comes from neither the old nomenklatura, nor a specific ethnic group, nor the sphere of economy. Rather, he **originates from the organized underworld**: he had been a crime boss before he entered the political sphere, linked to numerous illicit activities like money-laundering, racketeering, and human trafficking.[138] He became an oligarch under Voronin by seizing control over a number of factories, airports, hotels, as well as railway, communication, media and natural-resource companies in Moldova, among other businesses.[139] Second, while "chief patron" is a fundamentally informal title, those who want to achieve it typically become head of executive, a formal title that fits the most in its competences to the role of chief patron and also signals his leading role to elite groups.[140] Yet **Plahotniuc became chief patron without becoming head of executive**, or holding any major function in the state for that matter. Indeed, there was a moment when he was nominated prime minister, but he never reached a position higher than First Deputy Speaker of the Parliament. Yet, uniquely in the countries discussed, he assembled a single-pyramid patronal network with the informal means of **kompromat and state capture** for a considerable period of time: he systematically extorted and/or "bought up" political actors important to achieving his goals. Using these techniques, **he managed to patronalize** as a poligarch a large number of autonomous actors, most importantly **(1) the Democratic Party of Moldova**, which entered the ruling coalition of prime minister Vladimir Filat after 2009 elections, **(2) the Constitutional Court**, and **(3) the chief prosecutor**.[141] He used these instruments to neutralize his rivals, especially Filat, who too had oligarchic goals and fought numerous fights with Plahotniuc but was eventually led out of parliament in handcuffs by the prosecutor on money laundering charges in 2015.

In the period between 2016-2019, Moldova was a patronal autocracy, informally headed by Plahotniuc "from the backseat." On the one hand, he achieved power monopolization, albeit not by formally gaining a constitutional majority but by becoming the informal patron of key people who operated checks and balances. Bankrolling members of government and parliament from his own private wealth, Plahotniuc achieved one-sided changes in the electoral system, too, changing the proportionate system into a mixed one before the 2019 elections. Plahotniuc extended his control to prosecutors, judges and the Central Electoral Commission, as well as the National Investigation Inspectorate and the National Anticorruption Center, which were used to collect kompromat.[142] On the other hand, Plahotniuc excelled in personal-wealth accumulation as well. A systemic analysis of Plahotniuc's network is offered by Sarah Chayes, who has been involved in a project at Carnegie Endowment for International Peace to map out the structure of kleptocratic states around the world. She enumerates the elements of Plahotniuc's network as follows: (1) government elements, including Ministry of Economy that used "customs and tax audits to discipline, handicap, or punish competing businesses;" (2) private sector elements, including banks, construction contractors, media, tourism, real estate and public utility intermediaries; (3) criminal elements, including smuggling and offering money-laundering services to Russian networks; and (4) active facilitators, including numerous shell companies and economic front men.[143] Several reports describe him using power over the state, judiciary and prosecution to carry out grey and white raiding as well,[144] adding predation to the portfolio of a state that had already become criminal, clan, and neopatrimonial under him. In short, Plahotniuc successfully instituted a mafia state.

However, **in 2019**, Plahotniuc did not manage to get an absolute majority in the elections, while the two major opposition parties had enough seats together to achieve a constitutional majority and remove Plahotniuc's people from key state positions. They eventually agreed to form a coalition against Plahotniuc, supported even by Plahotniuc-protégé President Igor Dodon, but the Constitutional Court ruled the coalition illegal and Dodon was removed. At this point, **Plahotniuc's mafia state seemed immune to internal attacks—but it was apparently unable to overcome the country's vulnerability to foreign intervention**. U.S., European and Russian interests coincided in this dramatic moment for very different reasons.[145] Plahotniuc was eased out and an unlikely coalition of geopolitical and governance adversaries, Maia Sandu's ACUM bloc and President Dodon's socialists took over. It turned out to be temporary and, in November 2019, the coalition indeed broke. President Dodon crafter a minority government, supported from outside by the remnants of Plahotniuc's Democratic Party. It is unclear how much control the now fugitive Plahotnicu still wields over his party. However, **Maia Sandu's democratic breakthrough** that had aimed exactly and explicitly to overcome the mafia state has, at least temporarily, finished. It is unclear how far the more patronal Dodon will be able to rebuild the patronal pyramid in an international environment where the Europeans and the U.S. actively oppose regime restoration and civil society has gained valuable systemic experience during Plahotniuc's reigning. In the 2020 elections,

Sandu was able to defeat the incumbent Dodon, opening the way for further democratic and, potentially, anti-patronal transformation. The successful implementation of Sandu's victorious regime alternative is still a long way to go. **Receiving the status of candidate of the European Union** under the commitment of structural reforms should have a positive effect on this process, although Moldova was granted that status under the shadow of the 2022 Russian invasion of Ukraine.

Georgia: An Attempt to Break the Regime Cycle

Finally, we may turn to the peculiar case of **Georgia** (Figure 37). Just like Ukraine and Moldova, Georgia was a member state of the Soviet Union until its dissolution in 1991. **After becoming independent, the country faced state failure and civil war**, with law and order in jeopardy and high levels of street crime and violence. To stabilize the country, local warlords Jaba Ioseliani and Tengiz Kitovani invited former general party secretary and Minister of Foreign Affairs of the Soviet Union, Eduard **Shevardnadze** to help put down the uprisings and become head of state after a military coup against then-sitting president Zviad Gamsakhurdia. Formally, Shevardnadze was Chairman of Parliament from 1992 and elected president **in 1995, which was the year he started instituting a single-pyramid power network with himself as chief patron**. Hale notes that already as Chairman, Shevardnadze started "the process of running his formal power into informal power. Aiming for the next elections, he created a party, the Citizens Union of Georgia, that could serve as an institutional vehicle for his coalition [...]. Emphasizing his own centrality, he also threatened to resign, prompting parliament (fearing more chaos) to grant him additional formal powers and even to suspend its own activities for a period. [...] Shevardnadze sought other powerful allies and gave each reason to be invested in his rule[, including] Aslan Abashidze's regional machine in the autonomous region of Ajara [and the] shadow economy business operations of Kakha Targamadze's Interior Ministry."[146] According to Mizsei, the state under Shevardnadze "worked like most of the CIS countries, with people close to Shevardnadze, including his family members, acquiring large monopolistic economic rights, including in the oil and gas trade."[147]

However, Shevardnadze achieved **only autocratic breakthrough but no autocratic consolidation**. That is, civil society remained very active under his role, with relatively strong autonomy of the media, entrepreneurs and citizens. This made **the Rose Revolution in 2003** possible, which broke out after Shevardnadze's electoral victory was announced before the votes were properly counted. Two days after large-scale legitimacy-questioning protests started in Tbilisi, opposition leader Mikheil Saakashvili and his supporters stormed the parliament building. Shevardnadze was evacuated and soon resigned, leaving the country for Moscow. Saakashvili won the re-run elections in 2004 with 96% of the vote.[148]

Figure 37: Modelled trajectory of Georgia (1964-2022).

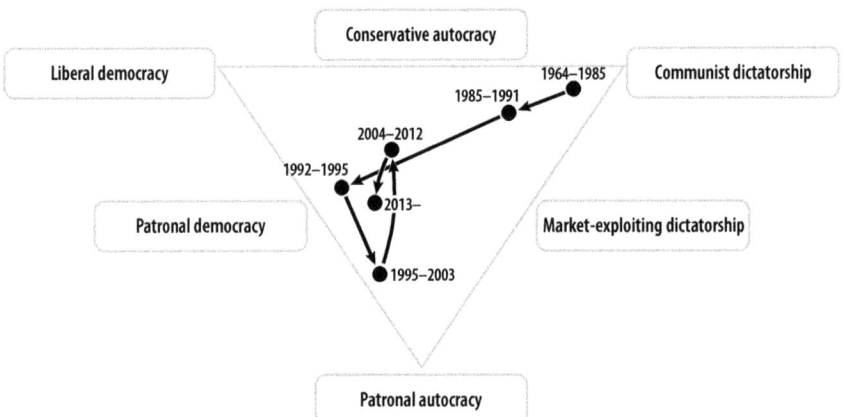

While patronalism did not perish after the revolution, the **Saakashvili government made a unique attempt at an anti-patronal transformation**. Indeed, he himself was not completely devoid of patronalism, having been supported by major oligarchs like Bidzina Ivanishvili. But after the Rose Revolution, Saakashvili "combined […] the genuine and brave fight against organized crime and corruption, and a libertarian drive to shrink the scope and extent of the state."[149] **Clearly ideology-driven**, Saakashvili's program proved to be anti-patronal because it **reduced the system of power&ownership by eliminating the power component**.[150] Realizing that power is automatically infused with ownership and public institutions are prone to be captured by informal networks, Saakashvili "brought sweeping deregulation that the Western partners didn't always understand, as they lacked appreciation of the context of those reforms. Two very visible measures occurred in 2005–2006, when the car and food safety agencies were eliminated, since they did not take care of car and food safety but were purely hotbeds of corruption. […] The early shocks of eliminating these dysfunctional, parasitic institutions, as well as other agencies, were often treated as 'excessive' and even 'lunatic' by international partners. In fact, it was exactly this radicalism that was a core factor in reforms that triggered real—not merely cosmetic—change."[151] In addition, "authorities were very strict with crime and corruption. Sentences were harsh and the prison population grew. This was crucial to break the expectation of the criminal state's eternal survival; it sent the message that there would be zero tolerance of crime and corruption."[152] The reforms succeeded in reducing free-market corruption and cronyism, too, particularly in dealings with state bureaucracy, education system, healthcare, law enforcement, and the judiciary.[153]

On the other hand, **anti-patronal transformation was not combined with democratic transformation**, resulting in **a sequence toward conservative autocracy**. Mizsei reports, "this period did not produce [...] the clear separation of executive and judicial power, a key component of the rule-of-law. [...] Media pluralism suffered after the 2007 Imedi case, where the police used force to disperse a demonstration, then the government ordered the closure of the Imedi television stations and police damaged equipment in their central studio. [Businesspeople] associated with the previous regime were often put in jail and released after a pledge to pay. At that point, it was purely informal and could even be justified by the urgent financial needs of the new, revolutionary state. This arbitrariness, however, never really ended. [...] Saakashvili [...] thought they could take shortcuts to reforming the state."[154] While Saakashvili's judicial reforms—which, in the initial phase, resulted in such centralization that the President personally presided over the council of the judges—were not only self-serving but responded to the local reality of massive organized crime, they ultimately became the source of significant abuses of power.[155]

The competitive authoritarian regime of **Saakashvili was eventually defeated by Ivanishvili himself in 2012, returning the country to a somewhat more patronal status**.[156] As Mizsei notes, it is a rare phenomenon in the post-Soviet patronal world that a peaceful, election-based transition of power occurred from Saakashvili and his United National Movement (UNM) party to the opposition.[157] With Saakashvili rendered an unpopular lame-duck, Georgia emerged—as Hale writes—with a "pronounced competing-pyramid situation."[158] This seemingly changed when, after modifying the electoral system toward a strongly majoritarian direction, the ruling Georgian Dream party achieved constitutional majority in 2016. However, as of 2022, **this has not been followed by autocratic consolidation, nor a clear attempt to establish a single-pyramid patronal network.** The intensity of competition and numerous (legitimacy-questioning) demonstrations suggest patronal democracy rather than autocracy.[159] In addition, the three-wave reform of the judiciary (2012-2019) increased transparency of system and judicial independence, limiting the rules of transferring judges from one court to another and introducing electronic random assignment of cases.[160] In spite of criticisms from the side of civil society,[161] and also that the government employs strong populist rhetoric, demonizing Saakashvili,[162] the aforementioned reforms indicate steps toward normativity instead of widening the realm of discretion as it would be typical for a patronal actor with supermajority.

Notes

For a full list of the literature used, see the bibliography of *The Anatomy of Post-Communist Regimes* (available on the authors' website, and via the QR-code on this page).

Estonia

1. David Smith, *Estonia: Independence and European Integration* (Oxford ; New York: Routledge, 2013).
2. Dorothee Bohle and Béla Greskovits, *Capitalist Diversity on Europe's Periphery*, 1st ed. (Ithaca: Cornell University Press, 2012), 96–137.
3. Smith, *Estonia*, 65.
4. Steven Levitsky and Lucan Way, *Competitive Authoritarianism: Hybrid Regimes after the Cold War* (Cambridge University Press, 2010), 14.
5. "Freedom in the World: Country and Territory Ratings and Statuses, 1973-2019 (Excel)" (Freedom House, 2019), https://freedomhouse.org/sites/default/files/Country_and_Territory_Ratings_and_Statuses_FIW1973-2019.xls.
6. Michael Coppedge et al., "V-Dem Country-Year Dataset 2019" (Varieties of Democracy (V-Dem) Project, 2019), https://www.v-dem.net/en/data/data-version-9/.
7. Henry E. Hale, *Patronal Politics: Eurasian Regime Dynamics in Comparative Perspective* (Cambridge: Cambridge University Press, 2015), 459–60.
8. Vello Pettai, "Understanding Politics in Estonia: The Limits of Tutelary Transition," in *Pathways: A Study of Six Post-Communist Countries*, ed. Karin Hilmer Pedersen and Lars Johannsen (ISD LLC, 2009), 69–87.
9. Evald Mikkel, "Patterns of Party Formation in Estonia: Consolidation Unaccomplished," in *Post-Communist EU Member States: Parties and Party Systems*, ed. Susanne Jungerstam-Mulders, 1 edition (Aldershot ; Burlington, VT: Routledge, 2006), 23–49.
10. Rein Taagepera, "Baltic Values and Corruption in Comparative Context," *Journal of Baltic Studies* 33, no. 3 (2002): 243–58.
11. Vello Pettai and Pille Ivask, "Estonia," Nations in Transit 2018 (Freedom House, 2018), https://freedomhouse.org/sites/default/files/NIT2018_Estonia.pdf.
12. Ott Lumi, "Comparative Insight into the Status of the Lobbying Regulation Debate in Estonia," *Journal of Public Affairs* 15, no. 3 (2015): 300–310.
13. Mikkel, "Patterns of Party Formation in Estonia: Consolidation Unaccomplished."
14. Martin Ehala, "The Bronze Soldier: Identity Threat and Maintenance in Estonia," *Journal of Baltic Studies* 40, no. 1 (March 1, 2009): 139–58.
15. Vassilis Petsinis, "Identity Politics and Right-Wing Populism in Estonia: The Case of EKRE," *Nationalism and Ethnic Politics* 25, no. 2 (2019): 211–30.

Romania

[16] Stephen D. Roper, *Romania: The Unfinished Revolution* (London: Routledge, 2004).

[17] Roper, 13–64.

[18] László Nándor Magyari, "The Romanian Patronal System of Public Corruption," in *Stubborn Structures: Reconceptualizing Post-Communist Regimes*, ed. Bálint Magyar (Budapest–New York: CEU Press, 2019), 311.

[19] Hale, *Patronal Politics*, 462. Also, see Milada Anna Vachudova, *Europe Undivided: Democracy, Leverage, and Integration after Communism* (Oxford: Oxford University Press, 2005).

[20] Magyari, "The Romanian Patronal System of Public Corruption," 309–10.

[21] Magyari, 311.

[22] Dragoș Dragoman, "Post-Accession Backsliding: Non-Ideologic Populism and Democratic Setbacks in Romania," *South-East European Journal of Political Science* 1, no. 3 (2013): 27–46.

[23] Magyari, "The Romanian Patronal System of Public Corruption," 311.

[24] Silvia Marton, "Regime, Parties, and Patronage in Contemporary Romania," in *Brave New Hungary: Mapping the "System of National Cooperation,"* ed. János Mátyás Kovács and Balázs Trencsényi (Lanham: Lexington Books, 2019), 357–78.

Kazakhstan

[25] James Minahan, *Miniature Empires: A Historical Dictionary of the Newly Independent States* (Westport: Greenwood Publishing Group, 1998), 136.

[26] Hale, *Patronal Politics*, 139–40.

[27] Sally Cummings, *Kazakhstan: Power and the Elite* (London ; New York: I.B. Tauris, 2005).

[28] Hale, *Patronal Politics*, 140.

[29] Rico Isaacs, *Party System Formation in Kazakhstan : Between Formal and Informal Politics* (London: Routledge, 2011).

[30] Hale, *Patronal Politics*, 250.

[31] "Nazarbayev's Christmas Tree," accessed November 21, 2018, https://www.elka-nazarbaeva.net/en/.

[32] "The Chart of N. Nazarbayev's Family OCG," accessed November 21, 2018, https://www.elka-nazarbaeva.net/en/scheme1.jpg.

[33] Sebastien Peyrouse, "The Kazakh Neopatrimonial Regime: Balancing Uncertainties Among the 'Family,' Oligarchs and Technocrats," *Demokratizatsiya* 20, no. 4 (Fall 2012): 345–70.

[34] "In Kazakhstan's Street Battles, Signs of Elites Fighting Each Other," *The Straits Times*, January 8, 2022, https://www.straitstimes.com/world/in-kazakhstans-street-battles-signs-of-elites-fighting-each-other.

[35] Hale, *Patronal Politics*, 243–48.

[36] Hale, 243.

China

[37] Samuel P. Huntington, *The Third Wave: Democratization in the Late 20th Century* (Norman: University of Oklahoma Press, 1993), 105–6.

[38] Susan L. Shirk, *The Political Logic of Economic Reform in China* (Berkeley and Los Angeles: University of California Press, 1993), 38.

[39] Minxin Pei, *From Reform to Revolution: The Demise of Communism in China and the Soviet Union* (Cambridge ; London: Harvard University Press, 2009), 84. It is worth mentioning the Tiananmen Square Massacre three years earlier, which unambiguously indicated that economic liberalization in China will not be accompanied by political liberalization. See White, "Democratization and Economic Reform in China."

[40] Iván Szelényi and Péter Mihályi, *Varieties of Post-Communist Capitalism: A Comparative Analysis of Russia, Eastern Europe and China*, Studies in Critical Social Sciences (Leiden ; Boston: Brill Academic Pub, 2019), 198.

[41] Robin Brant, "Why Is Jack Ma a Communist Party Member?," *BBC News*, November 27, 2018, sec. Business, https://www.bbc.com/news/business-46353767.

[42] Brant.

[43] Sebastian Heilmann, ed., *China's Political System* (Lanham: Rowman & Littlefield, 2016).

[44] Roya Ensafi et al., "Analyzing the Great Firewall of China Over Space and Time," *Proceedings on Privacy Enhancing Technologies* 2015, no. 1 (April 1, 2015): 61–76.

[45] Xiao Qiang, "President Xi's Surveillance State," *Journal of Democracy* 30, no. 1 (January 9, 2019): 53–67.

[46] "China Invents the Digital Totalitarian State," *The Economist*, December 17, 2016, https://www.economist.com/briefing/2016/12/17/china-invents-the-digital-totalitarian-state.

[47] Qiang, "President Xi's Surveillance State," 53–54. Also, see Rachel Botsman, "Big Data Meets Big Brother as China Moves to Rate Its Citizens," *Wired UK*, October 21, 2017, https://www.wired.co.uk/article/chinese-government-social-credit-score-privacy-invasion.

[48] Elizabeth C. Economy, "China's Imperial President: Xi Jinping Tightens His Grip," *Foreign Affairs*, no. 6 (2014): 80–91.

[49] Sebastian Heilmann, "3.1. The Center of Power," in *China's Political System*, ed. Sebastian Heilmann (Lanham: Rowman & Littlefield, 2016), 161.

Czech Republic

[50] Hale, *Patronal Politics*, 60.

[51] Hale, 459.

[52] "Freedom in the World: Country and Territory Ratings and Statuses, 1973-2019 (Excel)."

[53] Coppedge et al., "V-Dem Country-Year Dataset 2019."

[54] Tim Haughton, Tereza Novotná, and Kevin Deegan-Krause, "The 2010 Czech and Slovak Parliamentary Elections: Red Cards to the 'Winners,'" *West European Politics* 34, no. 2 (March 1, 2011): 394–402.

[55] Andrew Roberts, "Czech Democracy in the Eyes of Czech Political Scientists," *East European Politics* 33, no. 4 (2017): 562–72.

[56] Abby Innes, "Corporate State Capture in Open Societies: The Emergence of Corporate Brokerage Party Systems," *East European Politics and Societies* 30, no. 3 (August 1, 2016): 594–620.

[57] Seán Hanley and Milada Anna Vachudova, "Understanding the Illiberal Turn: Democratic Backsliding in the Czech Republic," *East European Politics* 34, no. 3 (July 3, 2018): 285.

[58] The term "dead soul" refers to Gogol's novel of the same name, but it was used even by the Czech Constitutional Court for the phenomenon. See Ústavní soud,

"Nález II: ÚS 1969/10 z 27. Prosince 2011.," 2011, http://nalus.usoud.cz/Search/ResultDetail.aspx?id=72560.

59 Michal Klíma, *Informal Politics in Post-Communist Europe: Political Parties, Clientelism and State Capture*, 1 edition (Routledge, 2019), 10.

60 Hanley and Vachudova, "Understanding the Illiberal Turn," 284.

61 Hanley and Vachudova, 285–387.

62 Hanley and Vachudova, 277.

63 Hanley and Vachudova, 288.

64 Hanley and Vachudova, 287.

65 "Billionaire Czech Prime Minister's Business Ties Fuel Corruption Scandal," DW.COM, June 25, 2019, https://www.dw.com/en/billionaire-czech-prime-ministers-business-ties-fuel-corruption-scandal/a-49351488-0.

66 "Czech Election Front-Runner Charged with Subsidy Fraud," POLITICO, October 9, 2017, https://www.politico.eu/article/czech-election-front-runner-charged-with-subsidy-fraud/.

Poland

67 A. Kemp-Welch, *Poland under Communism: A Cold War History* (Cambridge: Cambridge University Press, 2008).

68 Jan Kubik, *The Power of Symbols Against the Symbols of Power: The Rise of Solidarity and the Fall of State Socialism in Poland* (Pennsylvania State University Press, 1994).

69 Kemp-Welch, *Poland under Communism*, 361–90.

70 Aleks Szczerbiak, "Power without Love: Patterns of Party Politics in Post-1989 Poland," in *Post-Communist EU Member States: Parties and Party Systems*, ed. Susanne Jungerstam-Mulders (New York: Routledge, 2006), 91–124.

71 Leszek Balcerowicz, "Poland: Stabilization and Reforms under Extraordinary and Normal Politics," in *The Great Rebirth: Lessons from the Victory of Capitalism over Communism*, ed. Anders Åslund and Simeon Djankov (Washington, DC: Peterson Institute for International Economics, 2014), 17–38.

72 Wojciech Sadurski, *Poland's Constitutional Breakdown* (Oxford: Oxford University Press, 2019).

73 Piotr Kozarzewski and Maciej Bałtowski, "Return of State-Owned Enterprises in Poland" (Paper presented at Seventh Annual Conference of the Leibniz Institute for East and Southeast European Studies, Regensburg, Germany, May 30, 2019).

74 Robert Sata and Ireneusz Pawel Karolewski, "Caesarean Politics in Hungary and Poland," *East European Politics*, December 19, 2019, 1–20.

75 Sadurski, *Poland's Constitutional Breakdown*, 140–43.

76 For a more detailed, comparative analysis of Poland and Hungary, see Bálint Magyar, "Parallel System Narratives: Polish and Hungarian Regime Formations Compared," in *Stubborn Structures: Reconceptualizing Post-Communist Regimes*, ed. Bálint Magyar (Budapest–New York: CEU Press, 2019), 611–55.

Hungary

77 József Ö. Kovács, "The Forced Collectivization of Agriculture in Hungary, 1948-1961," in *The Collectivization of Agriculture in Communist Eastern Europe: Comparison and Entanglements*, ed. Constantin Iordachi and Arnd Bauerkamper (Budapest–New York: CEU Press, 2014), 211–47. For the sake of simplicity and

because our purpose is only illustration, not historical documentation, we do not depict the Revolution of 1956 in the triangle as a new point.

[78] János Kornai, "Paying the Bill for Goulash Communism: Hungarian Development and Macro Stabilization in a Political-Economy Perspective," *Social Research* 63, no. 4 (1996): 943–1040.

[79] Péter Vámos, "A Hungarian Model for China? Sino-Hungarian Relations in the Era of Economic Reforms, 1979–89," *Cold War History* 18, no. 3 (July 3, 2018): 361–78; Mária Csanádi, "The 'Chinese Style Reforms' and the Hungarian 'Goulash Communism'" (Discussion Paper; Centre for Economic and Regional Studies, Hungarian Academy of Sciences, 2009), http://econ.core.hu/file/download/mtdp/MTDP0903.pdf.

[80] András Bozóki, "Hungary's Road to Systemic Change: The Opposition Roundtable," *East European Politics and Societies* 7, no. 2 (March 1, 1993): 276–308.

[81] Quoted by Tamás Sárközy, *Illiberális Kormányzás a Liberális Európai Unióban: Politikailag Igen Sikeres Túlhajtott Plebejus Kormányzás – a Harmadik Orbán-Kormány, 2014-2018 [Illiberal Governance in the Liberal European Union: Politically Very Successful Overdone Plebeian Governance – the Third Orbán Government, 2014-2018]* (Budapest: Libri Kiadó, 2019), 62–65.

[82] Magyar Bálint, "Magyar polip – a szervezett felvilág," *Magyar Hírlap*, February 21, 2001.

[83] Takis S. Pappas, "Populist Democracies: Post-Authoritarian Greece and Post-Communist Hungary," *Government and Opposition* 49, no. 1 (2014): 1–23.

[84] Attila Mong, *Milliárdok Mágusai: A Brókerbotrány Titkai [Mages of Billions: The Secrets of the Brokerage Scandal]* (Budapest: Vízkapu, 2003).

[85] For a comprehensive discussion, see Bálint Magyar, *Post-Communist Mafia State: The Case of Hungary* (Budapest: CEU Press, 2016).

[86] Kim Lane Scheppele, "Orban's Emergency," *Verfassungsblog* (blog), March 29, 2020, https://verfassungsblog.de/orbans-emergency/.

[87] András Bódis, "Amíg Ön a Járványra Figyelt, a NER Bevette Az Országot [While You Were Being Occupied with the Pandemic, the NER Took over the Country]," *Válasz Online*, January 28, 2021, https://www.valaszonline.hu/2021/01/28/amig-on-a-jarvanyra-figyelt-a-ner-bevette-az-orszagot-leltar-a-hazavitt-strategiai-agazatokrol/.

Russia

[88] Peter Pomerantsev, *Nothing Is True and Everything Is Possible* (New York: Public Affairs, 2014), 71.

[89] János Kornai, "The System Paradigm Revisited: Clarification and Additions in the Light Of Experiences in the Post-Communist Region," in *Stubborn Structures: Reconceptualizing Post-Communist Regimes*, ed. Bálint Magyar (Budapest–New York: CEU Press, 2019), 23–35.

[90] Csaba László, *Válság-gazdaság-világ: Adalék Közép-Európa három évtizedes gazdaságtörténetéhez (1988-2018) [Crisis-economy-world: Additions to the economic history of the last three decades of Central Europe (1988-2018)]* (Budapest: Éghajlat Könyvkiadó, 2018), 53–55.

[91] Cf. Anders Åslund, *How Russia Became a Market Economy* (Washington, D.C: Brookings Inst Pr, 1995).

[92] Hale, *Patronal Politics*, 110–15; David E. Hoffman, *The Oligarchs: Wealth And Power In The New Russia*, Revised, Updated ed. edition (New York, NY: PublicAffairs, 2011).

[93] Hale, *Patronal Politics*, 135.
[94] Hale, 270–74.
[95] Ben Judah, *Fragile Empire: How Russia Fell In and Out of Love with Vladimir Putin* (New Haven ; London: Yale University Press, 2014), 55.
[96] Judah, 43.
[97] Richard Sakwa, "Putin and the Oligarchs," *New Political Economy* 13, no. 2 (June 2008): 185–91. Browder also describes the chilling effect the Khodorkovsky case had on other oligarchs, who reportedly had to give a significant portion of their property to Putin's *de facto* ownership. In addition, Browder's own crusade against Russian oligarchs was supported and used by Putin, but only until the latter could subjugate the oligarchs, "[consolidate] his power, and, by many estimates, become the richest man in the world." Bill Browder, *Red Notice: A True Story of High Finance, Murder, and One Man's Fight for Justice* (New York: Simon & Schuster, 2015), 157–63.
[98] Hale, *Patronal Politics*, 276–91.
[99] Julia Gerlach, *Color Revolutions in Eurasia* (London: Springer, 2014), 22–24.
[100] Grigory Yavlinsky, *The Putin System: An Opposing View* (New York: Columbia University Press, 2019), 66–80.
[101] Alexei Navalny, Дворец Для Путина. История Самой Большой Взятки *[Putin's Palace. History of World's Largest Bribe]*, 2021, https://www.youtube.com/watch?v=ipAnwilMncI..
[102] "Data Scientist Claims 'Staggering' Fraud at Russia's Constitution Vote," *The Moscow Times*, July 3, 2020, https://www.themoscowtimes.com/2020/07/03/data-scientist-claims-staggering-fraud-at-russias-constitution-vote-a70769.
[103] Françoise Thom, "What Does the Russian Ultimatum to the West Mean?," *Desk Russie* (blog), December 30, 2021, https://en.desk-russie.eu/2021/12/30/what-does-the-russian-ultimatum.html.
[104] Amiah Taylor and Tristan Bove, "Meet the Russian Billionaires and Elites Who Just Got Hit with Sanctions," *Fortune*, February 23, 2022, https://fortune.com/2022/02/23/meet-the-russian-billionaires-elites-sanctions/.

Ukraine

[105] Mikhail Minakov, "Republic of Clans: The Evolution of the Ukrainian Political System," in *Stubborn Structures: Reconceptualizing Post-Communist Regimes*, ed. Bálint Magyar (Budapest–New York: CEU Press, 2019), 220–28.
[106] Minakov, 228–34.
[107] Kálmán Mizsei, "The New East European Patronal States and the Rule-of-Law," in *Stubborn Structures: Reconceptualizing Post-Communist Regimes*, ed. Bálint Magyar (Budapest–New York: CEU Press, 2019), 537.
[108] Hale, *Patronal Politics*, 148; Valerie J. Bunce and Sharon L. Wolchik, *Defeating Authoritarian Leaders in Postcommunist Countries*, 1 edition (Cambridge: Cambridge University Press, 2011), 115–22.
[109] Hale, *Patronal Politics*, 182–90.
[110] Yushchenko was in power until February 2010, therefore we include 2010 to the period of Yanukovich who replaced him and ruled in the larger part of that year (the figure has, due to the illustrative nature of the regime trajectory, only years, not exact dates).
[111] Hale, *Patronal Politics*, 325–31.

[112] Vladimir Dubrovskiy et al., "Six Years of the Revolution of Dignity: What Has Changed?" (Kyviv: CASE Ukraine, June 2020), 23, https://case-ukraine.com.ua/content/uploads/2020/06/6-years-of-the-Revolution-of-Dignity_v-02_06.pdf.

[113] Dubrovskiy et al., "Six Years of the Revolution of Dignity," 61–81.

[114] "Despite Violence and Threats in East, Ukraine Election Characterized by High Turnout and Resolve to Guarantee Fundamental Freedoms, International Observers Say," OSCE, May 26, 2014, https://www.osce.org/odihr/elections/119081.

[115] Wojciech Konończuk, "Oligarchs after the Maidan: The Old System in a 'new' Ukraine," Policy Paper, OSW Commentary, 2015.

[116] Mizsei, "The New East European Patronal States and the Rule-of-Law," 584. Mizsei also discusses the initial invitation of reformists (including Georgian ones) and the later blocking of their reform attempts in detail (pp. 583-599).

[117] Dubrovskiy et al., "Six Years of the Revolution of Dignity," 52.

[118] Andrew E. Kramer, "Oligarch's Return Raises Alarm in Ukraine," *The New York Times*, May 16, 2019, sec. World.

[119] Vladimir Dubrovskiy, "Ukraine after 2019 Elections: Prospects for the Rule of Law" ("Partners in Eastern Europe: Multiple Crossroads" Conference, Budapest, December 9, 2019).

[120] Dubrovskiy et al., "Six Years of the Revolution of Dignity," 13–15.

North Macedonia

[121] The country was officially renamed North Macedonia in 2019, while earlier its official name had been Former Yugoslav Republic of Macedonia.

[122] Hale, *Patronal Politics*, 641.

[123] William Crowther, "Ethnic Condominium and Illiberalism in Macedonia," *East European Politics and Societies* 31, no. 4 (2017): 743–44.

[124] Levitsky and Way, *Competitive Authoritarianism*, 124–28.

[125] Crowther, "Ethnic Condominium and Illiberalism in Macedonia," 749.

[126] Crowther, 745.

[127] Hale, *Patronal Politics*, 641.

[128] Crowther, "Ethnic Condominium and Illiberalism in Macedonia," 751.

[129] Ljubica Spaskovska, "From Feudal Socialism to Feudal Democracy - the Trials and Tribulations of the Former Yugoslav Republic of Macedonia," *OpenDemocracy* (blog), July 23, 2014, https://www.opendemocracy.net/en/can-europe-make-it/from-feudal-socialism-to-feudal-democracy-trials-and-tribulati/.

[130] Crowther, "Ethnic Condominium and Illiberalism in Macedonia," 751–54.

[131] See also Cengiz Günay and Vedran Dzihic, "Decoding the Authoritarian Code: Exercising 'Legitimate' Power Politics through the Ruling Parties in Turkey, Macedonia and Serbia," *Southeast European and Black Sea Studies* 16, no. 4 (2016): 529–49.

[132] Crowther, "Ethnic Condominium and Illiberalism in Macedonia," 754–56.

[133] Shaun Walker, "Anti-Asylum Orbán Makes Exception for a Friend in Need," *The Guardian*, November 20, 2018, sec. World news, https://www.theguardian.com/world/2018/nov/20/anti-asylum-orban-makes-exception-for-a-friend-in-need; Eva S. Balogh, "Further Thoughts on the Gruevski Affair," *Hungarian Spectrum* (blog), November 17, 2018, https://hungarianspectrum.org/2018/11/16/further-thoughts-on-the-gruevski-affair/.

Moldova

[134] Hale, *Patronal Politics*, 168–69.
[135] Hale, 170.
[136] Mizsei, "The New East European Patronal States and the Rule-of-Law," 541–42.
[137] Mizsei, 566.
[138] Aaron Miller, *Moldova under Vladimir Plahotniuc: Corruption and Oligarchy* (Tel-Aviv: Studio Igal Rozental Ltd., 2018).
[139] Miller, 44.
[140] Hale, *Patronal Politics*, 76–82.
[141] Miller, *Moldova under Vladimir Plahotniuc*, 52–61; Mizsei, "The New East European Patronal States and the Rule-of-Law," 566–76.
[142] Sarah Chayes, "The Structure of Corruption: A Systemic Analysis," in *Stubborn Structures: Reconceptualizing Post-Communist Regimes*, ed. Bálint Magyar (Budapest–New York: CEU Press, 2019), 507–30.
[143] Figures C.2-5 in Chayes.
[144] Miller, *Moldova under Vladimir Plahotniuc*, 97–124.
[145] Vladimir Solovyov, "Moldovan Regime Change Is Rare Example of Russian-Western Teamwork," *Carnegie Moscow Center* (blog), June 19, 2019, https://carnegie.ru/commentary/79333.

Georgia

[146] Hale, *Patronal Politics*, 152.
[147] Mizsei, "The New East European Patronal States and the Rule-of-Law," 547.
[148] Gerlach, *Color Revolutions in Eurasia*, 6–9.
[149] Mizsei, "The New East European Patronal States and the Rule-of-Law," 547.
[150] Mikheil Saakashvili and Kahka Bendukidze, "Georgia: The Most Radical Catch-Up Reforms," in *The Great Rebirth: Lessons from the Victory of Capitalism over Communism*, ed. Anders Åslund and Simeon Djankov (Washington, DC: Peterson Institute for International Economics, 2014), 149–63.
[151] Mizsei, "The New East European Patronal States and the Rule-of-Law," 550.
[152] Mizsei, 548.
[153] Huseyn Aliyev, "The Effects of the Saakashvili Era Reforms on Informal Practices in the Republic of Georgia," *Studies of Transition States and Societies* VI, no. 1 (2014): 19–33.
[154] Mizsei, "The New East European Patronal States and the Rule-of-Law," 547–55."
[155] Dubrovskiy et al., "Six Years of the Revolution of Dignity," 33.
[156] Hale, *Patronal Politics*, 208–10.
[157] Mizsei, "The New East European Patronal States and the Rule-of-Law," 559.
[158] Hale, *Patronal Politics*, 212. Also, see Scott Radnitz, "In Georgia, Two Machines Are Better Than One," *Foreign Policy* (blog), September 27, 2012, https://foreignpolicy.com/2012/09/27/in-georgia-two-machines-are-better-than-one/.
[159] Tatia Nikoladze, "Protests in Tbilisi Continue after Dispersal – Demonstrators Plan to Disrupt Parliament," November 20, 2019, https://jam-news.net/protests-in-tbilisi-continue-after-dispersal-demonstrators-plan-to-disrupt-parliament/; Aaron Genin, "Georgian Protests: Tbilis's Two-Sided Conflict," *The California Review*, July 25, 2019, https://calrev.org/2019/07/25/russian-impiety-georgian-riots/.

[160] Ekaterine Oniani, "Towards Strengthening the Rule of Law through Independent Judiciary: Georgian Experience" ("Partners in Eastern Europe: Multiple Crossroads" Conference, Budapest, December 9, 2019).

[161] Ana Abashidze et al., "The Judicial System: Past Reforms and Future Perspectives" (Tbilisi: Coalition for Independent and Transparent Judiciary, 2017), http://coalition.ge/files/the_judicial_system.pdf.

[162] Ani Chkhikvadze, "Georgian Dream's Pyrrhic Victory," *The American Interest* (blog), December 18, 2018, https://www.the-american-interest.com/2018/12/18/georgian-dreams-pyrrhic-victory/.

About the Authors

BÁLINT MAGYAR is a senior research fellow of the CEU Democracy Institute. Magyar is a sociologist and a former liberal politician. An activist of the anti-communist dissident movement since 1979, he was one of the founding members and leaders of the Hungarian Liberal Party (SZDSZ). He was a former Member of Parliament (1990–2010) and Minister of Education (1996–1998, 2002–2006). His previous English-language books include *Post-Communist Mafia State: The Case of Hungary* (2016) and *The Anatomy of Post-Communist Regimes* (2020).

BÁLINT MADLOVICS is a junior research fellow of the CEU Democracy Institute. Madlovics is a political scientist, economist, and sociologist. A visiting professor at Corvinus University of Budapest (2022–), he is the author of numerous book chapters, peer-reviewed publications, and commentaries for online media such as Project Syndicate (in English) and printed media including *Élet és Irodalom* (in Hungarian). He was a visiting professor at Eötvös Loránd University in Budapest (2021). His previous English-language book is *The Anatomy of Post-Communist Regimes* (2020).

Lightning Source UK Ltd.
Milton Keynes UK
UKHW020808031022
409835UK00012B/1491